BURBIA MAN
Life as a Civil Servant

Illustrated

To
Paul Jr. (P.J.)
You are in a word, wonderful!
A constant joy to me, always,
a man of respect. Love you
much - DAD

By Paul Steucke Sr.

Paul

This writing is a continuation of the memoir, *Burbia Boy*, ©
published in 2006 and revised in 2012.

Copyright © **2012,** by Paul Steucke Sr.

Published by Amazon.com/creatspace

ISBN : 1470151456
        9781470151454

Biography – Steucke – Blacksburg, Alexandria, Annandale,
Reston, Virginia. US Department of Agriculture, Virginia
Extension Service, Agricultural Research Service, U.S. Forest
Service, Sylvania, US. Water Resources Council, Joint Federal
State Land Use Planning Commission for Alaska, Federal
Inspector for the Alaska natural gas pipeline, Federal Aviation
Administration, unidentified flying objects, UFO, KAL flight
007, JAL flight 1628

The layout and design of this book, including the illustrations
and photographs, unless otherwise noted, are by the author.

356 pages

◈

*This book
is dedicated to civil servants
in America, who through their daily work
keep the functions of government moving smoothly,
through one political administration
after another.*

◈

My father,
uncle, aunt, brother, son,
granddaughter, and I have worked,
or are working, as civil servants for the federal
government. My father once told me, "When you work
as a civil servant you will never be rich, but you
will never be poor."
He was right.

I
know a man
whose friendship
is like Alaskan sunrise
which stands above darkened peaks,
glowing concentrated rose
in the cold morning air,
tendrils of warmth stretch out
touching color to drab slopes,
expanding, reaching
to tint the farthest hill.
it does not fade
till every ridge and valley
partakes and then reflects
the joyous dawn.

Ivy P. Moore
© 1984

Paul Steucke Sr.

Table of Contents

"All you have to do,
is decide what to do,
with the time that is
given to you."

J.R.R. Tolkien
Lord of the Rings

Introduction

As in life, the writing here is comingled with stories about family, love and work. These memories are intertwined chronologically, weaving from one to the other and back again, the emphasis being on my career as a civil servant for the United States government. At the age of 21, while a junior in college, I married my high school sweetheart, who in a short previous marriage had born three children. Her husband had left her alone with no financial or child support; I adopted them legally two years later. This emotional and financial responsibility moved me to choose a safe and risk free employment to insure the basics of living. I never left or quit a job until I already had another one.

With over 2.0 million civilian employees, excluding the Postal Service, the Federal Civil Service is the largest employer in the nation. Eighty-five percent of those employees work outside Washington, D.C. Most, but not all, civil service employees are beyond the reach of political influence. This arrangement, necessary to maintain a consistent workforce that is dedicated to the nation, and not a political party or the *spoils* system, was created by the Pendleton Civil Service Reform Act of 1883.

Over 1,500 top-level appointments are made by every new president. These are not additions; they replace people in existing political positions. There are also about 1,500 additional lower-level political appointments made at the beginning of each political cycle.

There is a significant difference between working for the public/government sector and working for the private/corporate sector. Corporate executives who come to Washington with the belief that the only thing government needs in order to function more effectively is a dose of business leadership are usually surprised and annoyed to discover that business and government require two different types of management.

For example, public service requires openness that is frequently enforced by the news media and the Freedom of Information Act of 1966. Budgets, job descriptions, salaries, expenditures, grants and policy actions are considered public information. The glare of publicity, called accountability by some, is often difficult for corporate executives in government positions to accept. This openness in a competitive marketplace is rarely a part of private management policies. Executives from the private sector expect the fairly rational decision-making process they have customarily employed to be equally effective in the public sector. They are often dismayed to find out how much bargaining and compromising is involved in each policy decision and how political the entire process is. The result of public policy decisions may not be the most cost effective, but it will probably satisfy most of the actors who built the consensus necessary to justify the use of public money.

> Two years is the average length of public service for politically appointed officials.

The private executive is also uncomfortable with the inability of government managers to freely change their minds. The public sector manager is changing policy direction out in the open, where the media, not to mention Congress, is almost certain to question the action. Like corporations, government organizations are organized in a hierarchical arrangement.

Every civil servant reports to someone further up the two million-employee ladder all the way to the White House. Decision-making is executive centered. A public policy or program based on two million individual decisions would be a disaster. Few government managers have the authority to make unilateral decisions affecting major policy areas. In government, there is a constant give and take on issues of equity and reciprocity, often replacing those well accepted business concepts of efficiency and effectiveness.

In high-level government, executives rotate in and out of positions according to the decisions made by the voters, and their political appointees rotate in and out with them. This turnover in leadership is a sore issue with career civil servants because their political supervisors, some good and some not so good, are constantly changing. The civil servant not only has to train each of these in/out supervisors, but also then has to stand aside as they make changes in policy and personnel that have taken years to build and develop into a smooth working operation.

Some appointees are knowledgeable and highly effective, but many do not know the program operations, personnel or history, and others do not seem to care. Two years is the average length of service in the federal government for new top officials. Their assignment is to install new policies that can be credited to those who appointed them-- not to the account of political opponents. This frequently involves the removal of personnel, offices, building space, mission, direction and budget for ongoing programs. When such politically motivated decisions fail, the appointed leadership can just move back to the corporate world, leaving the civil servant to spend years trying to get the system operating successfully again. Recent examples of inept public/political leadership come to mind:

Hurricane Katrina wiped out the city of New Orleans in September of 2005. Mr. Mike Brown, the top manager of the Federal Emergency Management Agency, appointed to the job by President George W. Bush, is an attorney who prior to the federal appointment, spent nine years as Commissioner of the International Arabian Horse Association. His management of the crisis soon became a disaster in itself and on September 9, 2005, he was relieved of his duties regarding the damage and emergency response to the hurricane. He subsequently resigned from federal service.

Here is another example from the Associated Press, dated Friday, May 28, 2010:

"The head of the troubled agency that oversees offshore drilling resigned under pressure Thursday as President Barack Obama moved more aggressively to take charge of the BP Gulf oil spill. The departure of Minerals Management Service Director Elizabeth Birnbaum was announced by Interior Secretary Ken Salazar at a Congressional hearing where Birnbaum had been scheduled to testify but did not show up. Birnbaum, who had led MMS since July 2009, left after she and her agency came under withering criticism from lawmakers of both parties over allegedly lax oversight of drilling and cozy ties with industry. Salazar recently announced he was radically restructuring the agency into three separate parts."

I am sure that the numerous civil servants who worked for Birnbaum cheered, because their efforts to protect the nation from oil spills had been thwarted at every turn by corporate lobbyists and Ms. Birnbaum.

It frequently takes months or even years for the decisions made by political appointees to be revealed. In December of 2010, the McClatchy Newspaper syndicate released information from their 2005 investigation that the Federal Reserve Board rejected requests from one of the nation's top banking regulators, a professional accounting board and even their own staff, to curb the banking industry's use of trust-preferred securities that allowed the banks to continue to issue unstable loans. Leaving the rules, unchanged allowed Wall Street investment firms the freedom to encourage community banks to take on huge debts which lead to the development of complex mortgage bonds that in 2008 nearly brought down the national and international financial systems. The Federal Reserve's decision to ignore what was happening allowed 324 banks to fail, along with the default of over five *billion* dollars worth of these *special* securities.

The failure of federal regulatory action, chaired by political appointees, provided for the continued creation of unsecured loans, which allowed people who could not afford to buy a house, or make loan payments, to purchase one. The result was a real estate market crash that left millions of homeowners with foreclosed homes and banks with no other option than to close or be bailed out with federal funds. The price and sale of homes nationwide plummeted. The lobbyists and political appointees who created this mess walked away from it with no punishment or negative repercussions. Some, particularly those in the real estate business, became millionaires.

The corporate industry spends millions of dollars hiring ex- political appointees as lobbyists with insider knowledge, to influence Congress and other political employees to support their clients' agenda. For example, British Petroleum, the oil company responsible for the massive oil spill in the Gulf of Mexico, spent $16 million in 2009 for lobbyists in Washington, D.C. One assumes this money was not spent entirely in vain.

Managers in the private sector earn a pass/fail grade with the financial success of their business. Their decisions, if poorly chosen, may cause the demise of the company and the employees' jobs. Detroit and the American auto industry is an example. Their mission is clear and unchanging: stay solvent. On the other hand, the government manager is often in the awkward position of having to administer imprecise laws. Public agencies have their goals and objectives set for them by legislative bodies that create and fund agencies; legislation that is often deliberately vague and ambiguous because only broad mission statements will garner enough Congressional votes to become a funded reality. Contrary to all rules of good management, Congress and the White House interfere constantly with the day-to-day management of federal agencies, yet the civil servants manage to keep the system going with little or no public support or praise. That is their job in the public sector.

My father, uncle, and aunt all worked for and retired from service in the federal government. I interviewed them before they died and obtained some wonderful stories that are in my first book, *Burbia Boy*, but my interview questions centered on their family history, not their government careers. I failed to ask questions that might have revealed their opinions about civil service. My older brother, Wally, who completed a full career with the U.S. Fish and Wildlife Service, is available; I asked him to share his thoughts about work as a civil servant. Here is what he said:

> I worked 35 years for the U.S. Fish and Wildlife Service, a career that provided me with awards, training and promotions. It also provided me with an opportunity to see government at its best and its worst. I started as a fisheries biologist and eventually, like Paul, ended up in management.
>
> My experience within the Service for the first ten years was limited to technical roles, and I had absolutely no experience with the political system. I received two years of very specialized training and became a practicing fish doctor. The job was fun, challenging and fulfilling.
>
> My first rub with politics came when my boss took another job and I applied for his position, only to find out that some upper management folks did not want me because I had, on several previous occasions, disagreed with them over proposals that would damage or destroy the natural resources we were supposed to protect. Even though the position was advertised as competitive (for the best-qualified person), they offered someone else the job before it was ever advertised. However, this story has an interesting twist. They did not know their man was also my weekly tennis partner. He told me

about the offer, and I suggested he get it in writing, which he did. I told him I was also interested in the position and I then took that letter to the Regional Director and filed a complaint regarding the blatant violation of hiring procedures. Something that I now realize was naive on my part because telling management they are cheating the system may gain something in the short run, but will eventually come around and bite you at a later time. The letter was withdrawn and I got the job. A lesson learned: if you get wronged, do not hide it. If you bitch about it make sure you have your facts together. My life and my work again became placid. I loved my job and was good at it.

> They did
> not know
> he was
> my
> tennis
> partner

Eventually, for financial and moral reasons I wanted to become part of the management team. The man who had tried to keep me from getting the lab job moved out of management, and I applied for and got the job. Like Paul and others moving up the career ladder, I found myself in a position I knew very little about. Worse, the system had no clear idea about what I was supposed to do either. The job turned out to be boring because accountability practices had not changed within the agency for many years. I tried to be innovative and introduce some new systems, but change was not in the wind. The Service was not prepared for me to be innovative, nor did I have the patience to wait years for change.

In about three years, I took the same step as my predecessor and moved back into the field, although not into the same technical area I had moved from. The federal government was setting up a program using students from local colleges and universities to increase their awareness of conservation actions. The program, the Youth Conservation Corps, was an excellent idea, and we had a small community college in the immediate area. Unfortunately, the person I chose to head up our YCC program did not meet the standards established by my immediate supervisors--The same people who attempted to prevent me from getting the technical job a few years back. The battle of wills got so bad that I was called to the *head shed* and threatened with firing. That is a big deal in the federal institution,  because it is very hard to remove somebody from his or her job without documented proof of failure.

Luckily, for me, somewhere in the past the Regional Director had become impressed with something I had done, and he overrode that decision and instead transferred me to the lovely city of Bismarck, North Dakota. This was not a place for a lot of fishery expertise, but I ultimately became a member of a team working on a special project for the International Joint Commission, which accomplished some worthwhile objectives. The price of doing a good job is to be promoted, and so I went to Washington, D.C. I was not happy with this geographical change, but I did find the job rewarding and challenging.

Two years later, I applied for and was accepted as the management head of all U.S. Fish and Wildlife programs in Montana and Wyoming, a great job. Unless you really screwed up, it was your show. I got close to the political folks in both states, and they gave me support even though the politics sometimes got in the way; I learned to navigate around or through them. There were bumps in the road, such as when the D.C. office supplied me with formal testimony for a public hearing that I refused to present because their proposed testimony was technically and socially unacceptable. After I complained, they had a change of heart and let me give my own testimony. That kind of give and take between the political folks in D.C. and the management people on the ground was then, and remains, perfectly acceptable.

It was while in this position that I fell afoul of the fourth estate, the news media. A major waterfowl disease struck Montana. The Service was very active in trying to manage the birds and the disease, and still provide some hunting opportunity for duck hunters.

Wally, giving a speech at the dedication of the Lee Metcalf National Wildlife Refuge in Montana, 1985.

Given this conflict, the press had a wonderful time writing and reporting about a situation that as yet had no single right answer

I discovered that quotation marks were of no value, and *off the record* meant nothing to reporters competing with each other for a story. Television reporters (a misnomer if there ever was one) were worse than any others, because they had no time to check facts; they simply reported as fact what they hoped was correct, even if their information came from a disreputable source. They seldom, almost never, reported corrections. (Have you ever heard a television reporter admit a mistake on air?) I did learn that if you can get two TV reporters to report different versions of the same story, you could whipsaw one of them into a least eventually providing the real facts.

The local Federal Fish and Wildlife management program in Montana and Wyoming was so successful and became so intertwined with the state programs, that the managers in Washington became concerned that too much power was being established at the local level, even though a sister agency, the U.S. Bureau of Land Management, had individual state managers for years.

An example of the power struggle between local managers, such as me, and our Washington managers, occurred when management of an endangered species, the Black-footed Ferret, was removed from the state and taken over by the Fish and Wildlife Service, even though I had signed an agreement with the State of Wyoming to manage the animals. I did this because the species lived only in a very small area of Wyoming and the state biologists were already doing an excellent job of managing the situation. The state biologists and management had also cultivated a highly cooperative arrangement with state politicians and the ranchers who owned the property the ferrets lived on. That decision was very unpopular with my staff and the state biologists, and it became a turf war with the result that our state offices were closed, and this time I was without a job.

Again, through people in different parts of the country, I was offered a position in the Pacific Northwest. I liked this new job, did it well, and retained some contact with my technical training while still having some policy activities. As a result, I was promoted in place to the deputy position for the Service in the Pacific Northwest. For two years, all went well. Then a different administration within the political arena caused the new management team to decide on a number of changes.

For years, federal employees at a certain level were protected from political impact. If you did not conform technically or politically, you could not be fired, but you could be transferred. My boss got tangled up with the political environment surrounding a number of endangered species and he was eventually removed from his job by creating another lesser job for him. This is a common ploy for getting rid of someone; the employee looses everything but pay. This process also-illegally--side steps the routine personnel rules and regulations for hiring and promotions. He appealed that transfer and eventually won a significant settlement from the Service. Of course, the people who tried to get rid of him did not have to pay anything. The government paid the bill.

While he was doing battle, someone had to do his job. That person was me. I felt a certain loyalty to him for my job, and I certainly did not agree with the political policies that were being made in D.C. and directed to the field as so-called biological decisions. I objected loudly and often, knowing that I could not be immediately replaced, because if that occurred there would be no one with any technical experience on the job. Lastly, the political and natural resource management systems in the seven states that made up our region were very supportive of my efforts.

And so a number of temporary supervisors were moved to our region. I knew most of them and they knew me, and given the state support, they were quite happy to just let things ride. Eventually the political forces in D.C. began making personnel decisions I simply could not live with. They were selecting incompetent people for key positions simply because these folks were loyal to their political system. I objected, and eventually I went to various congressional representatives and senators to try to prevent these people from becoming part of the top management. It worked, but I was told that my future with the Service was now limited, or in other words, they would get me. Fortunately, I had sufficient time in service and age to qualify for retirement.

One Monday morning I received a telephone call from our D.C. office. I asked my secretary if she had any idea what the call was about, and all she would say was, "I think you might want to consider retiring…now." I immediately went to the Office of Personnel and implemented my retirement plans, called a staff meeting and told everybody what was going on, and then called the local newspapers. The eventual result of all this hanky panky was that the Service got a new director and staff in D.C., and I retired after 34 years of service with the taste of skunk in my mouth.

For people who have an interest in the attributes of a government organization, be they technical, moral, or social, use caution with regard to upward mobility. My ego eventually caused me to leave the technical bench side and take a management position. I rationalized those decisions by saying I could do more good for the organization by assuring that good people were in place to make good decisions. The fact is, in the end I became one more person who reached a position where he could not bring positive actions to bear because of incompetent political supervision. The system does indeed reward for incompetence, particularly at the highest levels.

The American public often voices its displeasure with actions taken by the government. Beginning with President Ronald Reagan, there has been continuous pressure brought to bear on the worker bees within the federal institution. To remain competent, a middle or upper manager must develop protection between him or her self and upper management, or endure pressure to perform some action or actions that are not in the best interest of the nation. I am an excellent example of a person who spent 35 years attempting to protect wildlife species that were in harm's way, and to protect habitat from destruction from a variety of developers, only to find that regardless of the fact that I hold the two highest awards given to civilians within the Department of Interior, when I became a political problem I was told to leave.

It is critical that new federal employees establish their own personal goals and boundaries beyond which they will not go, especially those who go to work for agencies that are in constant pressure from outside forces to utilize the resources that they are charged with protecting. They become the last bastion of reasonableness in what is becoming a totally political world. Those pressures must be alleviated in a very short time or this country will become a company/corporate owned government run organization.

To solve that problem several actions are needed. We must take the money out of the election process and use public funds for that purpose. Elections should only be two months long and a cap should be placed on funds expended. Senators should be elected for *only* two terms, and congressman for six terms (12 years maximum for both). Until those minimal actions are taken, big business will continue to unduly influence our elective process and money will be the determining factor in what government actions are taken. Let's face it, the Supreme Court in a five to four decision has determined that corporations are, in the legal sense, people, and so multi-national corporations can spend as much money as they want to influence our elections. When told of the action on this vote, one of the Supreme Court Justices mouthed the words *not true*.

However, it is true, and in my opinion, he needs to be impeached.

We must take the money out of politics and eliminate the corporate lobbyists, like Karl Rove and others who exist to manipulate government actions through the use of corporate money. Use public money, with a cap and a maximum time limit for elections. There are those who argue that such measures are an infringement upon their constitutional rights. I suggest we are very close to having those rights subjugated to large corporations.

In the meantime, the United States of America is following down the road taken by the Germanic people in the 1930's, and most people in the country are too busy to care. It is in such conditions that democracy, the government of, for, and by the people dies, and fascism, a consortium of big business, the media, and government, flourishes. We have become a country where big business and government run the country together, and the media, both print and visual, have joined hands, because information, which keeps the

government and business honest, has now become the purview of the very few and the very rich. Almost all TV stations are owned by six corporations. I expect that within my lifetime, the number will be even smaller.

There is a name for this type of government: fascism. Our government will continue to function only as long as middle class workers draw that moral line and remain devoted to believing in the American dream. In a critical election year, it is estimated that about 50 percent of eligible voters will actually vote. The American people must make up their mind as to where they want to go--the way of Thomas Jefferson, or the way of Benito Mussolini. After watching the election process of 2010, with, bank frauds, liars, cheats and people who cannot even spell Constitution running for public office, I am no longer sure what the future holds for this country-- democracy of, for and by the people, or fascism for the wealthy, the politically powerful and the media.

Like Wally, working as a civil servant for the government provided me with opportunities to learn about management. It also allowed me to transfer from one job to a better paying one, as there is no penalty for changing agencies since everyone works for the government. My basic philosophy was this: work the first year learning the job and the new agency policies, the second year doing the job the best that it can be done, the third year learning your boss' job, and the fourth year, if they do not promote you, looking elsewhere for a job with higher pay, As a result of this philosophy, I worked for six different agencies in 30 years, and had 18 different supervisors in that time. I learned from watching the great ones and learned what not to do from the not so great ones. I went from an entry-level pay grade of seven to the top of a grade fifteen, as high as one can go without moving into political appointment.

This book, *Burbia Man* , volume two of my two-book memoir, focuses on my adult life and career in federal employment, beginning with my marriage in 1960 and continuing to 1994, when I retired from the federal government at the age of 55. My wife's and my post-retirement life is also included. As of this writing, I am seventy-two years old.
Burbia Boy (ISBN 1470183838) is volume one of my memoir, which portrays my grandparents, parents, and my youthful life up until I married.

Chapter One

When I was twelve my family moved from a small house in Alexandria, Virginia, to a two-story brick home just south of Annandale, where most of the roads were made of gravel and the houses were on half-acre lots to accommodate a septic system. It was rural, but to me it was suburbia and I thought of myself as a *burbia boy*. When I graduated from high school, I went to work for a survey outfit in Springfield, Virginia. Nine months later, I realized I did not want to be the office errand boy all my life, so I saved my money and went to an art school in Richmond, Virginia, Richmond Professional Institute, then a branch of the College of William and Mary, now a part of Virginia Commonwealth University.

I was fortunate to have drawn an inventive college roommate, Malcolm Carpenter, who hailed from Falls Church, a place about 30 minutes drive from my parents' house. Carp, as he was know by his friends, and I dubbed Richmond the Gritty City because most of the old homes throughout the place were still being heated by coal furnaces. After a snowfall, you could actually see a light dusting of black soot on the snow, and the air smelled a lot like soap. Carp was my roommate for two years, until love intervened and I married Annette Hagaman, the girl I had shared a table with in high school biology class. The nation was in an economic depression when we got married.

Dwight D. Eisenhower, who led the allied effort to defeat Hitler, was elected President for two terms starting in 1953. When he became president, the country was in the dumps. Unemployment was high and jobs were disappearing as firms were laying people off due to high interest rates and declining sales. It took years to pull out of that recession, and we were still affected by it when we got married.

At the beginning of summer 1961, the on campus apartment we were renting was purchased by the school for faculty offices, so we moved to the other side of town into the ground floor house where the upper flat was rented by a fellow art student. Of course, we looked at the place briefly during the day, but we did not have an opportunity to see it at night until we moved in over the July 4th holiday.

During the day, the place was fine, but at night, it had a surprise for us. Soon after going to bed, we heard lots of scratching about on the floor. Turning on the light revealed an army of black beetles, so big they walked a quarter inch above the floor. Fortunately, they did not climb up the bed legs, but that racket did not make for sleep. We cringed, watched, listened to the scratching and skittering noises on the hardwood, and rested as best we could. Calling the realtor in the morning solved nothing, as it was a three-day holiday, so for three nights we listened to the Olympic Bug Games on the floor.

While waiting for the bug exterminator, I explored the basement, especially the outside stair entrance, and noticed several places where the wood around the door had rotted away leaving an insect super highway to the inside of the house. That night, armed with an aerosol can of bug killer; I walked to the basement entrance and watched as the roaches swarmed into the old concrete stairwell near the basement door. The walls and floor were moving, throbbing with them.

I was revolted, but I had to do something. I started spraying here and there, watching the bugs run every which way--including a few who decided the safest place to hide was up the inside of my pant leg. Annette, watching from the bedroom window above, could not stifle screams of horror and maybe a laugh or two, as I jumped around like a lunatic, trying to get them off me. The next day I repaired the doorjamb, plugged up the holes with concrete, and the exterminator came and did the clean up. However, as long as we lived in that place, almost every morning there would be one of the bugs trapped in the kitchen sink, unable to crawl up the slick sides. How they got into the sink I do not know and I do not want to know.

When school was out for the summer, Annette and I both worked various jobs to pay for the rent and groceries. After several interviews, I got a job working for a very small company that made odd advertising stuff such as pens and small drafting tools. Their strongest seller was a plastic hat stamped out to imitate woven straw. The big selling gimmick was that the plastic supposedly contained a chemical that helped protect the wearer from the ultraviolet rays of the sun. Considering the size and junkshop status of the company, I think that was a hoax, but they sold well, particularly in the bright Richmond summers.

With no air conditioning, this was a true sweatshop, operating out of a warehouse that was nothing more than a large converted garage. Along one wall were two large mechanical machines that used a combination of hand operated levers to heat and create 12 plastic hats at a time. The operator of this device stood on a raised platform and pulled a large sheet of colored plastic off a roll that was above and behind the hat molds, which were arrayed at an angle in front of the operator. Each sheet of twelve, once laid onto the heated molds, was cut with a long wire, and the newly made hats, still in a sheet, were laid aside on a pile. When a dozen or so of these sheets had been collected, another person took them to a cutting area to be machine-cut into individual units. Advertising tags touting the ultraviolet protection were then placed with each and they were boxed for shipment.

The fifth day I was there, one of the other workers and I got into an unspoken competition to see who could produce more hats. We stood side by side, each with a hat machine in front of us, bare to the waist and sweating while we pulled the plastic sheet down, pulled levers to drop them onto the molds, cut, and place them in the pile. Hour after hour, we toiled without a break--until finally he gave up.

After I had been working this prestigious job for three weeks, I had to go off to National Guard camp. I became a member of the Virginia Guard in high school, encouraged by two friends who had already joined up. In addition to meeting once a week in the evening, I was required to attend an annual two-week summer training camp. I knew that Federal law requires employers to rehire or take back any guardsman who goes to duty. Though obviously, I thought, if it takes a law to enforce this civic duty, it must be a problem. And sure enough, when I came back to the sweatshop, I found myself out of a job.

Realizing that finding any work for the remaining summer would be impossible in the recession, we took the opportunity to visit Annette's aunts in Rochester, Minnesota. Being young, foolish and poor, we decided to make the trip non-stop to save motel fees, and for sustenance, Annette packed a cooler with enough ham sandwiches to last the whole trip, which we ate, accompanied by our gallon jug of sweet tea, until we got so sick of ham that we could not eat it for years.

We arrived at Annette's parents home in northern Virginia late one afternoon and left after dinner, to start a 1,200-mile trip. Driving all night is physically more difficult, but also quieter and cooler. It began beautifully. I can still recall the fireflies lighting up farm fields as we drove through northern Maryland on our way to the Pennsylvania turnpike. After 15 hours of continuous driving we crossed the Mississippi River at Onalaska, went through La Crescent, headed up to Winona and west toward Rochester. Shortly after leaving the Mississippi hills, the two-lane road ran through farm country decorated with small towns, grain silos and massive lilac hedges.

The road, with the exception of small rises, was flat with gentle hills going up and down with the highway. It was daylight again, and looking in my rear view mirror, I noticed a pick up truck behind us with two young men in it. They tailed us closely and then passed us on a flat stretch of highway. There was no other traffic in either direction. After passing, they slowed down in front of me until we were barely moving, so I moved into the passing lane to go around them, but as soon as I got even with their truck, they sped up, pacing my speed so that I was unable to get out of the oncoming traffic lane. When I jammed on my brakes to get behind them, they did the same. I was trapped on the wrong side of the road.

They thought my predicament was hilarious

We started up a hill side by side, without knowing what might be coming over the top toward us. They found my predicament hilarious, and they laughed. As we came up over the crest, I could see the road ahead was clear, so I floored the gas pedal on the Buick, but the tired engine, combined with an automatic transmission, could not outrun them. It was a sad attempt at escape. Finally, I realized I could not risk going up another hill on the wrong side of the road, so I stopped on the highway in the middle of a flat area. They slowed down, and tired of the sport, shifted to a lower gear and raced away, laughing all the time. I eased back into the right lane, slowly gained speed, and was relieved to find them gone when I crested the hill.

When we got to Rochester, we were very tired and so was the Buick. I took it to the auto dealer in town and asked them if there was anything they could do to get life back into a ten-year-old car. They told me it was wearing out and without a complete engine overhaul would not last much longer. I could barely afford gas and oil, so I thanked them, and a week later we drove back to Falls Church and parked it on the street in front of Annette's parents' house, where it sat throughout the winter until purchased by two young girls for $100. (A 1950 Buick Roadmaster convertible is now a rare collector car worth over $100,000 in 2011 money.)

To help us out, Annette's father offered me the 1952 Cadillac limousine he had inherited from his former employer. The car had originally been a part of the White House limo fleet. The two of us went to the vehicle registration office, where I signed the paper work and paid him one dollar. My first ownership chore was to replace the leaking dual exhaust system; it cost me $80 in parts ($350 in 2011 money.) I did the work in his garage, jacking the car up one wheel at a time and placing a crisscrossed stack of red building bricks under the axle beside each tire. When I finished the job, I noticed that all the bricks had cracked. The thought of those cracked bricks still gives me a sick feeling--they could have crumbled at any time pinning me under the car. The limo was black and extra-long, with power windows and fold down seats that pulled out of the back of the front seat for Secret Service agents to sit on. The floor of the back seat was so big that a full-size playpen could be set in the space, which we did on a regular basis a few years later. We drove the Cadillac back to school and used it for several years.

Early in my senior year, I discovered that the Dean of the college's commercial art school was still helping last years' graduates get jobs. I went to him and complained, saying they had had their chance, and now it was time he started helping the current senior class. Shortly thereafter, I received two helpful job leads. The first was designing monthly magazine covers for a cooperative that supplied electricity to rural farmers and homeowners, a program started by the US Department of Agriculture. Each month they published an 8-x10-inch free, newsprint style magazine , *Rural Virginia,*

Rural Virginia magazine cover

which required a two-color cover design. For over a year I provided the cover artwork for $35.00 per cover. Two of these were accepted for the Annual Richmond Art Director's Club show, a competitive juried show that included the best of the year's work for all the advertising companies in town. That was quite a coup for an art student.

The second lead was a part-time job with the Duplex Envelope Company in Richmond. Their primary product was church collection envelopes for member donations to the church on Sunday services. The small envelopes usually bore a small black and white image of the church building in one corner. My job was to convert a small photograph of the church building into an ink drawing suitable for reproduction on the envelope. This was easy for me because of my year's experience as a draftsman for the survey firm in Springfield, Virginia.

The envelope company was unusual for the time in that women filled all the top positions. The executive office, separated by antique glass window walls, was aligned along Richmond Avenue lying two floors below. The president and art director offices were next door to each other; we could see into them, but could not hear anything. I worked for the art

director, Mrs. Jansen, a woman with a teenage son a year or
two younger then me. The president of the company, Mrs.
Marshall, was six feet tall, thin, and as far as I could tell, was
not afraid of anything. She was a *General* before her time. One
day she came striding over to our office and said, "Paul, come
with me; I need you for a few minutes." I was not sure what
she meant by that, but without a thought I jumped off my
drafting stool and followed her disappearing form through the
office as fast as I could. The backside of the building contained
toilets and dressing areas for the men and women who worked
in the various shops, and we headed straight into the men's
dressing area without a moment's hesitation or announcement
while she hollered in an angry voice, "John Stuart, I know
you're back here. I need to talk to you immediately. Where are
you?"

I do not know what John Stuart had done, but I was glad
she was not looking for me. There was no response, except the
surprised looks of several guys who were half-dressed in front
of their lockers. We waited another ten seconds, and turning,
she said, "Well obviously he's not here. You can go back to
work." Yes'm," I said in my best southern drawl, and we left,
with me still trying to keep up with her purposeful stride as she
went around workstations, storage cabinets and corners. I
never found out what that was all about, but I was glad it had
been John Stuart and not Paul Steucke she was searching for in
the men's room. I kept that job and Annette worked several
part-time jobs right until I graduated.

My college classes, with the exception of philosophy, were
going smoothly. Even as art students, we were required to take
a core of basic college classes to graduate with a bachelor's
degree. One of the art students I made friends with suggested
that we take philosophy, because it could not possibly be a
difficult class. He was wrong.

The class of ten, of which four of us were art students, met
in an old dark paneled classroom that might have held 15
students comfortably. We were instructed by a short, droll,

gentle-mannered professor, who might better have been at Oxford.

We definitely were not in an art class. The appropriately titled text, *The History of Philosophy,* was a large book with small type that put me to sleep every time I read it. It was dry, boring, dull and hard to understand. Sometimes I had to read a page or paragraph several times before I could figure out what was being described. I worked hard trying to learn about the subtle meaning of Plato's shadows on the cave wall and managed to get a *D* grade for the year. But it was enough for me to pass and graduate. One of my friends did not make it and had to return the following year. I don't know what he took as an elective that next year, but I suspect it was not Philosophy,

In June I walked across the stage of the grand Mosque Theater in Richmond and received my diploma while my parents cheered, as did my wife, my brother and his wife, Joan. (I had attended Wally's graduation two years earlier in Montana.) Immediately after the ceremonies, all the visiting family left for Northern Virginia and other parts unknown. We, however, were headed for Blacksburg, Virginia in the morning. There was no celebration or festive dinner. Everything was oriented to earning a living, and thanks to Annette's jobs, my part-time work, and the scholarships, I had no student loans.

(Federal student loans did not exist. I received two art fellowships from the Virginia Museum, for $900 per year, which would be $15,000 per year value in 2010 money. I was grateful then and I am grateful now.)

* * *

The Virginia
Extension Service, VPI

Pestering the Dean of the School of Arts resulted in my getting a job interview with the Director of the Office of Information for the Virginia Extension Service, located at Virginia Polytechnic Institute in Blacksburg, Virginia. It was and still is the State's premiere school for engineering and architecture (among many other fine disciplines.) The interview took place in May at RPI in Richmond, four weeks prior to graduation. A few days later, I was offered my first full-time civil service job.

Three days before graduation I rented an enclosed U-Haul trailer along with a hitch device that temporarily clamped onto the rear bumper of the Cadillac limousine. Everything we owned, bed, television, chairs, tables, lamps and clothing was packed into the back of the Cadillac and the trailer. Anything that had legs or came apart was disjointed and stuffed into that trailer. It was packed from floor to ceiling, solid. There were no holes, airspaces or gaps.

Before sunrise the next morning we closed the door to our empty first floor apartment and headed due west 210 miles for Blacksburg. The Cadillac was a little sluggish, and the trailer felt like it was pushing us rather than our pulling it, but we continued out of the city until we reached the outer limits, where I thought I felt a thump-thump sensation in the car. I pulled off into an empty lot and took a look at our little caravan. Much to my surprise, I discovered that the left rear tire on the car had a large, unsightly bulge in it from the extra weight of the trailer pressing down on the rear of the car. We were fortunate that it was still inflated.

Half an hour later we were headed back into Richmond with the trailer parked alone on the vacant lot. Our cash supply was very low, and the only credit we had was at Sears Roebuck, a large all purpose national merchandise store that has been in existence for about a hundred years.

We limped back into town, parked the car in the Sears Roebuck lot, and walked over to a nearby restaurant for a breakfast of heavy unappetizing pancakes. When Sears opened, I purchased two new tires on credit and had them put on the car. We then went to the garage/gas station where I had rented the trailer and asked if they still had some one-way rental moving trucks that were there the day before. The owner said they were all gone, but that he had one large truck that belonged to him and that he would lease it to me and refund the lease cost of the trailer. This arrangement looked good except for one thing. We had to return the truck back to Richmond after unloading it in Blacksburg.

I needed help unloading the stuff in the trailer and getting it into the truck, so I drove downtown to an area where day laborers stood on the sidewalk looking for work. Annette and I pulled up beside the biggest person on the walk and asked him if he was willing to help me transfer furniture from my trailer into the truck for $20.00. He agreed and climbed up into the cab of the truck with me behind the wheel and Annette, who was four months pregnant, in the middle. After transferring the furniture, we headed back into Richmond to return the empty trailer now being towed by the truck. On the way, we said goodbye to the day laborer, dropped off the trailer and headed back out of Richmond, six hours after we started.

On Friday, just before graduation, I called an apartment rental business in Blacksburg and obtained an apartment on the edge of town, sight unseen. They told me to call when we got in, and they would put me in touch with someone who could help us unload the furniture. Four hours and 210 miles later, about 4 PM, we entered the outskirts of Blacksburg and I called the realtor who in turn told me to call Big John for help in unloading. John gave me directions to his place out in the nearby farm country so we could pick him up. It seemed to us that Blacksburg was nothing but country. We followed his directions and the road became narrower and narrower until it was for our purposes a single lane road. The truck took up the entire road, and I never knew as we approached a blind hill if I was going to have to put the loaded truck into the ditch to avoid hitting someone head on. Fortunately, we never met another vehicle. Big John was indeed big. He must have weighed 300 pounds and was well over six feet tall. Once again Annette was squeezed into the middle as we repeated our trip into town. At one point we came over a hill only to discover a baby robin right in the middle of the downhill side. Our truck cab was so high above the bird that it felt like we were one of God's angels looking down on earth. John got out and tenderly moved it off to the edge of the road where its noisy parents were waiting.

It was getting late in the day when we returned to the apartment. I stayed up in the back of the truck and pulled boxes from the inside to the edge, where John picked them up, one under each arm, and carried them into the apartment. Within a short time he was carrying the boxes in and returning before I had the opportunity or energy to get more boxes to the edge of the rear door. At one point Annette became concerned about John's health and suggested that I move the boxes out faster. I almost choked with laughter as I told her I was killing myself as it was trying to keep up with him. Eventually the job was done. We set the bed up in the small bedroom and I drove John home while Annette made up the bed, which we collapsed into upon my return. It had been a very long day.

Sunday morning dawned clear and warm. After breakfast in a nearby restaurant, we headed back to Richmond to return the empty truck and pick up the Cadillac. A short distance out of Blacksburg we encountered a long convoy of Army National Guard vehicles headed for Richmond. The normal three-to-four hour drive took seven hours, as it was impossible to pass them on the hilly two-lane highway. After returning the truck and picking up the car, we headed back to Blacksburg, arriving late Sunday evening. We had no groceries, no food or drink, and the electricity was not on yet, so we went to bed. The next morning I put on a white button-down oxford shirt and a necktie, washed my face and brushed my teeth in the nearest gas station restroom, and went to work. Not exactly a pleasant experience but workable. My pregnant wife had it a lot worse. Annette spent the day cleaning the refrigerator, which had been left uncleaned, door shut and power turned off, and was therefore chock full of black mold.

***

The gentleman who had interviewed me in Richmond was the Director of the Office of Information for the Virginia Extension Service, a State/Federal organization that provided information to rural citizens about the modern world of agriculture and home activities. Specialists wrote and created publications that explained the various activities of farming and home economics. Our task was to illustrate and design the publications. Two women artists in addition to two photographers were the staff. I supervised the two artists and reported to one of the photographers, who in turn reported to the director. Based on my college training I labeled myself as the Art Director, a term I later found out led to a discussion as to whether or not that was appropriate, as up to that time, the Director of the Extension Service was the only person whose job title included the word *director*. I guess they decided I was not a threat, so they let me keep my self-appointed title. My first brush with bureaucracy.

A month later, we found and rented a small brick house a few miles outside of town in a subdivision of sorts, carved out of a farm field. The road was dirt, there were no trees and the grass was sparse. The owner of the house had left three things, two of which were helpful. The first was an old, beat-up gas lawnmower, which I managed to get working sufficiently to cut the grass.

The second was a dismantled pool table, complete with a slate top that was stored under the basement stairs. The third was an unknown amount of heating oil stored in two 500-gallon tanks in the basement. The pool table was useless, but the oil in the tanks was a godsend.

The grassy back yard had a hill that dropped down from the house, eventually ending in a fifteen-acre grass field that was burned off in the late fall so new grass would grow up in the spring. There seemed to be no concern for the small animals that lived in the field, although they must have scampered off, since I never saw any little burnt bodies. The older couple who were our next-door neighbors were sweet and helpful when asked. He had worked the coalmines in West Virginia and had hands the size of dinner plates, which he said came from shoveling coal in the mine. They graciously let us use their telephone in times of urgent need, as we could not afford one.

We had been in the house about six months when our son, Paul, was born in the nearby town of Radford on November 22, 1961.

One morning in the middle of that winter, I went out to the carport to start the Cadillac for work and heard a very loud bang. It sounded like a broom handle had fallen on the car, so I got out and looked around, but could not find anything. By the time I drove half a mile and pulled into a local garage, the engine was making one hell of a racket. The mechanic took one listen and said he was certain the engine had thrown a broken piston and would have to be replaced at a cost of $250. It was quite a blow for someone who could not afford a telephone or a six-pack of soft drinks, but I had no choice but to have the work done. I remember that it took them one week to order and get the engine from Roanoke, truck it to Blacksburg and another week to get it installed in the car.

Blacksburg is located on a geographical plain that makes for hot summers and cold winters. In April the furnace ran out of fuel, and we did not have the money to fill the tanks, so we heated the one story, three-bedroom rambler by placing a window fan in the kitchen doorway and turning the kitchen oven on full with the door open. We lived in the house one year, and I am sure the owner of the property wondered how we managed to time our departure to coincide with the total depletion of both fuel tanks.

Author with children in Blacksburg: Stacia, Cathy, Susan and newborn son Paul Junior.

Below; bedtime stories

Working with the Extension Service gave me the opportunity to read several US Department of Agriculture employee newsletters. This gave me the idea that I might be able to secure employment in Washington, D.C. with the Department, so we piled into the limo and drove to my parents place near Alexandria to look for work. The job in Blacksburg was friendly, but we were going broke.

The Agricultural
Research Service, USDA

I lined up two job interviews in the Washington, D.C. area. One was for an artist position with the Agricultural Research Service, a part of the US Department of Agriculture. The second interview was with a new advertising agency that was searching for an art director. To test my skills, the advertising director asked me to develop a series of advertisements for a bank client of theirs. I did several proposals for them and a few days later they asked me to come to work for them, but just prior to their call, I had received an offer for the job in the Federal Civil Service at a grade level 7, and I accepted it. Pay grades at the time went from a GS-1 to a GS-18. * Each pay grade had within it ten pay increase steps that were tied to service years and satisfactory performance on the job. The first three came one year apart. The next three came two years apart and the remaining ones were three year apart. This also coincided with an increase in paid sick and annual leave, the first year being two weeks of each.

*see Appendix five, on page 336

Designs by the author for the USDA Agricultural Service. Left: The symbol for the successful screwworm eradication program. Right: Symbol for the grasshopper control program.

My new boss told me he could either hire me direct if I had a 3.8 college grade average or he could hire me off the national list of Federal job applicants if I was on the list, which I was not. So he hired me on a temporary status until I got on the list. I had to take a lengthy entrance exam, given twice a year, covering a variety of subjects, including algebra, which I barely passed in high school, English, geography, and science. It was, in short, a college entrance exam. The first time I took it, I flunked it due to my poor math skills. Annette found a study guide, about an inch thick, which we studied together and the next time we both took it and passed. This was the start of my 30-year career as a civil servant for the Federal government.

I told my supervisor in Blacksburg that I had accepted a job offer and would be leaving in two weeks. The next day they offered me $5,000 per year, a $1,000 increase to stay, but that offer was still short of the pay I would receive for the D.C. job. So after one year in Blacksburg, we moved to Alexandria, Virginia.

My parents and Annette's parents were delighted to have us near them again. Mother was working as the superintendent of nurses for a small hospital in Alexandria, Circle Terrace Hospital, where her nursing friend, Lou, was the manager. Lou had known our family for some time. She was the anesthesiologist who put me under when I had my broken wrist set at Alexandria Hospital, after a playground accident at Groveton Elementary when I was in the first grade. She liked to tease me later in life about how I came out of the anesthetic and threw up on her. Lou was always a generous person; when she heard we were transferring back to Alexandria she offered to rent us a two-story brick house that was owned by and was across the street from Circle Terrace. She also saw to it that the hardwood floors were refinished and a new Amana refrigerator was installed before we moved in. The rent was very reasonable.

It was an ideal location. I could take the bus to work in D.C. and on the weekends, we could visit both parents. We learned to play bridge from my parents and enjoyed many an evening playing cards with them while the children slept in the back bedroom. Both grandparents were kind and gave generously to the children, especially at Christmas. We had some very good times together.

When we moved into the hospital house, my brother Wally showed up from West Virginia where he was working as a fisheries biologist for the US Fish and Wildlife Service. He spent one very hot weekend helping us paint the kitchen just before we moved in. Wally is one of those people who can negotiate, wheel and deal, with just about anyone. He especially gets pleasure out of forcing salesmen to lower their price bit by bit until they wonder how they ended selling something at cost instead of making a profit. This is a talent I do not have. While we were trying to paint and settle the house, Wally took the Cadillac limousine to a nearby car dealer and managed to get us a used red and black Nash Rambler station wagon. He showed up at our door and asked, "What do you think about that car?" We were astounded. The Cadillac, with its cardboard and plastic window where the power window would no longer work, was gone and in its place was a cute little Nash station wagon, which we drove for the next five years. God bless Wally.

1963, Alexandria, Virginia, used Nash Rambler

The house was two-story brick with the front facing due west. In summer, the heat trapped in the brick was horrific because the afternoon sun faced the entire front of the house. At bedtime we sweated and slept fitfully until 3 AM when the place finally cooled down.

A city bus route two blocks from the house allowed me an easy commute to work at the Department of Agriculture, located on the south side of the mall in the District. I purchased two inexpensive suits, my first since high school, from Sears Roebuck for a total of $40.00. They were cheap but they did the job for several years.

The office had a full-time photographer, another artist a few years older than I and a middle-aged woman artist, who had bright red hair and was artistically flamboyant in every possible manner. I am embarrassed to say that we made fun of

Cover photo taken in "Sylvania", by the author

her dramatic shenanigans behind her back. About two months after I started work, they hired another artist and assigned him to design booklets for the Agricultural Research Service, our parent organization. With the exception of the redhead and the art director, we were all under thirty. A year later they promoted both the new man and me to a GS-9 and the next year they promoted him to a GS-11. I could find no reason for them to promote him before they promoted me, so I started looking for another job.

A fellow worker came in shortly after that and, waving the job advertisement in his hand, said that a GS-11 art director job for the U.S. Forest Service was available in Wisconsin. The next morning he announced that his wife said she was not about to move out of the Washington, D.C. area, so he gave the announcement to me. (A few years later they divorced.) A week later, I was interviewed for the job, and a month later, we were on our way to Milwaukee, with the government paying all the moving expenses including the family drive there. We were living high.

* * *

The U.S. Forest Service, Eastern Region, Milwaukee

We settled twenty miles west of Milwaukee in the small Midwest town of Waukesha, which provided me with the opportunity to ride in a carpool with several other Forest Service guys. The job was a dream. I supervised two other artists and became the official photographer for the regional office, which covered a nineteen state area. The Office of Information had eleven employees. They were all great people.

It is almost impossible to hire additional people in the government, but you can purchase additional equipment that will increase production and improve the product. This made the people working for you happy and made you look like an outstanding manager. So that is what I did. When I arrived, there was no system of keeping track of the many jobs we were doing. So I found a short memo form, printed by the government, which had a built in carbon copy that could be used as a job request form. I built a letter rack so I could put each of these carbon copy memo job lists in an individual location on the rack. This let everyone, including the two other artists, easily see what jobs needed to be done, and it showed the incoming client our entire workload at a glance, thereby reassuring them that their job would be done in the order that it was requested.

Author at work in Milwaukee

The work as a photographer gave me an artistic outlet that I had not enjoyed before. I had taken one college class in photography, but this was a new responsibility. My assignments included illustrations for publications, field trips to document agency work, and meet-and-greet shots of people getting awards. I learned how to operate new equipment, such as a big 4 x 5" camera that was great for outdoor photography.

The *Speed Graphic,* (no longer in use), was the classic camera used by press and sports photographers in the 1940's. It was big, heavy and required the photographer to carry a number of film carriers, each holding two 4 x 5" negatives. The flashgun used bulbs that were good for one shot only. By the time I got to use the camera, the Honeywell Corporation had created a battery operated repeatable flash that not only flashed but automatically read the amount of light coming back off the subject and shut down or opened the light system so that the exposure was perfect.

The 35-millimeter camera of the day was the Japanese made Nikon single lens reflex, which I used for taking color slides that were in turn used to illustrate presentations by the regional director and others. The Japanese cameras were taking over the market from the German made Leica, which had been the standard professional camera for years. The newest system for projecting slides was the Kodak Carousel slide projector, which had a round drum that held the slides and sat on top of the projector. The slides rotated around, allowing one slide to drop into the slot in front of the lamp lens assembly. This could be combined with a second Kodak Carousel projector, using a dissolve control box that plugged into each projector. The dissolve machine would alternate between the two projectors, turning one off as the other turned on, creating a fade in, fade out sequence that was very effective.*

On one occasion the regional director had a speaking engagement at the University of Wisconsin in Madison, 78 miles due west on the interstate highway. I went ahead several days prior to the speaking date, and scouted out the large auditorium and discovered that the Kodak slide projectors with the dissolve control would project from the glass projection booth in the back if I used a ten by twelve foot screen and telephoto projection lenses. We did not have a screen that large, so I rented one from a photo shop near our office. It came rolled up in a metal tube that sat on the floor. The screen inside was then pulled up to a heavy-duty center post that held it in place. The office had a talented handy man that had a fix-it shop, plus an official government pick-up truck that I borrowed to haul the screen to the university early on the day of the presentation.

The morning of the presentation, I drove to the photo shop with the pickup and found the 8-foot bed in the back a little short for the 12 foot screen. No problem. I put one end in the bed, against the tailgate, and leaned the other forward over the cab and tied it down in several places with twine cord so it would stay in place, and started west on the interstate. I barely got out of the city when I heard a scraping sound and a thump as the weight of the screen broke the twine and slid off the truck.

* Computers, digital photography, and PowerPoint presentations have eliminated the need for slides and projectors.

As luck would have it, the screen fell crosswise on the pavement in the lane I had just travelled. I looked in the rear view mirror and could not believe my eyes. Of all the vehicles that could have been following me down the highway, I was unlucky enough to have a cement mixer loaded with concrete right on my tail, and it ran over the screen with all four sets of tires; thump, thump, thump, thump.

I backed up and hauled the road-killed, flattened screen off the  road, loaded it back on the truck and returned to the photo shop. Fortunately for me they had a second screen, so the U. S. Forest Service bought the first one. We thought we could salvage it but after letting it sit in the shop for two years, we threw it away. The regional director's slide show went very well. I am grateful no one got hurt.

Author, in uniform, doing field photography using the Nikon 35 mm for slides and the Speed Graphic camera for black and white publication illustrations.

This was the first job that required me to do field work, so they purchased an official U.S. Forest Service uniform for me, something I was proud to wear. The Forest Service, like most other Federal and State organizations, has thousands of employees who consider it their job to protect the nation's resources, National Forests in this case.

Started in 1908 by Gifford Pinchot, the Service has grown in responsibility so much that its mission is now officially one of multiple use of the lands. This includes not only forestry and lumber harvest, but also research, and recreations such as camping and skiing. It is a difficult job because several of the missions conflict with each other (logging and wilderness for example).

The Forest Service is in the Department of Agriculture because harvesting timber is similar to harvesting corn. It just takes a little longer for the crop to grow. The National Park Service gets all the natural wonder jewels to manage and the Forest Service, along with the Bureau of Land Management, and the Fish and Wildlife Service, gets the other stuff. And when the Forest Service gets to manage a semi- natural resource jewel the Park Service comes along and takes it. This management relationship has been going on for some time. There have been political moves to force the Forest Service into the Park Service's parent organization, the Department of Interior, but so far, all attempts to accomplish this have failed. Forest service employees do not want to be a part of the Department of Interior, because they fear the primary mission of the Park Service to preserve will override the Forest Service's multiple use missions.

Most employees throughout government, no matter where they work, take great pride in providing outstanding service to the public. Like many public service employees, they put in many free uncounted overtime hours because they believe in what they are doing. Most taxpayers have no idea that the country is managed, not by bankers, lawyers or carpenters, but by hundreds of thousands of public servants who dedicate their lives to keeping the various systems that support our nation alive and functioning. The politicians, congress, governors, and mayor's get the publicity, but it is the everyday civil service workers who keep the wheels of society steadily and inexorably moving in the right direction.

Food inspection, aviation security, agricultural research, forest and land protection, air traffic control, military and national defense, judicial and supreme courts, immigration, drug testing, law enforcement, housing, public health, and security, are just a few examples that come to mind.

Paul Steucke Sr.

Publishing Illustration emphasizing clean water stored by the National Forests.

When I took the Forest Service job, we rented a house in a cute Midwestern town that also served as a bedroom community for people who worked in Milwaukee. Our commute of five employees was always driven by one fellow who had a permanent leg brace on his ankle. About two months after I started work, one of the other commuters mentioned that he was being transferred to another city and

Our own Waukesha house: 3 bedrooms, basement, one bath: $15,000, 1965

was having trouble selling his house in a weak housing market. He had only been in it for eight months, and he asked if any of us would be interested in buying it. I told him we would love to purchase it, but we had no available money. The next day he offered to sell us the house with no down payment, no exchange of money - just pick up his Veterans Administration loan and monthly payments. It was the housing arrangement of a lifetime, with an angel as the broker. We paid an attorney $100 to draw up the paperwork, took over the three-bedroom house and the $15,000 mortgage, lived in it for three years and sold it for $3,000 profit. It got us started. It was a true Godsend for a very poor family of six.

When we first moved to Waukesha, I mistakenly made a double deposit in our checking account that put us $500 in the hole - money we spent on the move. Money we did not have. So, like many young people, I asked my parents for a loan to cover the gap. They sent us the money, and then, later, told us we did not have to pay it back, a generosity we sincerely appreciated. We never had to ask them for a loan again, nor did we ever ask or receive money from Annette's parents.

An added benefit of moving was that we would be within a day's drive to Annette's three aunts in Rochester, Minnesota. They were not married, had no children, and were always delighted with our company. Like many women of the WWII era, they were without partners, largely, because over 400,000 American servicemen, potential husbands, died in the war. That is one price of war that is seldom mentioned.

That summer the aunts in Rochester wanted to go on vacation and take along our two oldest children, so Annette went up to Rochester to house sit and keep her grandmother company while they drove to the Grand Canyon National Park. Unfortunately, in their haste to depart they took Annette's luggage by mistake, so Annette called me in Waukesha and asked me to bring her some clothes to wear. The second weekend they returned, prior to my departure back home, and offered to let me drive their Volkswagen convertible home and bring it back on my return trip the following Friday. Annette and the children stayed in Rochester.

The afternoon was sunny, crisp and pleasant. I drove down to Winona, where the Fish House restaurant is located and then headed south on State Route 14, which parallels the Mississippi River. Everything went fine for about 45 minutes and then the car quit running in fits and starts. There was plenty of gas in the tank, so I saw no alternative except to drift off the road onto a side street, lined with five small houses. Here the car quit and would not restart. I walked to the nearest house and after explaining my situation, was invited into the house (where the family was eating dinner), called Annette in Rochester, explained my situation, and gave her the name of my location.

I went out and sat in the car and waited, and waited, and waited. The sun was beginning to set, and the air was getting cooler, so I put on my lightweight yellow windbreaker and started walking up and down the side road to relive the boredom and keep warm. The road was about three football fields long with a hump in the middle that was just high enough to block my view of the car.

After walking the road, I crested the hump to see a tow truck, with the Volkswagen attached, moving away from me toward the open highway. I ran, waved my arms, and screamed, "Wait!" only to see the truck pause briefly at the stop sign and then disappear down the highway. I was in shock. It was beginning to get dark, so I walked down to the intersection and faced the oncoming traffic, waiting and watching for Annette and her aunts to pick me up.

I waited and stared into the traffic, examining each car on the four-lane highway, until the cars came and went in a mind-numbing blur. I saw Annette and the aunts drive past on the *opposite* side of the highway headed back toward Rochester. It was a disappointing moment.

As the evening twilight faded into darkness, I stared into the oncoming headlights, thinking that surely my bright yellow windbreaker, along with the name of the place I had given them, was enough for them to find me. And I was afraid that the moment I left my place alongside the highway they would pass. Slowly the lights in the neighboring houses went out until they were all dark, and I was loathe to wake up the owner of a dark house just to use their telephone.

Traffic dissolved to almost nothing as the night continued, and finally at midnight I decided it was time to do something besides stand on the side of the road and shiver in the cold. I started walking north. The first little town I came upon, like the houses left behind, was totally dark. I looked, but could not find a public telephone, so I started walking again. The center grass median strip of the divided highway seemed safer than walking the edge, so I plodded on in the dark, with only an occasional car going past, until one car made a point of slowing down on the other side of the road, as if inspecting me. A few minutes later, the same car came up the other side of the road behind me, and driving very slowly, they asked me if I wanted a ride. There were three guys and two girls in the car, all under the age of twenty. I told them I was OK walking, but they continued to drive at my walking pace, laughing, and asking me where I was from and where I was going. I became uncomfortable with the situation and kept walking up the grass median. They continued to offer me a ride, so I finally said yes and got in the back seat between one guy and a girl. They laughed and joked and we drove off in the dark, with me laughing on the outside and praying on the inside,

Thirty minutes later, true to their word, they pulled into the parking lot of the now dark Fish House restaurant, and I called Annette from the pay phone. It must have been close to two in the morning. Everyone at the aunt's house was ecstatic that I was alive. I was pretty happy about it myself. Annette had called the police, who dusted the whole thing off by telling her that I was probably on a drunken spree and would show up in the morning. It was three AM before we all got back to Rochester.

The car? Well, the aunt that owned it decided to buy a new one so she called the dealer in nearby La Crescent and told him to go get it. When the aunts called the dealership to locate me, the tow truck driver said he had not seen anyone with the car, so, he just hitched it up and towed it away. Annette and the aunts thought I was dead for sure. There were moments when I thought I might be headed that way myself.

* * *

The little Nash Rambler my brother Wally found for us in Alexandra was giving out. One evening we left the Aunts' place in Rochester with four children and gear, and departed for home, a distance of 262 miles. After several hours on the road, the car started running rough and using huge amounts of gasoline. I closely monitored the gas gauge, evaluated the remaining distance, and finally decided we were not going to make it. I turned off the main highway and looked for a town, any town, which might have a gas station. Everything in town was closed. Finally, in desperation, I headed for the police station. There was no other choice. The police called the owner of the only gas station in town, and the nice man got out of bed, drove to the station and gassed up our little car. We made it home. I never had the problem again and still do not know what caused it to occur. The children, all under the age of seven, slumbered through it all in the back. The rambler served us well but it was wearing out, so I went looking for something newer.

A Ford dealer on the edge of town had several used station wagon style cars that I thought would work for us, so I signed a contract to buy one and told the salesman I had to go get a loan. The bank near my office in Milwaukee told me I should buy a new car, not a used one, because he could not loan money on a used car as they make poor collateral. The loan officer took out a little blue book listing car prices, chose a basic Chevrolet, full size station wagon (the only extra on it was a radio) and told me exactly what to pay for it. His calculated price included a $500 commission for the dealer. Anything above the price he gave me would be out of my pocket, money we did not have. The first new car dealer I went to was aghast at the price I offered. I told the dealer right up front that the bank said this car, their car, was worth just the amount the bank quoted and that included $500 for the dealer commission. There was no room for negotiation. It was take it or leave it. They took it, and we drove home in our first new car, a 1967 blue Chevrolet, full size station wagon that could seat seven. We were thrilled!

* * *

My reputation with the Forest Service's Eastern Region office grew with each opportunity. The graphic art training and newly acquired photography skills, along with my management philosophy of treating everyone kindly, resulted in my receiving a promotion from a GS-11 to a GS-12 in a year. The extra money was quite helpful.

I had a major assignment with one of our two writers to a place in Northern Michigan called Sylvania. A 640-acre area of pristine woods and lakes that had been purchased by a wealthy family a generation ago. They made it a private hunting and fishing retreat. Having transferred down to heirs it was now being donated to the Federal Government as a sizable tax deduction. The transfer was to take place in a few months, and the Service wanted photographs of the various lakes and lodges.

Mark Bosch, a recently hired Montana author, and I drove up to the area. While he interviewed local people and gathered a feeling for the place, I photographed the property with 35mm and 4 x 5 Graflex cameras. Several times the Sylvania family property guards raced across the lake with their boats to check us out. A month or so later, we went back to help document and dedicate the official takeover of the property. President Lyndon Johnson's' wife, nicknamed, Ladybird, along with the Secretary of the Agriculture Department and a caravan of Secret Service staff, came to the official transfer ceremony held on site in Northern Michigan.

As the singer-songwriter Pete Seeger wrote, "The times, they are a-changing," and the times were also a-changing in the employment world. We had a newly hired young woman in the office, a graduate forester. In preparation for the official ceremony, she was assigned to ride with me to the site, about a four-hour drive from the office in Milwaukee where we, as the staff working the event, were to stay several nights in a local motel. This was the first time I had been placed in the position of travelling alone with a women who was not family, and I was uncomfortable about having her ride up in the car with me. So I asked the only African American employee we had in our office to ride with us. Lou was a big, gregarious person who had two college degrees. I liked him, everyone did. I do not know what his job was at the event but I was glad to have him as a riding partner on the way up. He was also pleased at my invitation to share a motel room. Several years later, I met him and his family in Los Angeles while I was on a business trip and they had me out to their beautiful home for a family dinner. I always enjoyed his spirit and company.

Mark and I were informed, while on our Sylvania trip, that our attendance would be required at a one-week training seminar that started the day we got back. I do not know why we were not told about this before we left for Sylvania. The result, however, was that our wives would have to take care of the families while we were gone. A single parent chore that management does not take into consideration.

Ladybird Johnson; Sylvania, Michigan

One of the benefits of working for the government turned out to be training, which I was grateful to receive. One course, Management Grid, was the first of many that I would take over my federal career. Developed in 1964 by Robert Blake and Jane Mouton, it allowed each of us to determine our current management style, whether it was more or less effective on a continuum, and change it, if we so desired. They taught us about The Grid, which is a graph that has nine numbers up the left side and nine numbers across the bottom. Our answers to management questions placed our management style somewhere within the grid. The left side on a scale of 1 to 9 was Concern for People, and the bottom scale, again 1 to 9, was Concern for Production.

The first day the trainers put us into prearranged groups of ten, enclosed each group in a room, and gave each an assignment to produce a document – any document. This sounds, and should have been easy, but it was not, because we had no leadership and no guidance. I now believe the intent of the training was to teach us that someone in a group has to take the risk of leadership or nothing will get done. At least that is one lesson I learned. This class went all day, from breakfast to bedtime, for seven days. One group was smarter than the rest of us. The regional pilots and medical staff said screw the system and went home every night. That is what I call leadership!

Another exercise the trainers ran us through is now a classic training tool that taught me not to make quick judgments about people. Each of us filled out a questionnaire that asked us what we did for a living, past employment, hobbies, etc. Two days later, they split us into groups, put us in various conference rooms and told us we were part of a fictional group of people who had just survived an airplane crash in a remote location. No one died or was hurt, but our survival depended on what we did as a group. After about six hours, we managed to come up with a plan that might save everyone from dying in the wilderness. The objective of the exercise was to learn what ideas and skills could be found among each of us that might make survival possible. Like most of the other groups, we did poorly, because in our haste to solve the problem, we overlooked the many talents that each person revealed in the questionnaire.

For example, one person had training as a paramedic, another was a certified private pilot, yet we failed to find that out, and lost significant information that would contribute to survival.

At another seminar, we were given a test to determine our own, and others, management and personality traits. Meyers and Briggs, a mother- daughter team, developed a questionnaire to identify the best persons, (mostly women), who could do the jobs of men who went to war. It is an accurate management tool that has been used extensively since it was first published in 1962. Taking the test and determining one's own management traits is an eye opener. It does not change anyone, but it does allow you to see yourself and others in a new way that provides a reasonable understanding as to why people do what they do in management.

I was also given training in how to manage public meetings, the government's legal response to persons seeking information under the Freedom of Information Act, and government printing regulations, to mention just a few of the educational opportunities that were provided to me. These courses increased my ability to manage and perform as a government employee. I was, and still am, grateful for the training.

* *

In Milwaukee, we had eleven employees in the public affairs office; two artists, one photographer (me), two writers, two secretaries, an education specialist for schools, the division director and deputy, plus two specialists that handled the newly created Job Corp, a part of President Johnson's 1964 War on Poverty program. Based on the concepts of the Civilian Conservation Corps of the 1930's, the Job Corps has taught over two million adolescents between the ages of 16 and 24 basic vocational and social skills, as well as schooled them to pass the general high school requirements. There are currently 18 Job Corps sites operated by the Forest Service under the guidance of the U.S. Department of Labor. When I worked for the Service the program was just getting started, and the problems of building dormitories, classrooms, food service,

septic and water systems, providing heavy equipment shops and teaching the young corpsman how to behave, work, and study was enormous. All this took place in rural locations, which was a new experience for these teenage inner city kids. The Service was shocked to discover that 50% of the corpsmen population of 16 to 24 year olds, could not read or write. The city school systems had just passed them on or they quit school. In a very short time, the Service had to create a new curriculum to teach English, basic math, and social skills. The program helped thousands of inner city youth, including heavy weight boxing champion, George Foreman, who credits Job Corps with giving him a new start on life.

Our region covered 19 states, from the Atlantic Ocean to the Mississippi river, and at one time, we had 24 Job Corps camps in operation. I went on many field trips to photograph the camps for use in publications. President Nixon, for political reasons, closed half the sites when he came into office, a sad decision indeed.

The annual budget cycle for the Federal government was from July to July, but Congress could not easily do its job of approving the budget on time, so they shifted to October to October. Of course within a few years the same problem reoccurred, so moving it to October actually accomplished nothing. The federal government, with the exception of certain necessary functions like security and air traffic, control is not allowed to operate without a congressionally approved annual budget. If the budget is not approved by October first of each year, the government closes down. It has happened a few times, especially when a Republican controlled congress and a democratic president cannot agree on the budget.

Federal agencies have learned to use all the money that congress gives them each year, because, if you turn that money back in, then it obviously means you do not need that much money, and the next year congress will reduce the amount of money you get. This penalty for reducing expenses has eliminated any incentive to save, so agencies sometimes go into a spending spree the last two weeks of the budget year. This is bureaucracy at its worst.

I got involved in this one year, when the regional budget officer came to me and said, "We would like you to spend a million dollars purchasing printing, photo and art supplies for the two largest Job Corps sites in our region... in the next three days before the end of the budget cycle." He then sat a 24-inch high stack of vendor catalogs on my desk and left. This is an outrageous example of poor fiscal planning, but I did my best by going through the booklets and ordering stuff that was almost beyond my imagination. Stainless steel sinks for photo labs, expensive Nikon cameras (in multiple units), and printing presses. I had no time to make sure these items were compatible with each other.

I did not spend a million, but I spent a lot of money. Several years later I was in a conversation when someone said, "You should see the equipment that is warehoused at some of the Job Corps centers. It makes you wonder what they were thinking when they ordered it." It made me wonder too.

At this time, two new managers came into my life. One was the director of the regional public information office and the other was his deputy. They turned out to be outstanding supervisors that I worked with, on and off, for the next six years. Annette had them out to our house for dinner while they waited for their families to move to Milwaukee. It was a great evening that established a bond for a lifetime.

Three years later the director, whom we called The Bear, became the national director of public affairs for the Forest Service. He transferred to Washington, D.C., and about two months later called me at home and offered me a promotion to a GS-13 * position.

* Pay for a GS-13 at the time was $1,376 per month less: $96.32 for retirement, $190.76 Federal Tax, $44.58 State Tax, $11.00 Federal Life Insurance, $41.50 Health Insurance, $7.50 Savings Bond, $60.00 Allotment deduction, for a net monthly take home balance of $924.34. (Based on an actual pay slip for the author.) The average price for a new house was $18,000: a new car was $3,500: a movie ticket $1.00.

While in Milwaukee, I created several outstanding slide show presentations for the regional forester and he wanted me to do the same for the chief of the Forest Service in D.C.

I told him I would be happy to do the job, not realizing that his telephone call was an introductory conversation intended to see if I would accept an offer. Thinking it would take weeks, if not months to sell the house, I immediately put it up for sale and three days later received an offer for $18,000, three thousand over what we paid for the house three years earlier.

I called and told him my good news and he laughed saying he would have to work fast on his end to get the job set up, as it had not been advertised yet. I apologized about my naiveté and he went to work creating a committee of three to work on the job process and select me as the winning candidate.

One of my work philosophies was to try and think like the boss and anticipate what he needed before he or she had to ask for it. This not only provided me with training but also highlighted my ability to get things done in a timely manner. It also provided me with recognition and in some cases a mentor.

The Federal government, like many organizations, has supervisors who recognize talented, hard working individuals and want to help them when possible, with training, words of wisdom and promotions. This mentor relationship occurs in all institutions worldwide and is an important informal part of the work system. Of course, there is a negative side to this if the supervisor is just promoting a friend and not a hard worker.

* * *

Forest Service,
Washington, D.C.

A few weeks later, the De Bruin called and formally offered me the GS-13 job. We said goodbye to Waukesha at a generous party provided by the various Forest Service employees living in the area and drove to Washington via a circuitous route that included photographic assignments through several National Forests.

One of the photo locations was a wildlife farm in West Virginia, where Annette and I met two other fellows from the D.C. office that were there to photograph animals. At another location, I photographed a large strip mine coal shovel in southern Illinois. I decided that this immense piece of equipment might look even more impressive if it was photographed at night, so I set my camera on a tripod and, using two additional strobe lights for side lighting, told the operator to swing the arm of the machine 180 degrees. The resulting photo was used as the cover of a national coal magazine.

My new job was the Deputy Manager for the Audio Visual Branch. This was a position I was well qualified for, especially since I had regional experience, but I did not realize that another employee in the office had expected to get the job. An awkward situation, which I did not figure out for a year. I think

it was common knowledge that I had worked for the new director back in Milwaukee, something that did not endear me to my new boss, the director of the audiovisual branch (a GS-14 position). He thought he was going to get to choose his own deputy, his buddy, already working in the office. This man was a know- it-all, who had tapped out the top of his career by going to a national convention to set up and monitor a large Forest Service exhibit that did not arrive on time (he was also responsible for shipping). Therefore, Mr. Right put a sign in the vacant space that said, *Sorry, but the Forest Service exhibit did not arrive.* The Chief of the Service, while at the convention to give a speech, walked past the vacant spot and sign, and did not like the sign or the lack of an exhibit. Combined with past history, and attitude, it ended his career climb in the Forest Service. This is how the system works when a person is incompetent, you cannot easily remove him, but you can go around him. In this instance, I was used as the *go around.*

When I arrived, I discovered that there was a clique of good old boys who consisted of the branch chief, the exhibit guy and a writer. They had all been working together for some time and frequently congregated in the chief's office to swap stories and jokes. I was never a part of these jolly times, and it was clear that I was not part of their fellowship.

My new boss did not know what to do with me. I was not a motion picture man like him or his buddy, so they sent me to several Hollywood motion picture courses, which got me out of the way for a while. It was the first time I had been to Los Angeles, so I toured Universal Studios as part of my training. Perhaps they were hoping I would make a career out of filmmaking. Of course, they no longer made movie films either. This was being done by a separate office staff working directly for the Department of Agriculture, not the Forest Service. Our staffs were merely technical advisors.

In desperation, the manager assigned me the task of revising the 500-page manual of rules for the national and regional audiovisual offices - not a significant task. I worked in the regional office doing audiovisual work for three years and I never saw the manual. He gave me no instructions, no interim reporting, just rewrite it. I am sure he did not know what he wanted either. I spent several months slowly retyping the entire manual with a few format changes. I had no idea what I was supposed to be doing with it. Of course, when I finished he wondered what I had done, which was not much.

That project failed, so he next sent me off on a series of two-week photographic expeditions to provide our vast photographic files with outstanding photos of the services we provided the public.

If an executive or research person writes a paper for publication or presentation, they are given credit for their work. However, they do not own it, nor can it be copyrighted. All works created by federal civil service employees are the property of the government.*

* I later discovered an interesting development with regard to the creation and use of federal government work. A private legal organization in Atlanta, Georgia, The Collegiate Licensing Company has registered government names as Trademarks. Accordingly, they are allowed to charge a royalty or deny the use of these names. This is an entirely separate realm from copyright. I believe what they have done is unlawful, but it remains until someone takes the issue to court.

It is also common practice in the art world, as in a motion picture for example, to credit creative work. An executive or agency director that travels to Phoenix, Paris, or Minneapolis, (or wherever), is given credit for their presentation, even if they did not write it. Traditionally, artists are not a politically organized group of people. They tend to bend the other direction if anything. Writers and editors on the other hand, like lawyers, tend to be well organized, and hence they usually rise in the management career chain while artists do not.

All Federal government printing is controlled by the Government Printing Office, or GPO. It is not managed by artists; it is managed and run by writers, some who have not written anything for years, however they keep a tight hold on government printing nationwide. One of their many regulations (we are talking books of regulations) says that government artists and photographers shall not receive a by-line or credit for their work.

Even artists who do not work directly for the government but sell their work to the government cannot receive a credit line.

My position as president of the Society of Federal Artists and Designers gave me an opportunity to write an article related to this subject in the August 1971 issue of the *Industrial Art Methods* magazine. It did not make my Forest Service supervisor or his supervisor very happy as they received a verbal reprimand from GPO for the article, even though they had nothing to do with it. I did not write this article as a Forest Service employee, so I did not pass it by them for approval. The text is as follows:

From the Inside Out

By Paul Steucke, former President of the Society of Federal Artists and Designers, and a designer, photographer, inventor and administrator. Paul has been a federal employee in the visual information and communications profession for the past 10 years, with a B.A. in

Commercial Art from the Commonwealth University of Virginia, and is presently employed with the U.S. Water Resources Council.

Government art appears to have earned a connotation all its own. To those outside government employment, it seems to be an outdated style of art. To those inside government the style is the product of an environment that suppresses creativity, and encourages indirectly the trite oddity called "government art." The designer in government detests the image and the style; and he/she strives daily to change it. Changing it is not easy. Every successful piece of Federal visual media has had to surmount a mixture of obstacles that have been established to control the designer, producer, and photographer.

On the average, government designers must tolerate poor working areas, extremely strict printing and paper restrictions, unimaginative supervision, and the lack of creative atmosphere. Take creativity as an example. How can you create something new and exciting when the company wants an image of being conservative, staid, and reliable? After all, who wants willy-nilly unreliable government?

> **Government art appears to have earned a connotation all its own.**

Qualification standards and pay scales for Federal creative personnel have been set too low to recruit and retain talented individuals. Visually creative people, with the exception of a few, either leave the government within a year or two, or move up to a supervisory position where the salary pays enough to raise a family. In 1971, the approximate starting salary for most artists and designers was $7,794 with a top at the end of a career of $18,906 as a photo/art supervisor, and $22,328 as an art director.

It is interesting to compare different design departments in government. The Society of Federal Artists and Designers' annual exhibition competition indicates that some design shops consistently produce high quality work while others do not. Good creative supervision can cultivate creative thinking and teamwork. We all know the overall office atmosphere resulting from physical conditions and management is critical to creative production of any product. A quick look at the visuals produced by a federal shop or the winners in a show will tell you if the management supports creativity.

Teamwork appears to be an unknown method of production in government. Rough ideas, layout, selection of type, paste up, finished art, and in some cases even copy writing are handled by one or two individuals. This lack of interaction and varying opinions stifles the creative growth of the professional designer. This happens within agency as well as between agencies and departments. If a department selects a particular style or quality of illustration and they do not have the talent within the department to do the job, they will contract for the talent thru a commercial firm, even though there are equally talented personnel located in other federal agencies. There has been no effort by the federal government to catalog or coordinate the talents of the visual communication personnel in its employment.

High quality assignments which have built in requirements for color, good paper, quality printing, and design are sent from the government to a commercial firm because the agency does not trust the average federal designer to handle the job. As can be expected, office morale and experience goes down as the plush jobs go out.

Printing and paper restrictions, referred to as specifications, are an important factor in limiting the design capability of government art today. Congress, administrators, directors, and printers have established and closely supervise these restrictions, and they are difficult to change. When a designer has to write letters, draw up justifications, and plead to allow the use of type vertically on a page then it's time the designer is allowed to have a full voice in setting government printing and paper specifications.

Now you know why the visually creative individual in the federal government must break the tradition and the bureaucratic bonds of government art in order to become an excellent designer, artist, or photographer. It is not easy, but it is being done here and there.

The Society of Federal Artists and Designers recognizes the difficulty of achieving excellence in government design and so encourages individuals to be creative by rewarding their effort in the Society's annual competitive exhibition which displays the standards of excellence that are achieved and established by the creative individuals who know how to break out of government art.

This country was conceived with the understanding that people can and should challenge the establishment. If those longhairs,* Washington and Jefferson did it, so can we. That is about it – from the inside out.

* Long hair on men was fashionable when this article was written. The political statement made by long hair changed when construction workers started wearing long hair with hard hats. White-collar workers then went back to short haircuts.

The following year the people who created the society decided to transfer all the authority and funding to a new artist group. I voted no on this maneuver, but they did it anyway, and several years later, neither group was in existence. Two years later the National Endowment for the Arts started sponsoring national training seminars for federal artists.

* * *

My new Forest Service boss still did not know what to do with me, so he sent me out to photograph the western National Forests, in what was an eye opening adventure for a kid who grew up on the east coast. One memorable trip sent me to Albuquerque, New Mexico, to take photos of several Job Corps centers, and then to the National Forests on the West Coast until I ended up in Los Angeles on my last night before returning to D.C.. I wrote a letter every day to my wife expressing my awe in what I saw in the West.

Landing in Albuquerque in the late afternoon and renting a car, I drove to a small town that was near the Job Corps site. The late evening turned into night and the lights of towns showed clearly in the dry cool desert climate, which in my naive eastern way seemed to be just a few minutes away. The more I drove, the more I discovered that the clear air and flat country was deceiving me. Those brief minutes turned out to be 25 minutes or more. That is when I finally realized that the lights of the towns I was looking at were forty or fifty miles away. It was an *ah-ha* moment for me.

They liked my photos so they soon sent me out again for two weeks, this time to the Northwest. I arrived in Seattle, again late in the day, obtained a rental car, crossed Puget sound on a State Ferry and spent the night in a small motel near the Olympic National Forest. Two weeks later and 1,000 miles down the road, I ended up at San Francisco.

As a result of my regional slide presentations, I was asked to build and help put on an international slide show on Forest Service wildlife management. The Chief of the Forest Service was to present it in Austin, Texas. Someone located a wildlife

Half Dome, Yosemite

Grand Tetons

Photos taken by the author while on Forest Service photography trips

expert in Pennsylvania who over the years had collected a beautiful and comprehensive collection of color slides depicting big game animals. The local district ranger and I met this fellow, had dinner at his home, and after reviewing the slides, purchased them for a reasonable sum of money. They were worth every nickel. Good big game photographs are hard to find.

As I mentioned earlier, the Kodak Carousel slide projector system included an electronic device that allowed one projector to come on just as the other one was going off, creating the ability to dissolve one slide into another on the screen. The writer of this slide show had included numerous graphs and charts illustrating the wildlife patterns of the animals. As charts or graphs, they were boring, but it occurred to me that they could be made more interesting if the bars and numbers on the charts were dissolved from one projector to another, back and forth, thereby building the graph, as in a movie. We went to a commercial exhibit firm and using their outstanding artists created great animal cartoon characters to go along with the graphs.

I accompanied the Chief on his trip and handled the projection from the massive elevated glass enclosed booth in the rear of the auditorium. There was one scary moment that taught me something about travel and slide presentations. To protect the images I had mounted them between two pieces of glass. However, the east coast air trapped within the slide was more humid than the dry air in Texas, so as a slide sat in the projector, heat vaporized the moisture trapped within.

Each slide took a minute to heat up, and then water bubbles appeared on the slide and the projected screen image. It didn't look like boiling water, however; it looked for all the world like the slide was burning. There was nothing I could do but let the heat boil off the humidity and clear the slide, because each slide illustration was coordinated with the chief's talk about wildlife management. Fortunately, the ones that did bubble cleared themselves quickly, but I did have one or two people at the evening reception tell me how concerned they were about the slides burning up. The Chief received numerous compliments about his speech and the slides. I thought I had done an impressive piece of work, though I was grateful I did not have to pay for it.

There were many national and international correspondents at the conference and one from the *National Wildlife Magazine* wanted to interview the Chief about some of the agencies more controversial policies, particularly one called clear cutting.

The author on assignment, clear-cut in Oregon.

I sensed that the Chief did not want to be alone with the reporter, so I walked with him around the gardens for several hours while he was interviewed. I assumed the role of the dumb assistant by asking leading questions when appropriate, so that the Chief could answer my question and make his point. From that moment on, I was a friend of Ed Cliff, Chief of the US Forest Service.

Whenever an agency is criticized by the public and congress, they study it. The answers may be obvious, may have been already studied, but they will study it again in hopes that the criticism will go away or at least die down enough to be ignored. Perhaps the study will support additional funding to solve the problem, or identify other issues. After all, making a hasty decision based on poor research can lead to in inappropriate solution that can make the political leadership look stupid - a position that is to be avoided or one might end up testifying before a congressional committee about it. That is how I became involved in a multi state three-month review of tree harvesting procedures in the United States.

The Forest Service has always had a problem in selling the management process, called *clear cutting* to the public. Certain species of trees reseed and grow best when every tree in the area, except a few seed trees, have been cut down and taken to the sawmill. This is called harvesting, as in harvesting corn. The big difference between corn and trees is that corn grows back to its full height in one year, and trees take generations to grow back. In the interim, the area that has been flattened by clear cutting looks like hell-especially when you can see large areas with no trees on the side of a mountain. From a distance, a clear cut looks like someone took an electric shaver, and instead of shaving the entire mountain smooth, just shaved here and there so that it looks like the mountain has a disease. Also, the stumps that are left along a highway look terrible for generations, and streams clog up with the dirt that runs off the barren hillside, which in turn kills the fish in the streams.

The logging companies love the clear cutting policy because it makes harvesting easy, just bulldoze some roads back and forth across the mountain and haul the trees out. This method of harvest is best suited for the type of trees that grow in western states and the Rocky Mountains.

Trees in the eastern mountain ranges, from New England to Tennessee, are hardwood trees, the kind that shed their leaves in the fall. They do not reseed well in a clear-cut environment, so a forester will go into these forests and mark each mature tree with a paint splash, and just those trees are harvested. This method is called *selective cutting,* and does not leave an ugly scar on the side of the mountain for all to see, hence there is no hue and cry from the public to stop it.

With regard to clear cutting, the Forest Service is caught between nature and wildlife lovers who want pristine woods to walk in and the large lumber companies who want access to trees so Americans will have wood to build houses, thereby making a profit from trees on land the companies never owned or maintained. (By law, a portion of the profit from cutting trees on public land goes to local county governments who use it to support county school systems.) Both of these contrasting groups seek help in obtaining their objectives through political means via their US Senators and Congressman, who in turn apply pressure on the Service to change the policy one way or another. This is usually accomplished by giving a little something to everyone in hopes that it will reduce the political pressure. Sometimes this works and sometimes it just makes matters worse.

When I started working for the Forest Service in 1964, they were hiring professional landscape architects to design the clear cuts so they would be more esthetically pleasing and acceptable to the public. Of course, the cuts that had already been done years before on thousands of acres of public forests could not be improved very much as the visual damage was done.

I transferred to the Washington headquarters in 1967. In 1970 the Service instituted a three-month clear cutting study that sent me on a tour of the United States like never before. To accomplish the study they established a *blue ribbon* committee of Forest Service professionals, the directors of various divisions. These were the big name people of the agency. To make sure these important people could remember what they saw and whom they talked to, the Service's Office of Public Information sent a writer and a photographer to document the review. The writer was to compose the draft and final report, and the photographer's work would illustrate it. I was selected to be the photographer.

The prospect of this trip concerned me because it was to take place in the southern part of the States in May and end in the northern part of the country in July, a venture that separated me from my family at a critical time when my three, pre teen-age, daughters were growing up fast.

When I found out I was going to be gone for three months, I went to the Director of the Information Office and asked for compensation time for the hundreds of hours of time I would be away from my family. Comp time is an unofficial policy wherein a record is kept of the hours an employee *donates* to the agency and allows the employee to use those hours later as if they were vacation time. The director was furious; "This is a wonderful opportunity for you," he said. "You will see the agency from the entire country, work with top officials, and gain a reputation for outstanding work." He paused, "Maybe we selected the wrong person."

Maybe, but of course I could not just quit my job. We lived, like most people, from paycheck to paycheck. We were not poor, but putting shoes and clothing on a family of six was expensive. There was no Wal-Mart, Target or other big box stores with discount clothing. We had no savings, and I was not about to default on my house mortgage, lose my family medical coverage, and go through the process of trying to find a new job. That choice would have to wait for an opportunity to present itself.

Our trip started in Alabama, Louisiana, Mississippi, and slowly, day by day, week by week, we worked our way north; Missouri, Pennsylvania, New York, up to Vermont and then across to Wisconsin, and Minnesota, west into the Rocky Mountains and north. Each time we flew into a major city and took a commuter flight to a smaller city, where we were met by the Forest Supervisor for that particular National Forest and his staff. Day trips consisted of the group convoying into the forest and looking at how the trees were cut down, or how they were replanted, and interpreting the various sizes of growth, depending on how long ago they were planted. The writer listened, took notes, and stood elbow to elbow with the local and national specialists, while I documented the situation in photos.

I quickly realized that trying to coordinate the photos with the writing and the locations of the examples was going to turn the project into a quagmire of photo nonsense. I solved this problem by continuously taking photos of the printed agenda for the day, and writing the location onto a clipboard in large letters and photographing it. This is similar to a movie Clack board that is used at the beginning of each movie segment that is filmed. Thus, the identity of the location and its meaning was automatically fused into the sequence of the black and white film negative as we went along. This turned out to be significant, because I was not the person assigned to identify or edit the thousands of photos at the end of the three-month trip.

The last two weeks we were in Alaska, as far north as you could go in the United States. We flew from Washington, D.C. to Seattle, on to Ketchikan, and then landed on Annette Island, located near the southern tip of the panhandle created by the coastal mountains and Canada. At that time, Ketchikan did not have an airport for commercial jets, or other aircraft, so our large jet aircraft landed on an old military airport built in World War II on the Native Indian Island. The terminal consisted of one very old military Quonset hut, a large shack of sorts.

Parked on the airport was a small fleet of amphibious aircraft built by Grumman Northrop of Canada, flying boats as they are sometimes called. Northrop made several different sizes of these amazing airplanes, and we took a ride to Ketchikan in the largest model, the Grumman twin-engine Goose operated by Ellis Coastal Airways. Based on our schedule, the exciting adventure of taking off and landing in the water daily was something that lasted for almost two weeks.

The geography of the area consists of many long islands, stretching primarily north, and south, with long stretches of salt water, that also run north and south.

In the mornings, we would fly over these numerous islands, landing in logging camp bays where we would disembark by being portaged from the boat-airplane to shore. After several hours of looking at the logging operations, we would get in the Goose and hop to another site for more of the same.

My task was to photograph everything that was going on during our visits. The aircraft, which held 20 people, had a large window in the back right side that gave me a wonderful opportunity to photograph from the air.

One evening on the return flight, we detoured up a narrow fiord full of icebergs that had broken off from a glacier that flowed down the mountains. At the upper end we did several tight turns in a circle to look at the mountain goats on the ridges. Then we headed for Ketchikan by crossing the islands at treetop. The aircraft remained at a set altitude, flat, so to speak, but the mountains came up to greet us as we passed over the ridges. The view reminded me of a circus ride; the

1970: Sea Park at Ketchikan, Alaska. Note three other Grumman Goose aircraft parked in the background. The tide changes in Alaska are so large that docks must be capable of sliding, or riding, up and down on the long poles seen in the photograph.

water was down below, then the shore of an island came into view, then the trees got bigger and closer as we flew over the ridge of the island, and it then dropped off again into another water abyss.

After crossing several of these mountain ridges and waterways, my fellow passengers urgently hollered for me to sit down and buckle up. The next thing I knew we were landing upwind in the water with no power to either engine--a dead stick landing. If this had occurred earlier, while we were in the fiord, we would have crashed into the mountain or the icebergs. If it had occurred while we were approaching a mountain ridge at tree top level, we would have crashed into the mountain. There would have been no alternatives.

The pilot took a long wooden stick from inside the plane, got out of the aircraft as we sat bobbing in the water and walking along the wings, he stuck the stick into the fuel tanks to see if we had fuel. We did, at least in one tank, so he got back in the pilot seat, flipped some switches and valves, started the engines, and took off, arriving safely in Ketchikan harbor. Later I talked to several pilots who flew this type of aircraft and discovered that the pilot had forgotten to turn a valve that allowed fuel to transfer from one tank to another. It was years before I could share this story with my family.

The second week we flew north to Juneau, the State capitol, and Regional headquarters for the Forest Service in Alaska, and repeated our inspection process. The climate in Juneau is dryer. Of course, almost anything is dryer than Ketchikan, where the rainfall can exceed 150 inches per year.

The time zone difference from our offices in Washington, D.C. to Alaska was a difficult adjustment. The longest daylight day of the year is June 22nd and the daylight time difference was seven hours. That means that our 6 PM dinner time in Washington was 11 AM in Alaska; or if viewed the other way around; midnight in Washington is quitting time in Alaska.

People in Alaska are always gracious and they welcomed us with big dinners and refreshments, Of course at 6 PM Alaska time, it was already 1 AM in D.C., and by the time the dinner was over it was 4 AM our time! We were beat when we got back to the Baranof Hotel.

The second day in Juneau we were scheduled to take one of the large state ferries from Juneau to Sitka, via the long north-south waterway called Chatham Strait and Peril Strait, and then fly back to Juneau. This was a long trip as the ferry departs Juneau at 5 AM, arriving at Sitka at 1 PM. An eight-hour boat ride, not counting the return flight back to Juneau.

I shared a room at the hotel with our writer, who decided at 10 PM the night before our departure to check out the saloons in town. These were cute affairs decked out with sawdust floors, wood beam ceilings, peanuts in the shell, and stuffed animals heads on the walls. I reminded him that we had a 4 AM wake up call, but he said he would be back in an hour. I went to bed.

When I woke up, he was out cold on the bed with all his clothes on, even his shoes. He reeked of booze, and I was amazed that he even found his way back to the room. Shaking him did nothing. I got dressed, put my camera gear in order, and shook him some more. Applying a very wet, cold washcloth to his face resulted in a little stirring and some recognition. He got up, went into the bathroom, peed, came back, sat on the edge of the bed, and then slowly fell backward in a flop, his feet still on the floor, still dressed, shoes and all. I wrote a note, left it on the dresser, and went down to the lobby where everyone was waiting. The boss man went up to the room, came back down and said, "Let's go, we can't wait any longer, the ferry will not wait," and off we went. (Ten hours later when we got back to Juneau he told us he had spent the day interviewing important people in town, and that his interviews would be a good thing to put in the report. I don't know as I never saw a final copy.)

The ferry to Sitka was the size of a cruise ship and it gave notice of departure with a loud sounding of the ship horn. The auto deck plates were withdrawn, chains rattled, crewman shouted, sea gulls shrieked and swooped, thick ropes were cast off the pilings, and the boat, shuddering from the increase in engine power, moved into the pink and blue Alaskan sunrise.

Cruise ships also use this route and in the middle of the Peril Strait, our Ferry closed in on one. The Strait is aptly named as it is deep, but very narrow in places, and it may be called Strait but it is anything but straight. The ferry kept pushing the big white cruise ship in what was obviously becoming a race. The speed of both boats became so great that they were heeling to the left or right when making turns through various parts of the waterway. Finally, the cruise ship gave up the game in a place where the waterway was large enough to allow the ferry to overtake it.

Juneau might as well be an island, since there are only a few short roads into or out of the city. The surrounding mountains, covered with snow year round are too tall and plentiful to allow a road to cross. For Juneau, it is either boat or airplane. Locals like to tell the story of two not-so-bright guys who robbed a bank and tried to escape using a stolen canoe. It didn't take long for the police to overtake and arrest them.

Alaska has three major cities: Juneau with a population of 30,711, Fairbanks 35,252, and Anchorage at 374,553. Well over half the state population is in Anchorage and Fairbanks, yet Juneau remains the capitol due to politics and a single bullet that brought down two massive high power lines, one on top of the other, the day the State voted to move or not move the capitol.

The voters of Anchorage and Fairbanks could not agree to let the capitol be moved to either competitive city, so the state legislature compromised on a hiccup in the road north of Anchorage, called Willow, population 1,658. As there was nothing there but a few houses and a gas station, the legislature created a committee to inform the voters what it would cost to move the capitol and build an entire new city to house it in Willow. The committee inhabited by a majority of unbiased legislators, from Juneau, Ketchikan, and Sitka, came up with a move-the-capital price tag that was enormous, outrageous, completely out of sight. The quoted price, established by knowledgeable experts in Juneau, scared everyone, which is just what they wanted. But just to be sure, the legislature, having split Anchorage and Fairbanks into rival parties, went on a spending spree, putting up new office buildings for state workers--in Juneau, of course.

But now the story of the magic bullet. Someone, who hopefully will confess on his or her deathbed, walked into a snow packed mountain valley just south of Palmer, Alaska, on voting day, 1982. This person really knew what they were doing. They carried a high-powered rifle with a mounted scope, leaned against a birch tree, and with careful aim shot the highest power wire that at this particular spot crossed another series of high-tension power lines that were going in a different direction. These are the lines that carry electricity to locations that need large amounts of electrical power; like Anchorage, Palmer, and the Kenai towns of Soldotna, Homer, and Girdwood. These are the lines you see on the top of tall metal towers that could have come out of an Orson Wells movie. This person evidently did not feel comfortable with the out-of-sight building estimate. They wanted to be sure the capitol stayed in Juneau.

The top power line fell on the crossing lines below causing a massive electrical blackout, and instantly over 400,000 voters, half the population of the State, were unable to vote on the capitol move. This incident was investigated by the Alaska State Troopers who determined that the top power line had indeed been severed by a bullet, but no one knows who did it. Strangely enough, this incident is seldom mentioned by the news media or the people in Juneau. There was no opportunity to re-vote. Even so, the vote was 45 percent in favor of moving.

* * *

While in Juneau, at Forest Service expense, I took the opportunity to photograph Kodiak bears which hang out along the wild coastal mountains streams in the spring.

I talked to the regional public information officer, who in addition to helping me arrange the aircraft and Forest Service help, also invited himself along on the project. On the day of departure, there were four of us in the party: the pilot, the forest ranger, complete with rifle large enough to slow down a bear, the regional public information officer, and myself. Fortunately, the pilot was very knowledgeable about the habits of bears in June. They come down to the waters' edge along the swampy inlets and eat the fresh grass that has started to grow after the Alaskan winter.

The pilot explained that bears were spooky about airplane noise, having been hunted that way, and would run into the woods when they saw or heard the plane. So we flew at a high altitude, hoping to spot one that did not run, which even at our height spooked several. Finally the pilot saw one and maneuvering the aircraft down quietly on the far side of a wooded peninsula, landed in the water, taxied over to a small beach and tied the airplane to an overturned stump so it would not float away in the tide.

We gathered ourselves on the beach, me with my heavy telephoto camera gear, the public information man with his cameras, and the forester with the bear gun, and headed into the woods to cross the area between us and the other side. The pilot, having done this before, quietly displayed his vast knowledge and experience by staying with the aircraft. This was my first experience in a natural coastal wooded area, one that was not cleared of timber by a logging operation, and I was shocked by the difficulty in crossing through the forest. Hundreds of trees, some five feet in diameter, lay on the floor of the forest crisscrossing each other like jackstraws. It was climb three feet up onto one, walk most of its length and look for another that went in the general direction of where you wanted to go. The work was exhausting and all I could think about, other than trying to protect my expensive camera gear, was how long it would take a bear to cross this same distance with me as bait. Even with a big rifle, the food chain here was disturbingly obvious. A person could be dinner in seconds.

Eventually, after a great deal of effort, we saw the clearing and swamp on the other side, and there was the bear, all 1,000 pounds, munching on the green grass. He lifted his head once, but the pilot had brought us in on the downwind side, so the bear did not sense we were there until we started taking photos. Then all it took was one click from the first camera and he was off and running into the woods. One tiny almost silent click in the woods. Less than a twig snap. In retrospect, I am glad he ran away from us and not toward us, even though the ranger had the rifle loaded, cocked, and pointed at the bear. I got one- and I mean one- very expensive photo. The trip back across the jackstraw forest was very tiring. That was the only bear photo we got for our effort. My boss in Washington thought I was crazy, but he did not find out about my endeavor until the bills for the rental floatplane came in months later.

My air flight out of Juneau to Ketchikan in the heavy rain and dull overcast was a let down. As we lifted off the odd, lonely rural airstrip on Annette Island, I thought to myself that I would like to come back. Eventually I did.

While in Alaska I discovered that the public information officer in Juneau was going to retire, so when they advertised his job I applied, thinking that my three years of experience in the Milwaukee public affairs office, and my three years in the Washington office, along with my high level friends in the service, would make me an outstanding candidate for the job. However, they selected a forester, a person with a degree in forestry, a common issue with jobs in the forest service. The only staff discipline that could compete with a forester for a job was an engineer. The writing was on the wall, *Look elsewhere!* because I was not a forester. I foolishly sealed my fate by writing a letter to the Chief of the Service, and sending copies to about six other directors I had worked with, telling them in so many words that I was not surprised that they had chosen a forester, because a forester, as we all knew, could do anything.

I realized that my supervisor, the manager of the audio-visual branch, was a permanent part of the bureaucracy and had no intentions of retiring, so I started looking for something new. An opportunity came from an unexpected source and resulted in a major job change that gave me additional training and experience that would eventually result in even better career opportunities.

* * *

A year prior to my big trip for the Forest Service, I joined a volunteer organization that is designed to help people become comfortable speaking in public. *Toastmasters* is an excellent self-help course, that includes a weekly evening meeting with a group, including novices like me, and experienced members, who were the officers and led the Club. The program includes several written books, a notebook, newsletter, and the requirement that you stand up in the group when asked and give a prepared speech on occasion and an impromptu two-minute speech when selected by the chairperson of the evening. The club and the course material help anyone who wants to learn public speaking. It also helped me meet other great people who worked in the area. At one of our weekly meetings, a fellow I met and liked told me that his small federal agency in D.C. was advertising for a GS-14 Executive Secretary, and he thought I might qualify. I applied and in thirty days started work for the U.S. Water Resources Council. It was an enormous step for me, a commercial artist, to wade into the world of writing.

* * *

United States Water Resources Council

The U.S. Water Resources Council was created by Congress in 1962 to coordinate and plan the massive water development projects in the United States. It died in 1982 after making lots of plans but proving totally ineffectual in reeling in and coordinating the costs of these huge projects.

The Council, as the name suggests, consisted of representation from the Departments of Interior, Agriculture, Army Corps of Engineers, Commerce, Housing and Urban Development, Transportation, Energy, and the Environmental Protection Agency, plus four regional river basin commissions. The council director was a Presidential appointee.

This great and grand design for coordination failed because these departments (especially the Army Corps of Engineers with an enormous budget) were not about to coordinate with any other departments.

While the council was made of the actual department secretaries of the various departments, the real work was done on a bi-weekly basis by their designated representatives, aptly called the Council of Representatives. The deputy director was a GS-18 (the highest grade in the civil service system), and the two associate directors were GS-17s. I was a GS-14. When the Council was formed, there was a considerable amount of political maneuvering by the member agencies to get their

WRC logo design by the author

people into key positions. For example, the deputy director came from the Department of Agriculture.

The director was being pressured by the two associate directors to hire an executive secretary--ideally one they recommended, a person who would report to the director, but actually be a *good buddy* of the two associates. These two men knew each other well, played handball together at the gym and did everything they could to, essentially, run the Council. The deputy director, being outside the political loop, was neither a friend of the director nor anyone else on staff, especially the two deputies who thought so highly of themselves. In a way, they had every right to think of themselves as hotshots, since they were GS-17s at the age of 40, an amazing feat.

The Civil Service grading system for pay went from GS-1 to GS-18. In 2009 money, a GS-18 would earn about $180,000 a year. A GS- 14 would earn about $100,000. Richard Nixon, early in his presidency felt that he did not have enough political control of the government because some bureaucrats continued to run the government in a manner not sufficiently in accord with his policies. So he created a Civil Service pay commission and based on its recommendations removed the GS grades 16 through 18 from the regular Civil Service system and placed them in an Executive Service System. He removed part of their Civil Service job protection, (which meant they served at the pleasure of the President of the United States.) One of the benefits of being tenured in the original Civil Service system was that you really had to mess up big time to get yourself fired. You could be shunted into a closet job for the rest of your career, or in the case of a GS-15, get sent to a job in a remote Alaskan location, but an employee was seldom fired. This interesting system meant that every so often in one's career you would bump into one of these people who had crossed the political line in some manner. The system is still in existence.

The director was in a hurry to hire an executive secretary, but he did not want to hire the one recommended by the two associate directors. He figured an inside spy was not what he needed, so in his haste he hired the first candidate he could get...me.

My job was to take notes at the Council meetings, do a summary of each meeting for approval by the director and representatives, prepare and publish an agenda for the next meeting, and submit a variety of information or memoranda to the representatives. I was also the agency public contact person who handled the (very few) inquiries from the news media and the public, especially letters requiring a response from the director or agency. I gave myself the fancy title of Executive Secretary and Public Information Officer.

This job opportunity had to have come from divine intervention; I had no training or experience in writing and was politically very naïve. I was, as they say in the West, a greenhorn. However, it was a grade promotion and a way out of the Forest Service.

Robert, the associate director for administration--and one of the two GS 17 guys-- immediately assumed I worked for him, and the day I came to work he placed me at a desk that was eight feet from his desk. I had no privacy regarding telephone use and everything I did had to go through his secretary, who did not like me, even though she did not know me. It was an awkward set up that made me very uncomfortable.

I had been on board for only two days when I got a lucky break; he left for a weeklong vacation. The first day he was gone, I looked around the office and discovered a small storage room with a door opening into the hallway, but more important, a second door that opened right into the director's office. It was full of storage boxes that I did not even bother to investigate. I asked the director if it was all right with him if I converted that storage room into my office. "Yes," he replied, with a slight grin. I stayed late the next evening, and after everyone had gone, I moved the boxes, piling them next to the associate director's desk right where my desk used to be.

This action meant I did not have the services of a secretary, even an angry one, who was really furious the next morning. How she hated those boxes! My new room had no windows, but that was all right with me. I was politically naive, but I did follow my instincts. I knew I had been selected by the director, and now I henceforth reported directly to him. When Robert returned the following week, he swaggered into my now nicely decorated little office and asked me if I was sure that I wanted to be in such a small room. I told him that I was willing to give up the daylight so I could be of service to the director.

After his return from his vacation, Robert and the other associate suddenly started to be very generous and friendly, inviting me to go out to lunch with them almost every day. We had a good time talking about my past work as a photographer/artist, my family, our dogs, and more. It was very pleasant, and I began to feel at ease. But not for long, after a two-week love fest, I was never asked to lunch again. They knew all they needed to know about me.

The Council of Representatives met every two weeks at a large conference table that accommodated all twelve representatives and the director--with me sitting right beside him. The representatives' staff and our WRC staff sat in chairs around the room that lined the walls. There were about 30 people in attendance. Once a year they held a budget meeting, where the political push and pull regarding what each agency was going to spend its money on for the next year took place. This was big money stuff. Dams, reservoirs, river basin staff, the St. Lawrence Seaway, the Mississippi river barge and lock system, levee construction, dredging of ports, and more were discussed and agreed upon. And suggesting that someone else's project should not be funded or built as planned was political suicide as your pet project might be next on the list. It was without a doubt the most important meeting of the year. Unfortunately, it was my first.

The notes I wrote became blurry shorthand as I wrote as fast as my hand could write, but nothing they said made sense to me. Words, names of projects, even the names of the representatives or what agency they represented were so new to me that I was swamped with information overload. At times the discussion of a topic would plod along for twenty minutes and then suddenly reach a conclusion in one sentence. I did not even realize they had moved on to another subject.

I took my notes, prepared a draft summary of the meeting, and naively gave a copy marked draft to my new luncheon friends, the two associate directors. I thought they might be willing to help me out. An hour later, the director called me into his office and sat me down in a chair beside his desk. He had the drafts I had given to the associates on his desk, both marked up with lots of their red pencil marks, and he was not happy. Picking up the marked copies and looking directly at me he said quietly, almost too quietly, "I think I may have hired the wrong man." He was serious.

From that moment on I documented my work--what I did, who I saw, and what directions I was given. I followed that *cover your ass* procedure and kept it in a CYA file for the rest of my career. A written history has legal merit, whereas verbal history is considered hearsay. I also learned to be very careful about who I trusted in an office environment.

We had recently bought a new house in Reston that we could not easily afford, our three teenage daughters were doing lots of worrisome experimenting with life, and now I had a new job that I did not know how to do and a boss who could send me into Siberia on a moment's notice. I told him this was just a crude first draft that I had sent out to get some early feedback and that I would have my final draft for him in a few days. All of a sudden, I was ill with a terrible feeling in my stomach, and my head would not stop thinking about what had happened.

That night Annette and I went to a long anticipated Ella Fitzgerald concert at the Carter Barron Amphitheatre in Washington, D.C.. Ella was our favorite and the current primo jazz singer, with nine or ten LP vinyl records out, which we had danced to night after night in my in-laws' basement while Annette and I were courting. The seats were up close and expensive, the evening was warm and humid, and I am sure the show was great, but I hardly remember anything about it. All I could think about was *what am I going to do now?* I didn't tell Annette what the director said, for it would have ruined this very special evening, but I was in torment trying to figure out what to do about this disastrous development.

The next morning I mentioned my situation to Ernestine, the director's secretary, a brilliant person who in addition to knowing English far better than I, was politically savvy. Ernestine suggested I talk with the deputy director, who previously worked for the Department of Agriculture (my alma mater).

I did as she suggested. The deputy said he would be happy to review my drafts anytime, and for the next four years, he reviewed every one. That is how I discovered that, in addition to my inept grammatical and format problems, I would never have been able to decipher the politics of each meeting and each subject. The director, even after the deputy reviewed and rewrote my drafts, made changes in what was really now the deputy's draft. I did get more proficient at this task, but even after four years, he was still changing the deputy's work. So finally, I realized that the director used the summaries to mold the meeting results to his liking.

Shortly after I arrived at the WRC, I was given a four-page introduction to a publication the council was preparing to publish. I read that introduction over a period of several days, trying to understand what they were saying. After a week of work, I was able to edit it down to one page that made sense to me and most likely to every other voter who might have to read it. This was my first big lesson in government writing, which is exceeded only by some university academic writing for it's intentionally unintelligibility quotient.

I noticed right away that the agency had no recognizable image, what in the public sector is called a corporate identity. To fix this problem, I created an agency logo and applied it to everything, including the special stationary that went to the Council of Representatives. I intentionally included the words

United States as part of the Council's name to emphasize that although small, we were part of the United States Government.

One other chore I was unprepared for was writing letters of response to people who wrote the director or the agency for information. I had a friendly neighbor who worked for another agency in D.C., and I confided to him that I really did not know much about how to write a letter. He selected a sample of letters he had written at work, and made copies for me. I put them in a three-ring binder, tab marking them by subjects, and copied them until I could write a good letter on my own.

In addition to signing regular letters, every other week I sent out a thick agenda and memorandum packages to the Council of Representatives. These required my signature, and the more I looked at it, the less I liked it. I had been signing my name Paul T. Steucke with the same swooping letter P that I had been taught in grade school. I experimented signing it in different ways until I got one that looked professional, and have been using it ever since. It helped build my confidence, and I think the change had a significant effect on how others looked upon my work. It is amazing how something so small can have such an impact.

One of the most significant steps taken by the Council was an attempt to require the various federal agencies to balance *all* the costs of a water project against the benefits, including environmental costs. For generations most projects were approved based *solely* on the benefits of the project. The costs of relocating people, cutting trees, killing salmon streams, et cetera, were not considered to be part of the cost. The Council, in compliance with the Environmental Protection Act, created a complicated, all-inclusive set of regulations to make sure federal water projects would comply with these requirements. The document, *Principles and Standards for US Water Projects*, was printed in the *Federal Register* on December 21, 1971. I hand-carried the document and printing request to the White House for President Nixon to sign and then to the Government Printing Office for publication in the *Federal Register*. (No, I did not see or even get close to the president.)

A period was set aside for public comment, which, in addition to written comments, included seven days of public hearings split between San Francisco, St. Louis, and Washington, D.C., for a total of 46 hours of testimony. My job was to travel to the hearing locations, rent the needed space, sound equipment services, steno staff, arrange for advertising in the newspapers, and of course, attend the hearings in case any other services were needed.

After the public comment period, the Council staff collected and analyzed all 4,782 comments by category, and published them in a 338 page *Summary and Analysis* (1972). My only contribution to that document was the design of the front cover and arranging for the printing by the Government Printing Office. The cover design shows a jumble of red, white, and blue dots at the top being funneled down between the words Summary Analysis, where they line up neatly in rows of red, white, and blue. The dots were made with a three-

hole punch and arranged on separate coordinated sheets of plastic for each color. A crude but effective design technique.

Employment with the Council taught me skills in a very new area of work that allowed me to obtain future employment as a writer as well as a photographer, artist, designer, and public relations man.

The director who had hired me quit and moved back to California when President Nixon, at the beginning of his second term, required all appointees to submit a resignation and then, as in our case, forgot to tell many people that they would be kept on. Our director got tired of waiting in limbo and chose to leave. His replacement immediately hired a management consultant who came in and interviewed everybody about his or her job and the Council. I liked him and upon being asked told him about the political power of the two young associate directors. When I left the agency, the new director said he was sorry to see me leave, as he had great plans for me.

Reston, Virginia

About the time I started work for the Water Resources Council, my wife found a townhouse development under construction in Reston, Virginia, that she liked very much. The attractive multilevel condos were joined together, four to a bunch. The common walls were cinder block with two-foot empty firewall airspace between. This gap was sealed over on the outside, so while not an evident feature, the result was that we never heard a sound from a neighboring condo, not even from a loud party, children carousing, or some heated disagreement.

Each unit was constructed in two parts, like narrow houses side by side and joined in the middle at various places to create doorways or ceilings. These were large houses, approximately 3,500 square feet. The entry level comprised the living room, kitchen, dining room and family room. The kitchen faced out the back and opened into a high-ceilinged family room with sliding glass doors to a second-floor balcony. (I later built a large elevated wood deck on the back, with plenty of room to walk around and eat at a picnic table.) A powder room was a half-level up from the main level, and the stairs continued up to a master bedroom, bath and studio/sitting room suite on its own level. The top level had two bedrooms and a full bath. The bottom floor (walk out basement) had a large hobby room that we converted into bedrooms for two of the girls, and a family room with a sliding glass door opening onto the back yard.

We paid $48,000 and waited several months for it to be completed. (Present value is now over $500,000.) The purchase price and monthly mortgage payment pushed our financial situation to the brink. For months I worried about our ability, or possible inability, to make each payment.

Watching it grow day by day gave me the opportunity to install some things that the builder did not include in the purchase price. The stairwell and numerous landings from the various floors was a significant part of the house, and I installed floor level lights on each landing all the way up and down the stairwell. Each bathroom also had one of the lights so there was no need for a night light that plugs into an outlet. They automatically came on at dusk each evening and went off each morning because I wired them to a light sensitive switch that hung under the roof eave. Purchase of the townhouse required membership in a condo association that was responsible for all the property, including sidewalks, lights, parking garages, snow removal, and exterior surfaces of the units. The only thing each homeowner owned was the interior walls and anything inside that space.

Inlet Court Townhouses, on Lake Anne, Reston, Virginia

Reston, the first planned community in America, was created by Robert E. Simon in 1964 after he purchased 6,750 acres of rural farm and woodland from the Bowman bourbon distillery family. (The name RESton is derived from his initials and Lake Anne is named after his daughter.) Careful planning allowed acreage to be developed with high-density housing that left large open spaces of woods and parks, tied together with miles of paved bike and walkways for community use. Unfortunately for Mr. Simon he ran out of money. Most people do not realize that the houses they see are but the frosting on the development cake. The big money goes into the early development, such as planning, roads, underground water, electrical, sewers, streetlights and such. In

1967, the Gulf Western Company, a real estate subsidiary of the Gulf Oil Company, bought the remaining interest that Mr. Simon had and continued to develop Reston.

There were 62 units in our Inlet Cluster of homes, and when the sales reached the magic number of 31, the Gulf Western office called a meeting of all homeowners to establish a Homeowners Association that would henceforth be responsible for all the common areas within the cluster of condos. This would include care and maintenance of the carports, road and driveways, drainage systems, grass and tree maintenance and snow removal, and the outdoor electric lights that were installed throughout Reston by Gulf Western. These beautiful outdoor lights stood on a brass pole about nine feet high. Each light had ten bulbs covered with a large elongated clear glass two-foot globe over the bulbs. They were beautiful to look at, provided a very attractive light, but were very expensive to operate. There were at least a hundred in our cluster alone.

The meeting, chaired by one of Gulf Western's more experienced managers, was held in the local elementary school. He had a rough worn farmer's face, was over six feet tall, about 55 to 60 years old, and acted like this was a routine thing that he had been through many times before. He gave us a brief introduction about Reston and homeowner associations and then handed out a proposed budget for the next year. We all knew that we were required by our settlement agreement to fund and participate in a homeowners association; however, we were not prepared for the extensive budget proposal and subsequent monthly dues that were handed out to us. It also became apparent that Gulf Western wanted us to become the Inlet Cluster Home Owners Association that night, thereby assuming all cost and responsibility for the yet to be completed grounds, lights and more.

This bothered me because all the contracts for the lights, electrical supply, sewers and ground drainage were done with Gulf Western, not us. So we were being asked to inherit their contracts carte blanche. The more I read, the more I balked, especially at having to accept this all in one quick meeting. Several of us began talking about it, the Gulf Western man started to get nervous, and finally the issue of being railroaded came out in the open.

Based on my experience with the Water Resources Council, I stood up and told everyone that contrary to what Gulf Western wanted us to do, we did not have to accept anything that night; we did not even have to become an Inlet Cluster Home Owners Association that night. I said we could accomplish this by taking a vote to table and postpone, all action until the next meeting, to be announced, and that this meeting would be continued at that time. The Gulf Western man seemed stunned. We collected volunteers to meet at my home in two days to sort this all out and tabled all action until the next meeting.

If you purchase a newly built home, you walk through the house and property with the builder to see what still might have to be fixed before you go to the final signature closing on the house. We did this same thing on the common association property. Gulf Western was flabbergasted, but they had no choice. On the day of our association's walk through, the Gulf Western executive was met by six of us, three of which were attorneys who had purchased Inlet condos. The walk through went as planned, with everyone taking notes on what was yet to be done before we would become an association and sign off on the various contracts and agreements. Gulf Western was in a box. The longer we held out, the more expensive the situation would become for them. Meanwhile our group of homeowners collected the monthly homeowner assessments and placed the money in escrow.

Gulf Western fixed all our cited problems. We re-opened the tabled meeting, which put us in business; however, we declined to accept the expensive lighting bill which was now over tens of thousands of dollars. This issue remained open for several years until Gulf Western agreed to pay half the outstanding power bill and change the lights into a style that used only two bulbs.

The Joint Federal-State Land Use Planning Commission for Alaska

As I mentioned, one of the benefits of working as a civil servant for the Federal Government is that there are no penalties for transferring from one agency to another. I had always wanted to live in the Western United States ever since I went with my parents to my brother's college graduation in Montana. The furthest west I got was Milwaukee with the Eastern Region of the Forest Service. My supervisor there was John Hall, the best I ever had in 30 years of government work. In addition to being a boss, he liked to guide employees into doing good work: a mentor.

(Logo designed by the author. Symbolism: The outside circle is representative of nature as nature seldom creates pure straight lines, the triangle represents man and land planning, as man usually creates, divides and plans using straight lines, the triangle represents the mountains and land of Alaska, the waves at the bottom of the mountain represent the coastline and many lakes of Alaska, the sun and moon above the mountain represents nature, wildlife, the air, the elements.)

When I transferred to the Forest Service's Washington Office, he moved to Washington and started working for the National Wilderness Society, an organization that helped the Forest Service establish wilderness areas in the National Forests. I did some freelance art design work for them and picked up a little extra money.

Author's proposed logo design for The Wilderness Society

John moved back to Alaska and I did not hear from him for several years, until he called me one evening at dinnertime in Reston. He said that the agency he worked for in Alaska was looking for a public information officer. They were a small outfit and he thought my experience as artist, photographer, writer, public information officer, and executive secretary would fit their needs perfectly because, unlike most people, I was capable of providing multiple services.

The small agency John worked for had a very long name: The Joint Federal State Land Use Planning Commission for Alaska. The Commission was created by Congress to help settle the various conflicting land use issues that arose in Alaska as a result of the construction of the 800-mile oil pipeline that was to be built from Prudhoe Bay on the far north shore of Alaska to Valdez, an ice-free harbor deep enough for oil tankers. It was a massive eight billion dollar project that would take several years to complete

John Hall, acrylic on canvas

When John called and told me about the job with the Land Use Planning Commission, I was ecstatic. At last a chance to move west. When I called my brother Wally and told him about it he said, Well congratulations, you could hardly get any further west than that!" The State and Federal directors had a trip to Washington, D.C. scheduled, so they interviewed me while there. I gave thirty days notice to the Water Resources Council and put the condo up for sale. It sold in one week.

I called Duncan Reid, one of the associate directors, asked if it had snowed yet in Anchorage and said we hoped to get there before the winter set in (the District was still enjoying nice fall weather.) He laughed heartily and said, "You are too late; winter in Alaska has arrived." I later discovered that Alaskan winter starts in October. The sun is so low by that time that the ground on the shadow side of a fence is frozen solid, snow or no snow.

We shipped our car to Alaska and flew out of Washington, D.C., with a stop in northern Minnesota where my parents lived on a small lake. It was Christmas and my brother, his wife Joan and their daughter Karen were there. All ten of us celebrated in a small three bedroom rural cabin on a frozen lake. It was a Christmas like no other, a memory that will be with us for a lifetime.

Father had a small ice-fishing shack on runners out on the lake and illegal tip-ups set out at several holes in the ice. He had been making these homemade winter fishing devices ever since he was a boy. Built on a stout stick of wood, a tip-up consists of a spring bent over from the top down to a catch which is released when a fish pulls on the fishing line/rig that has been let down into the lake. When the catch is released a red cloth flag tips/pops up, signaling that a fish is probably on the line. Binoculars were available, along with hand held radio walkie-talkies to talk with someone in the icehouse. I was warned never to mention the tip-ups while using the walkie-talkie system, a fact I promptly forgot, but was quickly reminded of when I blabbed on the radio that a fish was on the tip-up, thereby possibly bringing us a visit from the state fish and game folks.

Dad also cleared a big rink on the lake, so we immediately ran out and bought ice skates for all of us--that we subsequently carried to Anchorage hanging over our shoulders because our suitcases were so tightly packed we couldn't have gotten in a deck of cards, much less a pair of skates.

The holiday ended, we drove to the airport at Brainerd and flew to Minneapolis on a North Central Airline, Convair turboprop plane, (Also called the *Blue Goose* airline for its logo of a blue goose flying through a circle.) From Minneapolis our party of five plus the maximum allowed baggage flew to Seattle and then on to Anchorage in an almost empty Boeing 747 aircraft.

The five-hour difference from Central to Alaskan time was starting to make the day seem very long indeed, as we flew over the snow covered Chugach mountain range bathed in the pink and orange afterglow of the setting sun. Winter sunset is about 4 PM in Anchorage, with sunrise at 10:15 AM. The

before and after glow lasts for another hour, just not direct
sunlight. We arrived in Anchorage about 6 PM Alaskan time
and were happily surprised to find John and his family waiting
for us in the airport lobby. They insisted that we come to their
house for dinner, and we agreed, temporarily forgetting that it
was already 1 AM Midwest time.

Anchorage was decked out in a fresh ten-inch snowfall;
the temperature was a balmy ten degrees, warm by seasonal
standards, when I went out to the airport parking lot to get our
rental car. The sky was overcast, deep gray, depressingly dark.
No one had plowed or cleared the parking lot. The frost on the
inside of the front windshield was so thick I had to scrape a
two-inch diameter hole in it with the edge of my plastic credit
card in order to see out. The car started because it had been
plugged into an electric engine heater, but there was no heat
yet to defrost anything, and it appeared to me that there would
not be any heat for some time. As I pulled around to the
terminal, the tires bumped and thumped in a steady rhythm
from the flat spot created by sitting so long in the cold. I pulled
up to the passenger loading area to pick up the family and
luggage, and the airport police officer walked over and told me
I had to clear the windshield of ice before I could drive off.
This would have been an impossible feat; the defroster
wouldn't have generated enough heat to accomplish this task
for several days. Ignoring his request, we loaded the car and
drove down the road behind John and his family to their home
for a dinner of moose meat and some entertainment. I found
that moose meat, like bear, is delicious when prepared like pot
roast.

Like many houses in Anchorage, their home was a split-
level, which I thought odd, considering the outside temperature
went below zero for weeks at a time. I also wondered why,
considering the vast amount of available land, houses in
Alaska, especially city houses, were crammed together in
subdivisions just as they were in the lower forty-eight. I later
learned that the increased cost of sewer, paved roads and other
utilities encouraged, if not dictated, that houses be kept close

together in the Alaskan cities. Also, it was friendlier to know in sub-zero weather that you had neighbors close at hand. There was a feeling of being vulnerable in the winters, a sense of danger hanging around to remind you that you really were living in the last frontier. This was first brought to mind when flying up the coast from Seattle. There were no city lights at all until Anchorage, a twinkling jewel, which came into view after hours of flying in darkness.

Electricity for Anchorage is created by several large natural gas power plants located on the opposite side of Cook Inlet. The gas reserves below Cook Inlet are so large that no one gives a thought as to the amount of gas that is burned to create the electricity, which is then routed through three large cables under the inlet to Anchorage. This particular winter, two of those three cables had ceased to function due to breakage, and the entire population of 350,000 was hanging on one electrical thread for the entire winter. Most residents quit worrying about it, realizing that they had no control of the situation. Fortunately, the remaining cable held power until the other two were replaced by a Norwegian firm in August.

After dinner, John hitched up his two Malamute dogs to a small traditional Alaskan dog team sled and gave the kids rides around the subdivision. By then it was almost 4 AM our time and we were tired. They led us back to our sparsely furnished second floor motel rooms and we went straight to bed. In 1980, most motels in Anchorage, with the exception of the two large hotels in town, were so old they did not have a central corridor, but had outdoor steps that led up to a covered deck, each room opening onto the deck. Not exactly a design suitable for Alaska. Ours was warm and had television, complete with a terrible picture and news footage that was 24 hours old. With the exception of local news, all shows, news and TV entertainment was shipped up to Alaska on airplanes via large canisters of video tape, as there were no satellite communications. A cheechako (the native word for newcomer) could easily lose money betting on sports games that looked like they were being played today, but actually had been played the day before.

The next morning we were awakened to the sound of a freight train going right behind the building, which swayed and shook as the train went past. I was standing in the middle of the room and I thought, "Wow, that train can't be more than eight feet from the backside of this building." Then it came again, and I began to realize this was no train, but an earthquake big enough to shake the entire building. I ran outside to the kid's room next door and was immediately run over as they leaped out onto the deck and down the snow covered stairs in bare feet. The quake made several more jolts for what seemed like forever and then stopped. We were without speech for a moment, just feeling the tremors.

During the night, we received another ten inches of snow along with wind and drifts, an unusual combination for Anchorage. The car was covered with snow again and the temperature during the night had dropped to zero. Welcome to Anchorage.

Fortunately, the motel had a restaurant attached to the

1992 Winter Olympics

building, so our food service was a treat because we did not have to drive anywhere in the snow. None of the roads were clear, and there was no sign of them being cleared soon. We discovered two things about restaurants in Alaska; the food was plentiful, almost falling off the plate, and the people, like all the service people we ever met in Alaska, were so friendly they were almost like family.

Later that morning I let the engine in the rental car idle for two hours before it got warm enough to defrost the glass on the inside. Then I drove slowly north on Spenard Road until I came close to downtown and a long park strip that ran east and west for eight blocks. The Commission's office was somewhere on 4th Avenue, so I parked the car along the park strip and walked four blocks through the snow until I found the office. I was wearing the only boots I owned, soft Italian leather dress boots that zipped up the side, and a coat that was not remotely right for the weather. The boots did not last the week and the next day I walked down from the office until I found a construction/army surplus store and bought a lightweight parka with a hood and fake fur ruff.

When I got to the office, I found out that this much snow, all at one time, and combined with wind, was unusual for the city, especially downtown, which was barely alive with people. The office was small, maybe forty people in total, who were friendly and generous. A relaxed humor permeated every work day.

I saw John every day, and he was a big help in guiding me into the system, especially how to pronounce the mostly native place names. Most of the staff went next door for lunch at a wonderful hole in the wall restaurant, packed with patrons whose chatter made a cozy and warm hub-bub noise and ambiance, and topped off with a 40 foot antique mirrored bar. The food was hearty and good. The building they were in was later purchased by a Japanese businessman who gutted it to create a new Japanese restaurant, which burned before it could even open.

I started work on a Monday and by Tuesday discovered that one of the several research specialists was going to Hawaii for two weeks, starting on the following Saturday. She asked if we wanted to live in her house while she was gone. We jumped at the chance to get out of the motel. Annette now had a kitchen and we got to eat home cooked food and live in a real house. While we looked for a home to buy.

The third day at work I was interviewed by a young reporter from the *Anchorage Times*. I thought it odd to be interviewed by a newspaper for this kind of job at my pay scale (I was not the director) but I gave a good interview, telling her how impressed we were with the kindness and warm personality of Alaskan people. The article ran at least 6 column inches, a lot for a warm fuzzy story. I later found out that the reporter had applied for my job and was, I think, vetting me for a fatal remark that never came. In 17 years, my impression of most Alaskan people never changed. They are great.

Our little Ford Pinto station wagon car arrived at the dock in Anchorage while we were in the house. I turned in the rental car and we started looking for a home to buy. Searching for a home in Anchorage was disappointing because all the houses were stuck near each other on very small lots. We started looking further out of town and ended looking at houses in Eagle River, a small growing bedroom community that was separated from Anchorage proper by the Army's Fort Richardson, a gap of about twenty miles.

Eagle River had a few stores, a couple of churches and lots of dirt roads. The river, aptly called Eagle River, came out of the nearby Chugach Mountains, and created the narrow valley that the various houses were built upon. These were not slow meandering rivers like those in Minnesota, but were mountain rivers full of large boulders and thrashing water that froze solid in the winter.

Skinny birch trees lined the bank and valley. The main road, known as Eagle River Road went straight up the valley like an arrow until it reached, you guessed it, Eagle River Glacier in the mountains. The definition of a glacier is that the snow/ice that makes up the glacier stays about the same year round, even though it melts a bit at the bottom altitudes during the summer and then collects more snow and ice in the upper altitudes during the winter. Bears were known to wander up and down the area and one year a grizzly wandered onto the main road and was hit by several vehicles. Most pick up trucks in the area had a rifle rack in the back window, and it only took a search of seven vehicles to locate a rifle, and put the animal out of its misery.

"Raven Rocks", frozen river rocks, acrylic on canvas

Our search for a home ended on a side street downhill from the main road, where we found a split level house with a three-car open carport on a half acre of land covered with birch trees. There was very little flat land in the valley and the site of our new home was no exception. Everything sloped down toward the river, which at this time of year was frozen and so silent we did not know it was there. The house had a trail across the back lot that had been bulldozed for utilities. There was a gentle slope from there to the house site, and then a thirty-foot drop in the front to the road. The driveway came up this steep hill and turned sharply in front of the house, where it allowed us to park the cars in the carport, which in the previous earthquake was now flat on the ground in front of the house, covered with snow. It was difficult to recognize.

Annette liked the house, which had a small back deck, a split-level entry with the standard living room fireplace, dining room area next to the kitchen, two bedrooms upstairs with full bath, two bedrooms downstairs, with full bath, and a large family room with fireplace. The upstairs living room had a large picture window with a broad view of the North Fork of Eagle River--the same window through which I watched a black cloud from the eruption of Mt. Redoubt come at us and deposit a gray ash on everything. I liked the area and the true feeling of Alaska, with space between houses. The agent assured us the carport would be put back to normal. Annette was pleased because the house, being empty, allowed us to move in immediately. However, this was not quite as easy as we assumed it to be. The area was definitely rural.

 Several days later, the moving van arrived at midday with all our possessions. It was a warm fuzzy feeling knowing we were about to see our very own household goods again. The truck, a standard 18-wheeler, pulled past the driveway and started to back up the hill to the house so they could unload our stuff from the rear of the container. About half way up it stopped, the wheels of the truck spinning in the snow, unable to shove that weight backwards up the hill. They pulled out and tried again as we watched out the living room window. After several tries they determined that it would not be possible to push that load up the snow-covered hill called a driveway so they drove away and said they would be back to try again tomorrow. It was heartbreaking to watch them go in the late afternoon light.

 Fortunately, a neighbor happened by and said another neighbor had a small bulldozer that might be able to pull the trailer up to the house. The suggestion turned out to be workable and the next day the dozer came across the back of the property and down the backyard to the top of the hill where it hooked up to the trailer and pulled it up to where it could be unloaded. We had a home again.

 We didn't realize the main road was gravel until spring thaw, which did not occur until several months later. Part way up the Eagle River road is a large rock, painted yellow for a landmark, and forever known as *The Yellow Rock.* In our case

Moving in at Eagle River

it was turn right at the yellow rock, go toward the river for a short distance and turn left on Ptarmigan Street. We were the third house on the left.

* * *

The federal government bought Alaska from Russia for $7.2 million dollars in 1867. At the time, Alaska was so far removed and so out of mind that everyone thought the purchase was absurd. The Alaska native people have been living here for thousands of years, but had nothing to say about who owned the land. American Indians considered the owner of the land to be God, not some white man, so they did not participate in the sale or purchase of any property. However, by the twenty first century the Alaskan Natives were beginning to realize they needed to protect their rights regarding land, and when oil was discovered where they lived, they went to Congress and said, "Look here, if you want that oil you're going to have to deal with us because when you purchased Alaska none of that money went to us. We were never conquered, you hold no treaties or agreements with us, we were never asked. Now we want a part of what was and is ours." The Natives of the North Slope did not talk to the State of Alaska; they went straight to Congress because they knew they could hold up the removal of oil for years

The oil companies wanted to get that oil to market now, not later, so a deal was made. The Natives, the State of Alaska and the Federal Government would each get a portion of the profit, and the oil companies would do the work and get a very big portion of the profit. At the time, about 93% of the land in Alaska was owned by the Federal government, and Congress decided it was time to figure out how to divide up the land. The great wilderness and unique natural wonders were given to the National Park Service. Some parts were given to the Bureau of Land Management, the Forest Service, the US Fish and Wildlife Service, and other parts were given to the State of Alaska.

As for the Natives, a unique system was devised in which each Native village was given the entire township square, a six by six mile piece of land, where it was located, along with all the surface rights and resources that went with that land, such as timber, gravel and water. On a larger scale, the entire State of Alaska was divided into twelve Native Corporations that were responsible for the underground natural resources within their boundaries, such as oil, minerals, and natural gas.

Later, Alaskan Natives who lived outside the state formed a group, went to court and won the right to become the thirteenth corporation and also to receive a percentage of the Native profits, deducted from each of the other twelve corporations share,

Each village and regional corporation was required to establish a working corporation, complete with a board of directors and officers. Filling these positions the first time was difficult because the pool of available professionally educated natives needed to run the corporations was small. Some were fortunate in having several native people with the necessary experience who were willing to dedicate their lives to their community and take the risk of failing.

The Alaskan Land Use Planning Act
gave everyone a slice of the Alaskan pie.
Photo illustration by the author

Kotzebue had such a person in John Schaffer, who was also a colonel in the Alaska National Guard. He is a wonderful man; I consider lucky to have met. Other corporations had a difficult time in starting and maintaining an organization, but eventually succeeded.

When everyone was satisfied with the arrangement, the construction of the Alaska oil pipeline began. The teamsters union, Texas welders, and pipeline construction crews, were paid an enormous sum to agree not to go on strike at any time during the construction. The pipeline was completed June 20, 1977, and the first shipment of oil departed Valdez in an ARCO tanker in August 1977.

The natural gas, as required by Alaska State law, is being pumped back into the ground at the North Slope. Oil royalty money earned by the State of Alaska is placed in a Permanent Fund that pays a yearly dividend to each resident; man, woman and child. In 2007 that fund was worth $40 billion dollars. Over the years, each resident has received an average of $1,000 per year. There is no state income tax in Alaska.

Top: Prudhoe Bay work site, Mid: Valdez tank farm, Low: Prudhoe oil derrick

The land in Alaska, starting just north of Fairbanks and going all the way to Barrow, is frozen all year. We are talking about frozen dirt and lots of it.

Alaska pipeline: under construction, Brooks Range, Livengood Camp construction.

During the summer the surface might warm for a few feet, creating millions of puddles that breed billions of mosquitoes, but the underlying land is frozen in what is called permafrost, as in *it never thaws*. Nature prevents the permafrost from melting even in mid summer by covering the land with several feet of vegetation that acts as a form of insulation from the heat of the sun. However, anything that disturbs that thin layer of vegetation and allows the warmth to penetrate into the ground will create water-filled bogs from the thawed ice, areas that will eventually swallow even a bulldozer as the U.S. Army discovered when they built the Alaskan highway from the lower 48* states to Fairbanks.

* Prior to Hawaii and Alaska becoming states, everyone in Alaska referred to the other states as the lower 48. The phrase stuck and is still used, even though there are now fifty states.

The builders of the Trans Alaska oil pipeline had two big problems to solve before construction could start. First, how to get supplies, much of it very heavy and in large quantities, to the North Slope oil field, and two, how to hold the pipeline ten feet off the ground without the posts and the pipeline sinking into the permafrost ground. It is less expensive to bury the line than build it above ground, but large portions of the line are above ground for environmental and engineering reasons.

During the winter of 1967, Governor Wally Hickel of Alaska authorized an engineering exploration trip from Fairbanks to Prudhoe Bay to determine the feasibility of building a road. The resulting tracks, due to the thawing of permafrost where they travelled, can be plainly seen in this photograph. It will take a hundred or more years--if ever--to heal the scars in the tundra. It is now called the Hickel Highway. This photo was taken by the author in 1980.

The first task was to build a road that would permit large trucks to carry heavy equipment from Fairbanks to pipeline construction sites.   Amazingly the North Slope Haul Road, now called the Dalton highway, in some places is built on multiple layers of Styrofoam, chosen because it is lightweight, sturdy, waterproof, and acts as a fine insulator.

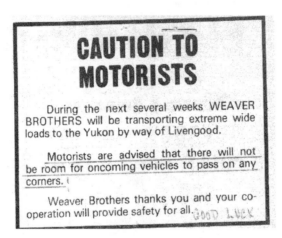

CAUTION TO MOTORISTS

During the next several weeks WEAVER BROTHERS will be transporting extreme wide loads to the Yukon by way of Livengood.

Motorists are advised that there will not be room for oncoming vehicles to pass on any corners.

Weaver Brothers thanks you and your co-operation will provide safety for all. GOOD LUCK

Warning about pipeline trucks, "The Fairbanks News Miner", 2-24-1975

Hundreds of flat bed trucks loaded with thousands of solid foam sheets two-feet by four-feet were hauled to the very end of the road as it was built. These sheets were then laid in an overlapping pattern right on the ground, several feet thick, and the dirt and gravel of the roadway was laid directly on top of the hard dry foam. The road literally created itself from the front edge, foot by foot. Culverts and bridges were built as necessary, and the road grew longer, day by day, until it reached the North Slope. Engineers solved the permafrost problem by creating a new type of double metal pipe post that kept the outside pipe cold, winter and summer. The pipe had a liquid between the two pipes and thin metal fins on the outside of the pipe at the top. The fins dissipate the heat into the air, thereby keeping the pipe cold and the ground around it stable. These pipes, invented for the pipeline, now hold up buildings as well as pipelines. For example, in Kotzebue and Barrow, buildings are kept cold underneath by inserting these pipes at a 45-degree angle under the foundation . This keeps the ground frozen and the building stable .

At the time there was a lot of controversy about the effect the line would have on wildlife, especially caribou that migrate across parts of the state seasonally. The herd has actually increased in size since the pipeline was built, but the controversy is still going on. Subsequent research has documented that not only do the caribou freely travel under the pipeline, but actually like to stand under it and eat the grass that grows there. The oil pipeline needs to be heavily insulated because the oil flows out of the ground hot and stays hot in the pipe all the way to Valdez. Approximately half the pipeline is above ground and half is under-ground. In some places, the ice and permafrost are so deep that the line was built over these areas.

The 48-inch diameter pipe is held off the ground with posts at regular intervals. The pipe itself, where above ground, rests on an eight-foot cross pipe that is attached to the posts on either side. This allows the pipe to adjust to temperature variations in the air by sliding back and forth on the cross pipe. The pipeline also zigs and zags as it crosses the land to compensate for any earthquakes that might bend or crack the pipe.

This summer, more than 300 transAlaska pipeline related vehicles will be travelling the Elliot and Yukon Highways EACH DAY For your safety Alyeska Pipeline Service Company urges you to avoid driving these highways if at all possible. Please exercise extreme caution on the road. Thank you

Display advertisement in the Fairbanks News Miner newspaper

The monthly meetings of the Commission were attended by the representative players in Alaska: the miners, natives, environmentalists, loggers, along with a few public spectators. Several of the members, appointed by the federal government, came from out of state. Adding to the mix was a significant political change in the office due to state elections two months prior to my arrival in January. The commission, by law, had two chairpersons, one from the state and one from the federal side. When I arrived Governor Jay Hammond had just finished an eight-year term, and the opposition was just starting to run the state government and we had a new state co-chairman, a young attorney who had just finished working on the state legislation setting up the limited fisheries program for commercial fisherman. The state made the existing commercial fisherman apply for a state fishing permit that then became the property of the fisherman, year to year. I think the permit originally sold for less than a thousand dollars, but because they were limited, with no new ones to be sold, the price quickly jumped to $100,000, from which the State did not profit one bit. I was not impressed with the lack of foresight, and the subsequent loss of revenue to the state. .

The Commission was beginning to draw boundaries on maps to show where various land activities might take place in the state. One boundary was the addition of property to enlarge the Mt. McKinley/Denali National Park. These chunks of real estate involved hundreds of thousands of acres of land, huge amounts, some almost the size of Rhode Island, all over the state, and some were controversial. It was a very large chess game, using millions of acres of federal land.

LUPC meeting, Anchorage, Alaska, Burt Silcock (far corner) Federal Co-chair, Walt Parker (head of table) State Co-chair, Fred Eastaugh, Celia Hunter, George Rogers, Jim Hurley, Phillip Holdsworth, Richard Cooley, Joseph Fitzgerald, John Schaffer, and Richard Stenmark, (LUPC staff in back corner)

Who would get what was very important to many people and the commission's recommendations were the first opportunity for the various factions to get their opinions into law.

The federal co-chairman decided to hold a public meeting in Cantwell, just south of the McKinley National Park, where there were a large number of private landholdings owned and lived on by the hearty and robust people of rural Alaska. Most people living in rural Alaska were there to get away from government of any kind or description. It takes a very strong person, man, or woman, to live without electricity, running water or nearby neighbors, but Alaska has a sizeable number of these people living in the rural bush.

We advertised our upcoming public meeting by placing display advertisements in the *Anchorage Times* and the *Anchorage Daily News and* also through the bush radio network, the *Tundra Telegraph*. (The word bush is used by all Alaskans to describe any place that is so rural that the only way people can get news is by listening to the AM or FM radio out of Anchorage or Fairbanks.) Messages were aired daily at the same evening hour, and would sound something like this:

To Mike and Ginger on the Delta: Meet me at the Crow River crossing on Tuesday noon. George
To David: We sold the truck and won't be able to get back with the new one until Wednesday.
To Janet and Jeff: Will bring medicine with me. Meet me Monday at the highway.
To Aunt Lizzie and Uncle Bert: It's a boy, 8 pounds, two ounces. Everything normal and healthy. Will send message tomorrow. John.

When the time arrived for the public meeting six of us got in one car, all bundled up in our double parkas, headed north on a clear, cold afternoon, and arrived at the Jack River Inn at the turnoff to Cantwell. John went in and checked on our reservations, and then we turned and went down the road to Cantwell. Everything was covered with snow including trees that were white with ice crystals generated by ice fog, the term for winter fog that floats through the air and sticks to anything already cold, like trees, cars, signs, posts, making the world look like a white fuzzy fairyland. The temperature was 20 degrees below zero and getting colder.

Downtown Cantwell consisted of one supply store and one adjoining restaurant bar, both made of logs. The neon beer sign in the front window, however, was a cheerful reminder of life in this remote cold location. The inside was one big room, at least as far as I could tell, but there must have been an adjoining outhouse, and the sound of the diesel generator was a constant reminder that everything in the place was dependent on it. There was a large fireplace with emergency wood stacked inside ready to light, a traditional bar in the back, and a stuffed moose head, whose large rack touched the peak of the ceiling. We carried our charts inside and started greeting people. The advertising evidently worked because there were about 25 people in the restaurant part. A good turnout.

The federal co-chairman presented the Commission's rough draft proposals showing boundary lines that surrounded the Park, but excluded private land holdings. People asked questions and, eventually the discussion wound down to a close. Some folks went to the bar. We packed up our stuff, put on all our multiple puffy clothing, went out into the cold and drove about a half mile to the motel.

The Jack River Inn was a light blue, two-story wood structure with twenty rooms along a central enclosed corridor on the second floor. The large restaurant was at one end on the first floor, complete with required moose head. The kitchen area had two, very large cast iron commercial gas ranges against a back sidewall and a waist high serving bar in front. The temperature outside was now down to 30 degrees below zero and still falling - not unusual for the area which is located just south of Mt. McKinley (20,320 feet high). Outside were numerous 18-wheel cargo trucks, loaded with a variety of materials, some enclosed and some not, all covered with frost, snow, and road dirt. All the tires on the trailers were spray painted with a four-inch white strip that ran from the outside tread into the central hub, creating a circus effect when they rolled down the road, each tire rotating at a different position. A white strip that was not whirling around meant that the wheel had frozen and locked while rolling down the ice-covered roads. A passing truck going the other direction would radio the driver that he had a wheel frozen up,

and the driver would stop and, using a blowtorch, thaw out the frozen brake assembly so the wheel would turn.

All the truck engines parked in the motel lot were on idle, and they would stay that way all night, sitting like half-asleep giants in the cold waiting for a master to come out and ride again. Shutting an engine off in minus 30-degree weather for several hours overnight meant it would not start again in the morning, so they rumbled on, filling the air and the building with the acrid smell of diesel exhaust fumes.

The motel had two large generators in a shed behind the restaurant. Only one was working, so all the lights in the building were at half power, giving everything an eerie cold feeling of dangerous expectation. The kitchen did not have enough electricity for the cooks to prepare a standard fare. Dinner consisted of big thick Alaskan truck driver steaks grilled on the propane fueled gas range. We took our parkas off and ate, heartily.

When we went upstairs, we were allowed to choose any empty room we wanted; they were all empty and nothing was locked. At this time of year, it did not need to be. The second floor was all ours, as outside, the truckers crawled into their truck racks, and slept as we did, to the tune of humming engines and the smell of diesel fumes. We took off our coats and realized that the temperature inside the building was dropping as the outside temperature was getting close to 40 below zero. We scrounged up and down the corridor, looking for anything to pile on the beds for covers. I ended up with six bedcovers and two blankets and went to bed with all my clothes on. In the morning, we ate fried eggs and steak with coffee, and went back to Anchorage.

Shortly after this learning experience, the federal co-chairman, prodded by my friend John, decided I needed to see what the world was like in northern Alaska, so they sent me to accompany our token native staff person, Willie, to Kotzebue for the weekend. (We always had a native person on staff, but I do not recall them ever inserting their native point of view into commission business. That was handled by John Schaffer, the native commission member who came from Kotzebue.) Every March the village held an annual snow machine race, complete with a significant winning purse. Willie had been the big winner the year before, and now he was going to defend his title.

We left Anchorage about noon via a twin-engine Alaska Airlines Boeing 737, arriving in the dark as we were above the Arctic Circle. Jet aircraft flying to rural Alaska locations always carried cargo that was placed in the forward section of the airplane ahead of the passengers. This was done to balance the aircraft, placing the heavy weight in the middle, with the not so heavy people in the back. It was starting to get colder and the wind was brisk, as I noticed they were unloading snow machines from the cargo area. This is a very expensive way to ship heavy objects, but of course, there was no other way to ship any object, heavy or not, in the winter. (In the summer, freight is shipped on barges.) We landed, deplaned and Willie disappeared into the blowing snow. I never saw him again until a brief encounter two days later.

I walked to the only two-story building in town, a restaurant, bar, and hotel, registered, dropped my things off in my basement room, and went to the upstairs restaurant, where I ate a hamburger with French fries and catsup, and drank a coke soft drink.

When I got to my room, I decided to take a bath and brush my teeth but changed my mind when I noticed that the water going into the bathtub was green with clumps of algae floating it. I got a coke from a machine in the corridor and brushed my teeth using a soft drink. A conflict in purpose if there ever was one. I decided to forgo the bath.

The next morning dawned bright, clear and cold with a bitter wind that did not seem to bother anyone but me. After breakfast in the restaurant, I took a walk around town in my new fluffy, yellow double parka--which I was grateful to have. When I first bought this coat, the hood did not have a fur ruff, a classic part of an Alaskan or Canadian parka, and for good reason, I discovered. As I walked around town with my hood drawn tight around my face, the wind felt like it was trying hard to sandpaper my skin from existence. Frequently, I had to turn my head away from the wind. The first thing I did on my return to Anchorage was to take the hood to an Alaskan tailor and have them put on a wolf hair ruff. (I still have the coat.)

Heida-Tlingit, "Storyteller", Babe Williams, acrylic on canvas

I discovered the native people lived in conditions I would not have been able to accept. They, of course, grew up in this environment. It is normal and it is home for them. The houses were very small wood structures, and behind each one was an outhouse raised on stilts. Under the outhouse was a 55-gallon metal drum, sans top. Anything deposited into these drums during the winter immediately froze solid. Before the spring thaw, the drums are loaded onto sleds, pulled out into the middle of Kotzebue Sound and set on the ice, where they eventually fall into the water when the ice melts. There are thousands of empty metal drums in the area, left over from

World War II activities, so finding another drum is not a problem.

Moving any water or waste material in a pipe above the Arctic Circle is a big problem. As explained earlier, the permafrost does not allow anyone to dig a trench because in summer it turns into a ditch full of water that slowly creeps deeper and deeper into the permafrost. The same problems occur in trying to tap fresh water or build a sewer lagoon. Eventually, the native corporations, using oil royalty money, started solving some of these and other northern engineering problems.

The snow machine race started on the frozen sea ice, in front of the main street that wound around the frozen beach. Where and how far the course went from there, I do not know. A gaggle of loud snow machines took off in a bunch and disappeared for several hours. Some of the locals sat on boxes along the beach and watched them go. I walked around town taking photographs. I am sure everyone in town knew who I was by this time. While walking I came across a man called Johnny, dressed in a traditional blue corduroy parka, working in an outdoor shed. He was kind and generous, and allowed me to photograph him. A few years later, I created this watercolor portrait of him, one of my favorite pieces, which now hangs in my granddaughter's law office.

Near sunset, the racers came back and everyone celebrated as the prize money was handed out. My friend Willie came in third. I went to the restaurant where the bar was doing a brisk business. I ate quickly and decided to get away before someone tried to include me in his or her side of an argument. Back in my room I read a book, and then got into bed only to be awakened an hour later by loud voices and screaming women from across the hall. I went to the door, slowly opened it a crack and looked out. The screaming--and I do mean screaming--continued, along with the sound of furniture being hurled into walls. It was disturbing.

Watercolor painting of Johnny

Seeing nothing I closed the door and pushed a large heavy chair against it for safety. I decided I might have to leave through the window that was draped with large heavy curtains, so I pulled the curtain aside and discovered a mattress had been nailed over a smashed window. At least it helped keep the room warm.

Walking around town the next day, I met an older gentleman in a traditional parka, who turned out to be Willie Goodwin Sr., my travelling companion's father. He was a lot like Johnny, friendly and warm, he reminded me of my father. The following October he died in a hunting accident. I heard about this one day at work, and it moved me so much....the loss of someone I met, the life, and hardship of living in the north. I wrote a short tribute, which was published in the *Anchorage Daily News*. It was also read at his funeral by the family. Actually, I didn't write it; God did. It just came through me as the medium, really.

Anchorage Daily News, Friday, October 24, 1975

A Tribute

Dear Editor:

Alaska! Brings to mind many ideas and visions: caribou, moose, golden sunsets, king crab, fishing nets, dog teams, deep snow, hooded parkas, bearded prospectors, lonely log cabins, bears, wolves, tundra, spruce, golden mountains, cold air, and Eskimos.

But those of us who live in Alaska know that beneath these romantic wonders lies an inner feeling that accompanies us with every breath we take. It hides in our gut and it draws the Cheechako to Alaska; it is the land, the sea, the air, the unknown side of nature.

We are familiar with it in the sunset, the animals, the wind, and the snow. We talk into the night around a fire that we beat it, that we made it through. Sometimes we plan with great care to beat it, sometimes we know the way, and sometimes…

In metropolitan areas, man has subdued nature by the simple weight of population. In rural Alaska, you have to live with nature and the elements, or not live at all. Occasionally someone will rescue you, but the chances of another person being around in a rural Alaskan crisis are slim.

I met a man in Kotzebue last spring. He was an Eskimo, a beautiful man, a man that knew the land and loved it. He was a leader, respected and wise, a grandfather, a man of wisdom and a man of jokes, a great hunter. He loved Alaska and he loved people. When you met him, you knew him, and you loved him.

While travelling from home to camp he crossed a frozen lake with his snow machine and broke through the ice. A trail of broken ice tells the story of his attempt to reach shore before he realized the futility of the effort. He went back to his sled and tied himself to it so the he would be found. His name is Willie Goodwin, Sr.

We all expect to see the sunrise, but sometimes we only see the sunset. Until we meet him again, we will miss him.

The federal co-chairman decided that some of the staff should drive up the recently completed haul road, to check on the construction of the oil pipeline. Work on the line was underway at various locations, and camps were built along the way to provide lodging, food and equipment motor pools. We were allowed to eat at any of the camps, but there were no available sleeping accommodations, as all the bunks were taken by construction workers.

We took tents and sleeping bags, and north of Fairbanks, pitched our tents in the open every night. This was August and the tundra was orange with vegetation. The early frost had killed most of the mosquitoes, thank God, and the grown baby birds, along with parents, were flocking for the migration south. The co-chairman was a birder, and every once in a while he would whip out a bird book, pencil, and spiral notebook and write in it. The farther north we went, the colder it got at night. The appropriately named Cold Foot camp was visible from a great distance because after crossing through the last pass of the Brooks Mountain Range, the North Slope appeared and everything was flat as far as you could see. When we got to the camp, we located a toilet area in the barracks and went in to relieve ourselves and wash up. The camps, built of prefabricated materials, were all similar in design. The toilet and shower areas were long and narrow, running along the backside of a hallway.

The room was a white tunnel with the entrance and exit doors propped open permanently. We zipped down and were standing in front of a long stainless steel urinal, when much to our surprise three women casually walked by just behind us. Everything was unisex! They never said anything and neither did we. I don't think they cared one whit, but we did. I really don't think they even looked.

*Tent camping on the North Slope. Author in
front seat heading up the haul road...*

I took lots of photographs using color and black and white film.* One was of an immense bulldozer going down the road with the driver sitting on top like a little bird steering it along. Right next to him, as tight as a tick, was a woman. Another photo was of the workers on line who rode to and from the camps in school type busses. When the grizzly bears showed up, workers would run and hide on the bus. The picture showed the workers feeding the bears out the bus windows, an

(*Now in the photo library: Anchorage Historical and Fine Arts Museum.)

"Sarah", Watercolor, Brooks Range, Alaska

act forbidden by the Alaska Fish and Game Department. I gave a copy of the photo to the *Anchorage Daily News* and it was subsequently published nationwide by the Associated Press. I declined a photo credit, as I did not want the all-powerful welders union seeking me out for a chat.

Fortunes were made and lost at haul road camps. Stories abounded about the nightly poker games in which ten and fifteen thousand dollars would be lost at each hand. Some people saw a great opportunity and took advantage of it. I heard about one man from Colorado who got a job on the line, and brought another family member up, then another and another, until all seven family members were working on the line. They took care of each other, watched to make sure they were not getting taken by others, and kept their money tight. After six months, they collectively had enough money to go back to Colorado and buy, with cash, several adjoining ranches.

Haul road, Atigun Pass, Brooks Range

We encouraged friends and family to come visit us in the Last Frontier, and in 1976, my parents made their only visit to Alaska. My father had retired from the federal government several years earlier, so there was no hurry for them to get back home. We, of course, wanted them to stay as long as they liked and enjoy everything.

Mom and Dad (Alice and Erwin) high up on the mountain behind our house, looking down into Eagle River with Anchorage in the distant background. Several years later, I learned that my father had a fear of heights.

Dad was anxious to go for the really big fish seen in all the Alaska travel brochures. The problem was that we could not really afford to charter a floatplane large enough to take all of us to Bristol Bay, famous for world-class fish and brown bears. This famous area is accessible only by floatplane or boat, the latter taking months instead of hours to reach the various lakes and rivers in the area. Instead, we took the pick-up camper and drove north on the Parks highway to a location I had checked out on the Sustina River near Talkeetna. It was a small state park, with pullouts for campers' right along side the river, and when we got there for the day trip, it was mostly empty. For that, I was grateful. The river is mountain clear water, fast running and twenty to thirty feet wide.

Several pools created by logjams were 20 feet deep and loaded with salmon; they were in layered schools, one group a few feet below another, and another, and so on as far down as you could see. I had never seen fish like this before, hundreds in each pool!

We broke out the fishing gear and started throwing silver spoon lures that had a single hook on the back. The fish paid absolutely no attention. We tried other lures with the same result. Then one of us caught a fish in the back with the hook

Salmon in an Alaska stream

part of the lure - snagged it. And that set off a series of scary events that kept me looking over my shoulder for the Fish and Game agent. Soon everyone was dragging a lure through the water as fast as possible until it snagged a fish somewhere, anywhere, on the back, the fin, the tail. I stopped fishing and began hauling the fish back to the camper. We had so many fish that I did not know what to do with them. They were hauling them in faster than I could unhook them; several were flopping around on the riverbank all the time. I looked around and discovered that the park management had emptied the large trashcans that were by each campsite and had just put in clean liners. I dumped the fish in the empty trashcan and went back for more. When the bag was full, I tied up the top, turned the can over to get the bag of fish out, and discovered extra empty bags in the bottom of the can! By the time I could get back and call a halt to the fishing frenzy, we had filled three trashcans.

I tied off all the bags, threw them into the back of the camper, and told everybody this little fishing trip was over because we had to get the hell out of there. When we got back, Dad and I hauled the fish around to the back yard, laid them out on sheets of plywood, cleaned and filleted them, put the meat in bags, and packed them in the freezer. It was the most successful fishing trip I was ever on, but not one I would recommend or repeat.

Our last trip with them was the highlight of their visit. We took the Alaska Railroad train to Mt. McKinley National Park, stayed at the lodge, rode the bus into the park, and had a great time – even the weather was pure sunshine. They went back to Minnesota with happy memories and many proud photographs, especially the one showing the fish.

* * *

The year following our arrival in Alaska was a constant stream of new experiences that I documented to our family and friends in the *Lower 48*, in a long letter written and mailed after our first year in Alaska.

January 1976

Dear Friends:

This is a long one. Get a coke or a cup of coffee, take your shoes off and settle down someplace comfortable. A years worth of love and news takes a little time to be set forth.

Alaska welcomed us in 1975 with two large quakes, a blizzard, power blackout, smog alert, record cold snap, extra heavy snowfall, ash fall from a volcano, late breakup, champion chuck holes, poor fishing, cloudy summer, hungry bears, lousy berry crop, record rainfall, a plague of caterpillars and mosquitoes …and we still like it here. That says a lot.

Well, that pokes a few holes in the myths of Alaska. The beautiful photographs are accurate. The country is beautiful, if you sit through two days of quaking, cloudy, mosquito-ridden days, with a rifle to keep off the bears, you will see that beautiful, full color magazine view. Frankly, we have not decided if we really like it here or not. We are about 50-50. [We stayed 17 years.] What do we miss? Well, we miss our many friends and family. We also miss the blooming dogwood, azaleas flowers, and the fall colors.

Bank sign, Fairbanks, Alaska, winter, minus 56 degrees

Spring in Alaska is synonymous with *breakup,* a term that refers to the frozen rivers breaking up the ice that has held them in its grip all winter. Melting ice and snow creates glacial silt-mud the consistency of bread dough, and the mixture coats dirt roads like ours ten-inches deep, making it impossible to use the Pinto for weeks. Interestingly enough, this same silt when dry turns as fine as ground flour, raising big clouds in the air behind the car and creating a form of air pollution for the city.

Breakup is a drip-drip time, with spotty days of 70 degree weather. Everyone welcomes it, except the ski buffs, since it is the end of winter and everyone is pretty tired of winter by then. Breakup this year was around the eleventh of April. But don't be fooled or misled by that date. Summer did not arrive until about June 15, and it lasted 2 to 3 weeks. My diary shows that on July 10, I could quote Annette as having said, "It's hot." Anchorage, being on the coast, keeps us living summer in a cool air-conditioned environment. Fairbanks is a different story, with summer temperatures reaching 100 degrees for six weeks or more, and winter temperatures dropping to 50 degrees below zero.

During our first breakup, all sorts of things appeared like magic in the yard as the snow melted. Piles of boards, shingles, plywood, pipe, garden hose, and firewood, and even a tin boat left by the builder or previous homeowner--that we sold for two hundred bucks!

With the exception of the American culture and language, it's a lot like moving to a foreign country. I never know what to expect from the season, the weather, the roads, and the  plants. Ravens are around all winter, but disappear in the spring to be replaced by sea gulls that in turn disappear in the fall so the ravens can come back. During the summer, you actually can read a newspaper outside at one o'clock in the morning, and if you hang around for a couple of hours, the sun comes up over the Chugach Mountains. Winter is, of course, cold and dark most of the time, but the layer of snow on the ground makes it easier to see and drive in the dark. You dress for it, buy proper equipment, and put a head bolt electric heater on your car engine so you can plug it in to an electric outlet at night. (Fairbanks, which can hit a minus 50 degrees in the winter, has electric outlets for every car in the parking lots.) Winter is pretty-fairyland stuff. The humidity in the winter air collects and floats around as ground fog where it clings to everything as white twinkle dust. A ground level rainbow--a *sundog*--occurs when this happens. Sometimes the ice crystals in the air at night send ground lighting, like streetlights, soaring straight up into the air. In winter, the Northern Lights, Aurora Borealis, flash across the sky almost every night, an awesome sight. In the brief fall, the leaves on the aspen and birch trees turn brilliant yellow, and the first snows, called *termination dust*, creep lower and lower on the mountains until finally snow stays even in the valleys, usually by the first week of November.

Our spring is the driest part of the year, and for Anchorage, the days with the most sunshine. The city is on a large alluvial plain flanked by the Chugach Mountains on the east and Cook Inlet on the west. (Eagle River, where we are, is in the mountains.) Clouds roll in from the western Pacific, push up against the mountains and stay there all day making life very dreary. Occasionally we would get a clear sunny day and the office staff would beg our chairmen to give us a sunday off with pay--which they sometimes did. About once every ten years, or so I've been told, there might be a spectacular summer of constant sunshine that everyone would remember for the next nine years. Fairbanks and the interior, boxed in by two massive mountain ranges on the north and south, would bask and bake in 100-degree summer heat. I must say that the hottest day and night I ever spent in Alaska was in Fairbanks when Annette and I pulled the mattress off the bed in the non air conditioned Holiday Inn and slept by the open sliding deck door where it might have been a few degrees cooler.

Our little Ford Pinto station wagon had a tough time getting around in the winter, even with studded tires on all four wheels, so we bought a used, full size pickup truck that had all wheel, all the time, four-wheel drive. The result of this odd arrangement was that it got about 8 miles to the gallon of gas, at 52 cents per gallon. We also decided to follow the Alaskan method of camping, secure from the bears, by purchasing a 12-

foot cab over camper that fit the truck bed. Well, actually it
rested in the truck bed with two feet extending over the cab
roof and two feet extending behind and below the truck bed. It
could sleep six, plus it had a propane refrigerator, stove, heater,
hot water, shower, and toilet. Some—but not all-- the comforts
of home in a 12 by 8 foot space on wheels.

   Seldom mentioned in the camping magazines is the routine
of shopping on Wednesday, loading on Thursday, departing on
Friday, the return on late Sunday, Monday
unloading the camper, and Tuesday spent
cleaning the camper. You get a vacation on
Wednesday, and then, if you are going to use
your investment, you start the process all over
again.

   There are only two main roads out of
Anchorage, one north to Fairbanks, Palmer and Tok, and the
other to Homer at the tip of the Kenai Peninsula. Our first trip
with this ponderous machine was south to the Kenai river
where we were going to do some real Alaskan fishing. I
cajoled one of my friends at work to advise us on buying
waders, fishing poles, and other gear for the family. He gave
us directions to the river campsite and told us to look for their
camper, as they would save us a spot next to them.

   We arrived at the camp late and by now, my nervous friend
had already fought off numerous other people who dearly
wanted to park their camper next to his, in what appeared to be
a really good empty campsite. Actually, campsite is not an
accurate description of our space. The campground was
nothing more than a big gravel parking lot along the river
where everyone parked within five feet of everyone else. Using
the wooden outhouses reduced the unpleasantness of emptying
the dirty water in the holding tank. Some sink water went into
it but that is not so bad to drain.

   Sport fishing for salmon is closely regulated by the state so
there will be enough fish to reach upstream and spawn.
(However, you can sit out at the mouth of the river, in salt
water, and catch all you want.) The result of these fishing

regulations is that everyone has to cluster on these streams and rivers at the same time. Anywhere a road gets near a fishing stream or river is where the fishing humanity packs in. That is not what we expected. In some rivers, on designated dates, the fishermen (and a few ladies, although most women are to smart to participate) actually line up along the river in waders, for miles, six feet apart, elbow to elbow, on both sides of the river. If someone catches a fish, people ten up and ten down have to reel in to give the fisherperson room to land the fish. We were shocked.

I grilled hamburgers on my little portable grill and Annette fed us dinner. Our friends liked to make everything go smoother in life by using a liberal amount of beer-which made them a little too friendly.

In the morning, we went fishing. I counted over 400 campers at this location. Six King Salmon were caught the entire weekend at this campground. We went home depressed.

Our next camper campout was to Mt. McKinley/Denali National Park, 230 miles north of Eagle River on the Parks Highway, a road so new that parts of it were still gravel north of Eagle River. Driving the Parks Highway cut three hours and 155 miles off the old trip that required a drive east to Tok and then north to Fairbanks, something no one wanted to do in the winter. Gas stations, even farms were few along these roads. Mt. McKinley National Park has two names. In addition to McKinley, the native Athabasca Indians called it Denali, "The Great One," the tallest mountain in North America. However, the white man explorers named it after President McKinley, and the Ohio congressional delegation has prevented any and all suggested legislation that would change the name to Denali. The National Park Service, however, did change the name of the park to Denali, and good for them!

The park provides free school buses called "Bluebirds" which run along the 92-mile dirt road into and back out of the park. They will stop anywhere to pick people up or let them off. Frequently, the bus stops to let people take photographs of the wildlife, such as bears, moose, wolves and fox out the

windows. But the travel is slow and in places difficult and
scary.

"Combat fishing" on the Kenai River, Alaska

After visiting about five churches in the Anchorage area,
we found an Episcopalian church that fit our needs. The pastor
was a big bear of a man with a classic Russian orthodox beard
and good sense of humor. Annette is now the superintendent of
the Sunday school; I am on the Vestry and sing in the choir.

That's it for now. Keep the fires burning. Love Paul

We were determined to find the great Alaska fishing experience that was advertised in all the brochures about Alaska.

About halfway down Cook Inlet, south of Anchorage, lies a spot on the road with the picturesque name of Clam Gulch. The razor clams along this beach, available at low tide, are six-inches long. We gave up on tent and pickup camping and tried what we called motel camping, camping that comes with flush toilets, showers and beds. Like sport fishing, clamming is closely regulated by the State fish and game department. The result, like combat fishing is that everybody congregates in the same areas at the same time. To guarantee us lodging, I called the Clam Gulch Lodge and reserved a room sight unseen.

Clam tides seem to come at odd times, usually very early in the morning, sometimes in the middle of the night, never at a convenient time. We packed our four-wheel Ford Bronco full of boots and gear, and did our clam thing.

Paul Junior with the Ford Bronco

After several hours on the beach, we went looking for the lodge at Clam Gulch and found a two-story log building all by itself along the main highway. The first floor was a bar, restaurant, and a large dance floor. I registered at the bar, and on the way up the stairs to our rooms, the innkeeper, with a touch of pride, mentioned that there was going to be a big bluegrass concert at the lodge that night. She showed us a bare bones room, directly above the dance floor, and I was concerned about the noise that would come up through the floor. The toilet was down the hall, and the clincher was that none of the doors locked--the owner told me that they used the "honor system." Adding it all up, I thanked them for the opportunity to see their accommodations, told them to keep our deposit, and drove to the small town of Soldotna ten miles north where we found a real motel for the night. I cleaned our six clams using the motels outside hose spigot and figured it cost us about $50 per clam. I like eating clams and oysters in chowder, but other than that, they are not my favorite choice of food.

Still we kept trying. People told us that to catch fish we had to walk into the bush, go off the beaten path, and take the road less travelled, to get where the fish are and people are not. A couple from church invited us to go fishing with them in an off-road area halfway between Palmer and Tok. We parked along the edge of the Glen Highway where a creek ran under the road. Not a nice big creek, a very small creek. There was absolutely nothing there but bushes and scrub alder-moose food, but the afternoon was warm and pleasant. I took down the dual Citizen Band radio antennas that stuck up from the roof of the Bronco so it would not invite a thief in the night, and followed our friends and their giant dog, Tok, into Alaskan nowhere, carrying our backpacks full of camping gear and food. Here and there, we noticed piles of bear scat along the trail. Tok was starting to look more valuable all the time.

After about an hour, we came to a creek with small pools of water that might yield a trout or two. We pitched the tents, leaned our fishing gear up against a tree, started a fire and cooked dinner. Their son, Chris, and our son played "splash you first" in the creek until their leather hiking boots and pants were soaked. Evening came (there was no real darkness at that time of year), and after hanging the food pouch high up in a tree, we climbed into our sleeping bags, even as the temperature dropped below freezing. About midnight Annette said she had to go outside for a nature call, and the moment she unzipped the ten flaps, Tok gleefully stuck his head in the opening to check us out. Due to the low ceiling of the tent we were on our hands and knees, a position Tok thought was ideal. Pushing him back was a real chore, but he was nothing but happy to see us in the night, and I was, ever mindful of the bears, glad to have him around.

When Annette came back said she had a big problem, namely a bladder infection, which was not going to go away by itself. So I woke up PJ and we packed everything up, woke our sleeping friends and told them that Annette was sick and we were going to the hospital in Anchorage. We tied Tok to a tree so he wouldn't follow us to the highway and hiked out, passing fresh bear scat on the way. PJ never complained, even though he had to walk out in boots that after getting soaked the evening before, were frozen so hard he could not tie the laces. Annette was in the doctor's office the next day.

I complained to one of my co-workers about our poor fishing experiences, and once again got invited to God's greatest fishing hole in the boonies. Annette, having gained wisdom about these ventures, declined to go. This time we caravanned in two cars north of Anchorage and past Wasilla to another remote creek culvert, where we parked and walked into another piece of the true organic Alaskan Bush. This definitely was the path seldom travelled. Six of us with lightweight packs and fishing gear walked several miles into the land of nowhere. In the process, we crossed several streams and small bogs, I in my waders and PJ in his well-trained hiking boots. I felt sorry for him, but he was stoic--just waded in, and got wet. If I had been forewarned, I would have borrowed or bought him a pair of waders. After what seemed like forever, we reached the magic fishing stream where six people caught six small trout for the entire trip. It was tiring, boring, difficult, hot, and the walk back took an eternity. I know that somewhere out there an Alaskan will read this and think, "Well you should have come with me; I know where the fish are." I am sure you do; show me the home video.

Every position in the government has a written job description. Early in my career there was always a catchall phrase stuck on the end of every one: *...and other duties as assigned*. Those five words covered a lot of territory, and they have subsequently been legally challenged and removed from all Federal job descriptions. When I worked for the Water Resources Council in D.C., I was, as in the other duties category, required to put on the very large food and open bar Christmas party for congressional staffers. This was a blatant form of lobbying, paid for out of the personal pockets of the Council members. The party budget in 1970 exceeded $500.00 (or $3,000 in 2010 money). It was a very popular, late afternoon affair, and the responsibility of pulling it off every year was on me. One year I deposited $400 of the Christmas money into the bank without listing all the checks and the cash. I got bank receipt from the drive up teller for $400, but later learned that a my receipt did not mean much to that bank, because they later said, my receipt notwithstanding, my deposit was actually $50 short--I assume the teller kept the cash. I quietly covered the loss ($300 in 2009 money) because I didn't want to admit to the office that I had messed up. Live and learn.

Although I was not aware of it when I started work for the Land Use Planning Commission, one of my other duties as assigned, was the responsibility for putting on Alaskan travel tours for congressional visitors.

Congressional staffers have a significant influence on congressmen and senators, so when several of them said they would like to visit Alaska and see the Commissions suggestions for land use, we responded with a ten-day tour of the state. I had never put on this kind of show before and did not know what I was doing, but I was willing to listen to my own intuition, which in turn opened some helpful doors. I learned quickly and I got lucky.

The federal agency representatives got together and called a meeting. My invitation to attend said 10 AM; however, it was evident upon my arrival that they had already been talking for some time. I entered the conference room, sat in the only vacant chair at the head of the table, and was surprised to discover that their reason for calling the meeting was to find out what I planned to do with the congressmen. Up to that moment, I did not have any idea, but looking at their expectant faces, I started to get some ideas fast. I went with my first thought and asked each of them to be responsible for one day of the trip. I would handle the lodging, morning and evening meals, and travel, but they would be responsible for lunch and, more importantly to them, the briefings, either in an office or in the field. They liked the plan, which worked out perfectly for everyone, and I used it when I put on several similar state tours.

My task was to move twenty people around the largest state in the union, and keep them happy. This was August, and I got lucky; we were about to be blessed with ten consecutive days of sunshine: an almost unheard of phenomenon in Alaska. We began in Anchorage shortly after their arrival with a press briefing. I set them up that first night in the prestigious Captain Cook Hotel, chartered a twin Otter aircraft and a Beech Baron plane to fly us around the state, and prepared a detailed hour-by-hour schedule, one page for each day, put into three-ring binders, one for each participant. Also in the binder was any information that the agencies wanted to include for their day of briefing.

Two days before our departure the Federal co-chairman called me into her office to inform me that I had to add one more person to the trip, a Democrat. Up until then I had not realized that everyone on the trip was a Republican (not that it mattered to me.) Now I had to solve the problem of lodging and travel for this extra person--without kicking someone off the trip. This was the prime part of the tourist season, and short-notice lodging at Mt. McKinley Park and similar places was impossible to get unless you knew someone--someone like

Senator Ted Stevens. Those words opened many doors for me in locations that had been booked for months. I was apprehensive about the new tour member when he showed up the first morning wearing a pair of leather, over the calf, explorer boots, but when he chipped in to haul luggage at the airport, I decided he was an all right fellow. He turned out to be a great asset, and at the end of the tour, I told him so.

The second day we took the Alaska Railroad train to McKinley-Denali National Park. The president of the railroad hooked up his private railroad car with a rear-viewing window and porch on the back, and entertained the senators all the way to the park. Everyone had a grand time, especially in the warm sunshine of mid-August.

The next morning we were all assembled on the grass by the airstrip waiting to fly to Fairbanks, when I realized the pilot of the twin-engine Beachcraft was not around. The Twin Otter was ready, but the Beach was not. I found him in his room asleep, but he did move fast after I woke him up, and we were in the air with both planes in an hour. That morning we held a public meeting in the Fairbanks Hotel, but due to tourists activities I could only get a very small conference room that was short on ventilation options. It was soon packed with a standing room crowd that set the temperature in the non air-conditioned room soaring. Several times, I walked to the front and turned off the two table lamps that were generating heat, and each time I did, one of the senators turned it back on. After awhile another senator lit up a big cigar. I thought that was very rude, but later he told me he had done it intentionally in hopes of cutting the meeting short--his strategy did not work; over half the population of Fairbanks smoked big cigars.

In the afternoon we boarded the three-deck, paddle wheel boat Discovery II, capable of carrying 400 passengers in comfort, and paddled down the Chena river for the afternoon, returning to the Pump House Restaurant, where the steamer dropped a gangway and let us off on the riverbank for a dramatic

From left to right: Commission Federal Co-Chair Esther Wunnicke,
Senator Ted Stevens,(Alaska), Senator Hanson (Wyoming) Senator Durkin,
(Mass.) reviewing Commission proposal in Fairbanks. ,

group entrance. The restaurant food, as usual, was great but the
service was extremely slow for a group of thirty. I had to
continually get up and prod the management into action. It was
my job to make sure everyone paid his or her share of the bill--
a truly thankless task--and moved on to the next scheduled
stop, even if that stop was to sleep in the hotel. The chartered
bus was on time and we rode back to Fairbanks in great spirits.

In the morning, I got everyone together for the bus ride to
visit the University of Alaska engineering department's
permafrost tunnel north of Fairbanks. This deep tunnel into the
side of a small mountain (hill in Alaskan terms) was done to
determine how deeply the ground is frozen. Created by miners,
under the direction of the University staff, a small railway line
inside is used to haul the soil outside. A string of bare electric
light bulbs provides illumination, and a heavy wood door on
the entrance insures that the tunnel remains frozen year round.
For a memento I picked up some small pieces of several
thousand-year-old wood

Our next stop was McCarthy, a great example of an
opportunity lost due to shortsighted bureaucratic politics.
McCarthy is an old mining area in the southeast corner of the
State above the lower panhandle of Juneau and Ketchikan. In

1900, two prospectors, Smith and Warner, wandering in the valley carved out by the nearby Kennecott glacier, spotted an immense green pasture up on a mountain hillside. It was so big that it could easily be seen from the valley below.

It turned out to be one of the largest deposits of copper ore ever found. J.P. Morgan and the Guggenheim brothers heard about it, bought the existing mineral claims, and in 1906 started the Kennecott Mining Company to get the ore to market. Not an easy task when considering the river, streams and mountains that had to be cut into and crossed. Short of using a helicopter or a small airplane, the area is still difficult to reach.

To get the copper out the owners built a railroad that went 196 miles from the upper valley alongside the Copper River to the sea where the ore was shipped to Tacoma, Washington. The CR & NW railroad was a construction marvel. They managed to bridge the Copper River and its numerous tributaries and carve space along cliffs without using modern gasoline or diesel powered equipment. The railroad transported over 200 million dollars worth of copper ore. The town of Kennecott quickly grew to 300 people, with an additional 250 miners working the mountain three miles away. (The area now has about 35 full-time residents.) Kennecott had a hospital, store, grade school, dental office, dairy, bunkhouses, recreation hall, and numerous mining buildings. Five miles down the valley another town sprang up, McCarthy, with restaurants, hotels, saloons, two newspapers, a dress shop, photography shop, garage, shoe shop, and hardware store.

In 1938 the bottom fell out of the copper market. The mine was closed and train service discontinued. The railroad and the right of way were given to the federal government, in hopes it would be converted into a public highway. It never was, and hence the sad tale of a government with no foresight.

When the mines closed, everyone left in a hurry. Perhaps it was a case of catch the last train out or walk! They abandoned vehicles right where they were last used or parked. There were clothes still on hangers, canned food on the shelf of the mess hall, dirty pots in the sink, plates on the table along with silver

Kennecott Mine, Copper River, Alaska

ware and cups. Machines were shut down with ore still on them, and on and on it goes, a complete town and processing facility left as though it was inhabited by ghosts--everything there but the people.

The government did not want it, and in the 1960's it turned into a hippie's town of squatters. The little stuff of leftover life in Kennecott and McCarthy slowly disintegrated and disappeared. The wood buildings remain like tombstones in a cemetery, testament to a lost opportunity. Eventually even the wood buildings will be powder. As the author Eckhart Tolle says, "All forms are unstable." Based on the Land Use Planning Commission's recommendations, the area was designated a National Historic Landmark in 1986 and the National Park Service acquired most of the land within the mill in 1998. Some of the structures and surrounding land remain in private ownership.

In 1916, a cannery building in Katalla on the coast near Cordova was moved up the railway to McCarthy where it became the McCarthy Lodge. The building, now over 100 years old, has a rural quaintness and charm both inside and out.

It also has a restaurant, so I called and asked if they could feed lunch to thirty people. They said they could, but everyone would have to eat the same thing--sandwiches and soup. The telephone arrangement worked great. I had the aircraft fly over the glacier and the town to give everyone a good view, and we landed on the gravel strip by the Lodge. During lunch, while chatting with the owners of the mine property, they generously offered to take our party up to see the mine. We piled in the back of a their flatbed truck with wood sidebars on all sides and watched the dust twirl behind us as we went up the three miles to the old mine. I was probably the only one on that truck who said a heartfelt word of thanks for the sunshine.

When we arrived, I took a moment to thank the owners for the opportunity to visit, and to remind everyone that the government did not own the property, and for them to enjoy, take nothing, and leave only footprints. An hour later, I rang a bell to collect my flock and we left the way we came in.

The next day our trip took us northeast out of Fairbanks to the Arctic Wildlife Range, an immense area set aside by Congress for preserving Alaskan wildlife in the north. Exploration for oil discovered the large reserve under the North Slope east of Barrow--oil that is presently flowing south in the Alyeska pipeline. At the same time, oil was discovered next door in the National Arctic Wildlife Range, and the situation has been controversial ever since. The wildlife environmentalists are adamant that nothing of modern equipment, buildings, or vehicles be allowed in the Range. The oil companies, state and other developers say that our nation needs the oil. Construction of the Prudhoe Bay oil field and the pipeline has shown that the work can be done with very little disruption to the wildlife.

If viewed from the moon, the oil line and development equipment would be so small in comparison to the size of the Range that they would be invisible. Truly, it is like laying a long single piece of sewing thread across an entire football field, the impact would be very small. But many people concerned about the environment think it would gradual destruction of the Range, so it remains undeveloped.

This sign over a doorway in Tok says it all

We flew over the vast landscape and then, much to my surprise, landed on an old WW II gravel airstrip just south of the Range. There was nothing there, not even an Alaskan tin shack--but there was a Boeing DC-3 parked on one end of the runway.

We taxied down to the aircraft, shut down our engines, and much to my surprise were greeted by Henry "Scoop" Jackson, (1912-1983), at the time the leading and most powerful Senator in the U.S. Senate. He wanted to talk to the senators and senior staff in our tour to see what they thought of the Commission's plans to divide up the state. Within minutes, were joined by several four-wheel tundra buggies operated by local Eskimos. Jackson was from the state of Washington, and the Eskimo people, especially the leaders, all knew him on a first name basis, he had championed their local native causes in the Senate on many occasions.

Left to right: Senators Hanson(Wyo), Jackson (Wash),Durkin (Mass)

I stood off to the side, consulted my schedule for the day to determine what we might be able to shorten, and waited. One by one, everyone sooner or later evaporated into the bushes to relieve themselves. It reminded me of the Alaskan Bush saying; there are four cans in Alaska to remember. Eat when you *can*, sleep when you *can*, and use the *can* when you *can*. That certainly was true here.

Our next stop was Barrow and the Arctic Research laboratory located on the edge of the Bering Sea, as far north on land as you can get in Alaska. It was late in the summer and the weather was already cold. Several vehicles were waiting for us and as we rode from the Laboratory airstrip through the town of Barrow, the Eskimos told us stories about the polar bears that wander into town. I had calculated flying times based on air speed and distance, but I missed this one by at least one hour, and we were late. All the local native chiefs and staff from the lab were waiting for us, so we were hustled out of the vans into the buildings.

Hotel baggage sticker, Barrow, Alaska

There were at least fifty people in the room. I stayed behind a few minutes to make sure the flight crews had arrangements for the night and then went into the building. I had to relieve myself soon or I was going to start doing the infamous "potty dance," so I went into a room just around the corner of the conference banquet hall and discovered what used to be a restroom--except the toilet was gone. The only thing in the entire room was an eight-inch waste pipe that stood up out of the floor about ten inches. In it, frozen solid due to the permafrost, was human waste that almost came to the top. However, I judged rightly that there was just enough room for a little more, and then I went into the banquet hall.

After dinner everyone milled about, a cocktail situation sans alcohol. I took the opportunity to relax, walk around, chat and listen to what was going on. At one point I overheard a suggestion that we skip Kotzebue, our next scheduled stop. This really concerned me because Kotzebue was the home village of the Commission's official native member. He had taken the time out of his busy schedule to travel on most of the tour with us. As I mentioned earlier, this well-educated man was an outstanding representative of the Alaskan Native community. He was a colonel in the Alaskan National Guard, president of his Native regional corporation, and was highly respected by everyone. He and his wife had adopted four children whose parents died in a house fire in Kotzebue (raising them along with the three kids they already had). I glanced over the shoulder of the staff member who was advocating we skip the only genuine native contact we would have and noticed my native friend standing just outside the conversation, listening to everything that was being said. It made me very uncomfortable.

The next morning we assembled for briefings that extolled the wonders of arctic research and the need for more federal funding. Everyone knew our schedule but wanted to make a pitch for more research funds. Every time one person sat down, another got up, until I, standing in the back of the room, began making throat-slashing signs and dramatically checking my wristwatch. Finally I stepped forward and spoke up, "Gentlemen, we are now two hours behind schedule and we have not yet eaten lunch or left. I will give you fifteen more minutes, and then we are gone."

We had two aircraft, the twenty passenger Twin Otter and the seven passenger Beachcraft King Air. I was in the smaller plane and my loud mouth friend from the night before was seated behind me. Someone on the other side of the airplane said the Kotzebue dinner might be called off, the local tour as well. I was in shock, but it did not take me long to figure out what had happened. I turned to my ignorant guest and said, "This is the result of your comment last night that we should not bother with Kotzebue. We stand to lose one of the most important visits of this trip. You need to apologize!" I was angry and I didn't care who knew it.

We landed in Kotzebue, and the next thing I knew everything was back on schedule, tour, dinner and all. The staffer had indeed apologized. He pretty much had to; when the truth came out everyone was mad at him. It certainly would not be a reputation I'd want to take back to D.C. The native demonstration in Kotzebue, which included the famous blanket toss, was outstanding, and the staff had an opportunity to talk with the native elders about the future land use plans. My much respected Commission member and Native corporation president put on a free steak dinner in their newly built corporation hall.

In the morning it was south to King Salmon, where we transferred in shifts to an amphibious Grumman Goose and landed at beautiful Lake Clark. We had been there only a few minutes when someone told me that Governor Hammond, who had a beautiful log home down the lake, was home, so I went down there in the lodge's floatplane and then flew back with the governor in his airplane. The lake was calm in the late evening air, so he had to do circles in the lake to create enough rippled surfaces to get the pontoon floats to release the suction and give us lift-off. We went down the lake at about 200 feet of elevation, splashed down by the lodge and went in for dinner. They served us fresh-caught silver salmon along with salad, bread and wine. The lodge was beautiful inside and out, with deep cream log walls and wood floors that shone in the light from the gas lamps and fireplace.

Lake Clark tour, 1977

Our extra political member increased the size of our tour just to the point that our group exceeded the accommodations at the lodge, so four of us went around the nearby waterway after dinner to the Alsworth family homestead, where we slept on the second floor in family beds with lots of feather comforters. I arose early the next morning. Looking out the second floor window, I noticed one of their sons walking a path through the vegetable garden to the small goat shed. By the time I got there, he had already milked the goat and was emptying his pail through a cheesecloth strainer into a galvanized can hung above him on a wall. I took a photograph, which I later converted into a painting. This resourceful family was almost totally self-sufficient.

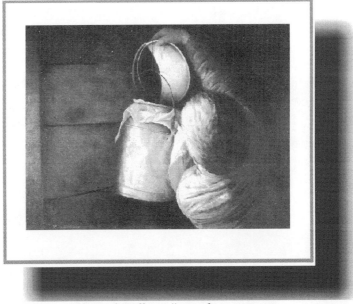

"Alsworth Milkman", acrylic on canvas

We had our breakfast with the family and then the whole group boarded the planes. Mrs. Alsworth asked me to tell the pilot to be careful when taking off, so as not to spray the garden with dust from the dirt runway. I do not know why, but even though I relayed the message to the pilot, that is exactly what he did when he turned the plane and headed down the runway. Go figure! I sure hoped she didn't think I had forgotten her request.

We left Lake Clark in the Goose and flew south to an area of large lakes north of Dillingham in the Wood River Tikchik State Park. This segment of our grand tour was set up by the State of Alaska and the US Fish and Wildlife Service, and it was a grand finale. The aircraft used King Salmon as the fueling and rendezvous site, so the two flight crews didn't have to stay with us until our scheduled departure. They set us down at the southern end of Lake Kulik, where three rubber boats were ready to float us down the river that joins two of the lakes. Again, the weather was clear and sunny, not a cloud in the sky; it was absolutely beautiful and the float trip was serene and leisurely. These lakes are joined by small rivers, draining water from one lake into another. While floating the river, we came across the world famous Royal Coachman Lodge, so we docked and walked in to say hello. They fed us lemonade and homemade chocolate chip cookies. Then it was back into the boats and another lazy drift until we reached the end of that connecting waterway, where the Alaska Fish and Game staff had set up tents and campsites. It was idyllic; even the mosquitoes were gone. Dinner was campfire-baked potatoes and steak, at a charge of $5.00 per person. That evening we sat around the campfire, enjoying guitar music, drinking brandy and singing along with a staffer's guitar. It was a wonderful ending to an incredible tour.

The Goose picked us up in the morning and after a brief rendezvous at King Salmon, flew us back to Anchorage. I had the pilots radio ahead to have the charter bus waiting at Lake Hood to take us to the Westmark Hotel for a closing press conference. From then on, they were on their own. I received several letters of appreciation, and two years later, a recommendation that would eventually lead me to a much-needed job.

United States Senate
WASHINGTON, D.C. 20510

September 28, 1977

Paul Steucke, Public Information Officer
Joint Federal-State Land Use Planning
   Commission for Alaska
733 West Fourth Avenue, Suite 400
Anchorage, Alaska 99501

Dear Paul:

The super job you did in planning and executing our tour of Alaska defies
comparison with anything I've done before. The logistics would challenge
any travel agent without adding such things as lunch at McCarthy.

It was so worthwhile. And despite my posing as a 10 day expert on d-2
lands, seeing some of the areas adds an important degree of understanding
to the excellence of the Federal-State Land Use Planning Commission
Report.

The concept of the problems and recognition of the fact that we can't
possibly know enough in anticipating future uses, needs and demands
makes your recommendations of a new classification system of Alaska
National Lands together with a permanent Federal-State commission most
sensible.

I intend to give careful, detailed consideration to the Commission's
proposals.

On a personal note it was a most enjoyable and exciting trip. Your
thoughtful concern for our every need made it one I'll long remember.

I look forward to seeing you from time to time. May our paths cross in
Jackson Hole. I'll report to Harry Byrd, Jr. about a great Virginian I know
in Alaska.

Sincerely,
Cliff. (Clifford P. Hanson)
United States Senate
Wyoming

* * *

Anchorage is built on a large plain with the Chugach Mountains to the east and the mud flats of the Pacific Ocean to the west. Before Captain Cook showed up, the area was full of moose that every winter came down to the low lands to feed on the more easily accessible vegetation. Many still do, undeterred by the houses, cars, roads, flowerbeds and people. They walk through back yards as peaceful as housecats. In the spring they disappear up into the mountains to raise baby moose. They are smart enough to avoid the mud flats that abound in the Anchorage and Cook Inlet area.

Alaska has the fourth highest tides in the world, and the twice-daily change in water is taken for granted by residents. In some places, such as Turnagain Arm near Girdwood, the bore tide is so powerful that when it funnels into the narrow water valleys it can be seen as a three-foot wall of water, a single wave, pushing itself *upriver* against the fresh water visible in low tide. When the tide goes out, it leaves mud flats far and wide.

Commonly referred to as mud, the substance is actually fine grains of sand mixed with glacier silt. While the tide is out, miles of it is hard enough to walk on and for a very brief time, hard enough to drive a small vehicle on. As the sea returns, it first comes in under the flats, fast and deep, not showing itself for vast distances--then all at once it is seeping in around one's feet. When that happens the formerly hard surface turns into mud/quicksand, unable to hold weight. The muck quickly surrounds the legs of a person or animal and secures them so tightly that it is impossible to withdraw. There the victim stands, feet as in concrete, while they watch the ice cold water rise around them until it is up to their waist, chest, chin and then over the nose and head.

Several people have died this way, including Adeana
Dickinson, who in 1988 was crossing the flats with her
husband in a small, four-wheel, all-terrain vehicle. The small
trailer they were towing behind their off-road buggy got stuck.
They were unaware that the tide was returning, because the
seawater's edge was so flat and so far away that the water
could hardly be seen. However, even at half a mile away, it
was beginning to percolate the mud from below.

One of her feet got stuck. Her husband spent two hours and
managed to get it free, but in the meantime, the other foot had
gotten stuck. Someone on shore saw them struggling and
called the fire department, but it took them half an hour to get
there. By the time they arrived, the water had risen over
Adeana's knees, and both her feet were firmly encased in mud.
The fire crews did their best, but could not get her loose and
finally--when they were in danger of getting stuck themselves-
-they had to withdraw. She drowned, the water closing over
her head even as she and her husband looked at each other. A
few months later the State of Alaska put signs all along the
road warning people not to go out on the flats. The fire
departments are now trained to handle this form of rescue.

* * *

We enjoyed our rural home in Eagle River, but the
twenty-mile commute into work and all our other activities was
beginning to get tiring and time consuming. Sunday morning
church, choir practice, other church activities and meetings,
socializing with friends, all entertainment such as movies and
the Repertory Theater, plus all but the most basic shopping
required a forty mile round trip to Anchorage. That and desire
to find the best high school for PJ, who was just finishing up at
the local junior high, led us to search for a home in Anchorage.

We found a builder who was starting to build
condominium units in Anchorage and after touring the model

condos, we bought one of the first scheduled to be built; we had to wait several months for it to be finished.

I learned a few things about the business of selling houses after putting our Eagle River home up for sale. We were on a septic system, so in order to list the house, we had to have it tested to prove that it worked. The city sent out a pumper truck, and the young driver backed it up to our tank and began pumping in water to test its capacity.

The house had two full baths, one upstairs and another directly below, both centered in the back of the house. I was shaving in the upper bathroom, heard a strange noise, and looked down the stairwell toward the lower bath, just as a column of gray water shot straight out of the toilet, four feet into the air. A sewer fountain. I screamed out the backdoor and the worker shut the water off and pumped the tank dry, but oh, the damage was done. Annette and I spent the next several hours mopping, cleaning, and disinfecting with chlorine. Then we rented a professional cleaner and went over the recreation room floor, and opened the house up so we could set out large fans to blow the air around until the house was relatively dry and odor free.

Shortly after this mess was pretty much dealt with, we had several people look at the house, and one Sunday morning a couple made an offer for several thousand dollars less than our list price, but within our acceptable range. That afternoon another realtor came to the door and asked to show the house to a different couple. I told them we had accepted an offer, but they insisted on just looking around, so I said, "Sure, come on in." They did a quick walk through, left, and an hour later the realtor called and said his clients wanted to buy it at the listed price. As this was several thousand dollars over the first couple's offer, I said yes, why not, and their realtor was out to the house an hour later with the papers, which we signed. Then I called my realtor and told him we had sold the house to another couple for several thousand dollars more than his clients' offer. Then my learning experience began.

It seems the first realtor, not wanting to drive from Anchorage to Eagle River on a Sunday afternoon, decided to wait until Monday to bring us the papers to sign--not a smart move. The house did sell to the second couple, but much to my surprise, the local real estate board censured and fined the second realtor, not the first one. That made no sense to me. According to the Anchorage real estate board, the agent who was representing me, the one who I was paying the commission to sell at our best price, was being fined for doing just that. That is when I understood that the realtor was really not working for me.

A few weeks after the new owner moved in, she called to ask if there was some reason the basement smelled rather like a sewer. I told her the whole story. She did some research and learned that the pumper guy who came to our house had made that same mistake with five other houses in the area, and *all on the same day*! Talk about a slow learner. She asked me to write our experience down on paper, which I did, and the city paid to have all six stinky houses professionally cleaned and re-carpeted.

I watched the new condo being built from the ground up in an area known as Baxter Bog, A bog forms where a lake retreats over a couple of thousand years, leaving behind a pond with a spongy ring of peat around the edge. In this case, the peat was fifteen feet deep. I am sure the people who owned the single-family houses across the street never imagined that their majestic view of the mountains could be blocked by a row of condos built in that kind of substrate, but this is how it was accomplished.

The builder drilled a series of two-foot diameter holes around the perimeter of each unit (four condos forming one unit), with each hole going fifteen feet down to solid soil. Then he set off a small dynamite charge in each hole to bell out the bottom area. A wood box form was built around the top of each hole, and steel rods, Re-bar, was set into the hole. Concrete was then poured in up to the top of the box where a heavy steel plate had been welded to the top of the re-bars.

After this dried, steel beams were set on top and welded to the plates around the entire foundation. So, instead of sitting on a concrete or cinder block foundation, our condos sat on pillars of concrete and steel. During earthquakes our building swayed on the pillar foundation, but nothing cracked or broke.

This construction technique also turned out to be advantageous a few months after we moved in, when high warm winds, a *Chinook*, from the west reached speeds of 100

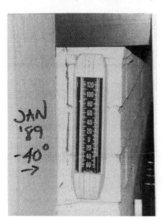

miles per hour on our side of town. Our condo afforded a splendid view of the mountains across the flat bog area, but the area also meant we received the full force of the winds. Our exposed condos and the split-level houses in our neighborhood were hit hard. Some homes across the street had the living room windows sucked out and the roofs partially torn off.

Indoor/outdoor temperature gauge inside the condo, showing 72 inside and -40 outside.

Our entire house shook over and over again, and the rear sliding patio door bulged in and out. I expected the glass to either explode or implode at any moment. Outside the air was filled with flying shingles and other debris, denser than confetti at a News Year's celebration. Thanks to our floating foundation, we wiggled but nothing broke.

Moving into town was good for the family. My work commute was cut to fifteen minutes, Annette began studies at the University of Alaska only a few miles away, and Bartlett, my son's high school did an excellent job of preparing him for college studies in chemical engineering.

* * *

My work at the Land Use Planning Commission was going along fine; then one day the federal co-chairman told us we all had to take a three-month, no pay "vacation" because the state co-chairman had spent large amounts of the commission's money travelling around the world to attend meetings. (Nice work if you can get it.) Frankly, I am still surprised that they told us the real reason. In his place, I would have resigned in embarrassment. He didn't.

Yes, our agency was so short of money that the only option was to shut the place down for three months. Fortunately for me, my good friend John found work for both of us with the Forest Service in Anchorage. They were producing an environmental impact statement on the Chugach National Forest and wanted John to help write it and me to help put the 150-page document together for the printer and get it to the Government Printing Office in Seattle. We did the work and three months later, with the start of the new fiscal year, went back to work for the Commission.

My job as graphic designer, artist, and layout-paste up artist meant I was always the last person in the line to work on the project before it
went to the printer. I *always* had a firm deadline. The writers had a deadline too, but would often let it slide until their allotted time ran into my time.

Sunny summer days were cherished like gold, and Annette and I had planned to take advantage of good weather to vacation for a week in McKinley National Park. Because of my work and the Commission's stature, I had been issued a photo pass allowing us to drive our Bronco anywhere in the park--a privilege the average visitor was denied. We loaded the Bronco on Thursday with everything needed for the trip: food, tents, camping gear, jackets and such, all ready for departure. All week I watched the weather closely. When I left for work on Friday, the weatherman was predicting ten days of pure sunshine.

As I got on the office elevator I said, "Good morning," to the federal co-chairman. She remarked, "We are supposed to get great weather all next week." "Yes, "I replied, we're going camping at McKinley for the week, so it is a wonderful co-incidence." She looked at me steadily and said, "You can't do that. You have to do the camera ready artwork for the annual report." I said, "I don't have the text yet," and she said, "Yes you do, it's right here; I just proofed it last night. You can't go without a leave slip, and I haven't signed one that I know of."

My heart sank to the floor as I realized that this trip was not going to happen. The writers had dumped on me big time. When I got to my office, I called Annette with the sad news, and then started work on the report. All week long I looked longingly out the window at Mt. McKinley shining in the sun, while I labored in the office.

The federal co-chairman continually expressed disappointment in the lack of media coverage about our meetings and studies. They would run a short blurb if I provided a news release, but that was it. I kept trying to encourage newspaper reporting, but our subject matter seemed rather dull to the reporters and the general public. I once arranged a breakfast meeting for my boss with the top reporter of the morning newspaper, the *Anchorage Daily News*. The three of us had a great breakfast at the Captain Cook hotel, but nothing newsworthy came out of our session.

Land Use planning Commission reports for 1975, 1976 and 1977, showing an Eskimo, logger, and wilderness camper.

A short time later, I tried to convince the co-chairmen to reproduce our next annual report as a tabloid insert in both city newspapers. This would have been a great way to reach over 400,000 people. The small page size, mock-up layout I did was very attractive, but they declined the suggestion.

* * *

Government regulations require that qualified companies be allowed to bid on government work. I had finished the layout and paste up of the 150-page, 1978 report, created a bid specification sheet and offered it to several printers in town. When the bids came back, the lowest one was from a very small printer, and I questioned their ability to handle a job this big. A visit to their shop did not convince me, but disqualifying them would involve the agency in a legal matter, so I arranged another meeting with them, only this time I took our attorney with me. We left the meeting still concerned, but with his legal advice, I went ahead and awarded them the contract. They ordered expensive glossy paper and cut it into two-page spreads--a big mistake. Printers who know what they are doing print four, six, or eight pages up at a time because this is the most economical way to print large publications. Then they fold and trim the paper to page size. Of course, this requires large printing equipment.

As we got closer to the distribution time, I visited the printer, only to discover they were closed. The paper, the press, everything was there, but the owners were long gone. They must have realized that there was no way they were going to make a profit using the printing methods they chose. They left Alaska, never to be heard from again, and we were left with no report. The paper company retrieved the paper, but it was useless because it had been cut down to such a small press size that no one would order it. As a result, the Commission's final report includes the complete 1978 annual report, two reports bound as one.

The Commission was meant to have a short lifespan, as dictated by Congress, but that was a detail that I failed to pay much attention to in my haste to get off the East coast. After two years the job was not yet done, so Congress extended the life of the Commission for an additional two years. It is amazing how fast time passes when you are having fun working at something you like doing. As the end of the second two years drew near, I sent out a few resumes in Alaska, but employment chances in government at the time were not good and it looked like I, along with everyone else on the Commission staff, was soon going to be unemployed.

Atlantic Richfield Company, known as ARCO oil, had recently transferred all its top executives back to Texas, and the result was economically devastating for Anchorage and Alaska. Within a year, we were in a recession. The real estate market fell so flat that people who had lost their jobs were walking away from their mortgages. They just went to the bank and said *here are the keys, the empty house is yours.* Our next-door neighbor did just that.

When the federal government hires someone from the Lower 48 to fill a job in Alaska and that employee subsequently loses their job through no fault of their own, federal law requires the agency to move the employee, the family and all their household goods back to their place of hire--in our case Northern Virginia. As the Commission deadline got closer, there seemed to be no other options for us.

When I was with the Toastmasters International group in Reston, a member gave a short speech about losing his job, and worrying about getting another. He was only unemployed for a month before he found new work, but in that month he became a nervous wreck from fearing that he would lose everything.

He said the one thing he would do different, if that should happen to him again, would be to take a vacation rather then worry about the future. Annette and I decided to heed his advice. We sold both vehicles and had the government pick up our furniture for shipment to Virginia. Using savings and money from the sale of our cars, I placed an order by telephone, with a Seattle dealership for a new 1979 Ford LTD Country Squire automobile, the largest model made, with a citizen's band radio, air conditioning and the works. I got Alaska tags for it and asked the dealer to meet us at the airport in Seattle.

Getting out of Alaska required one last task, the combined annual and final report. The writers, as usual, were very overdue in getting the text to me for layout. Their timing left me with one week to get the two-week job done, and in one week, I would be off the payroll. I could not walk away until the job was done. I worked many hours of unpaid overtime every day of my last week, and the day before we flew out, I worked all day and night, 22 hours straight, completing the paste-up and printing specifications just in time to take a cab to the airport, where I was met by Annette and PJ. We flew to Seattle, picked up our new car and went on a month's vacation up and down the West Coast and Rocky Mountains. When my boss realized all my last week's overtime, she kindly added three days salary to my last paycheck. Many months later, I finally saw a printed copy of the final report.

The Ford dealer picked us up at the Seattle airport and drove us to the dealership, where we signed papers, paid for the car and put our Alaska tags on the front and back. From there we went to dinner at the Space Needle. I felt great relief, and was happy to be on our way at last. We drove south for several days, visited the Redwood National Park and went across the Golden Gate Bridge into San Francisco. Annette doesn't like riding long hours in a car, even one as cushy as the LTD, so I planned and reserved our hotel accommodations to fit our daily drive of 350 miles. Our lodging at San Francisco was a disappointment. I wanted the Travelodge across from the Fisherman's Wharf, but based on misleading advertising, we ended up ten blocks away at a Travelodge that had advertised itself as being near the wharf. By the time we arrived, we were too tired to change locations.

I scheduled two days at San Simeon, the well-known Hearst castle. It was fairly interesting, but really not two days worth of interesting. Poor guy, it seemed to me that he had a lot of money but didn't know what to do with it other than buy boatloads of antique stuff in Europe and ship it to California to, one way or another, incorporate into his own mansion.

Annette at Disneyland

Our son had packed his favorite cassette tapes to play on the car stereo, but he worried about the music bothering us, so at the San Simeon motel I took the dashboard of the new Ford apart, wired a headset jack into the radio and put the whole thing back together, all in one day. In hindsight, I think I was a bit crazy, but it worked--although it turned out that we really liked most of his music (ABBA.)

Our next stop was Santa Barbara, where we hoped to sunbathe and swim. Surprise! The Pacific was so cold I couldn't even stand to get my ankles wet, and the beach was gibbered up with grape-size balls of tar from the passing oil tankers. When we registered at Disneyland, we found that our prepaid, preregistered bungalow was still occupied by someone else, so the management delighted us with a beautiful corner suite on the fifth floor of the high-rise hotel. We were booked for two nights and the entire visit was a pleasure.

An auto trip up, down and across the country did not seem like a good idea to most people at the time because of the current nationwide oil crisis and gasoline shortage. People had stopped all but essential driving, which benefited us in two ways: we had no problem getting enough gas and Disneyland was almost empty. I teased Annette about her fabulous good fortune. She has no patience for waiting in line, but we found no lines; we just went straight to the ticket-taker and got on the ride.

Our itinerary called for San Diego and the famous zoo, but we changed our mind and headed due east from Los Angeles for Carlsbad Caverns, which Annette had long wanted to see. We crossed the Mojave Desert and stopped for the night in Needles; the temperature was 120 degrees when we pulled into our motel. A young man came over to check us in, walking across the asphalt parking lot in bare feet. When I pointed that obvious fact out to him, he just said, "Yeah, you get used to it."

We registered and went for a swim in the outdoor pool. It was pretty warm water, but not as hot as the late afternoon air. When we walked back to our room, a distance of about a hundred feet, our hair was dry by the time we got to our door. We searched the phonebook for some good Mexican food and chose the only one of three single-line listings that also sported a big, fancy boxed ad. The motel man's directions took us to an industrial park, which at six in the evening was deserted, save for a few cars parked by a door marked with the correct address.

We walked in to find a very plain room containing five or six circa 1950 Formica and chrome tables, matching chairs with turquoise vinyl seats--and nothing else, not even one window. This was a real mom and pop Mexican restaurant.

We sat down at one of the tables and Pop walked out from the next room to take our order. As he came toward us, the only other customer, a man seated at a table against the far wall, called out an order for "the usual."

I first asked about a chimichanga, which meant nothing to Pop, because, as I now realize, that's the lingo for a gringo-style item common to less authentic establishments than our current eatery. Pop indicated he did not understand my query and before walking away, handed me a two page, single-spaced typed menu listing a staggering number of every possible combination of amounts and choices in a one-of-this-and-two-of-that, two-of-this-and-one-of-that form of the better known (even-to-gringos) possibilities: enchiladas, taco, soft and crisp, chili rellenos, and so on, ad infinitum.

We made our choices and in a short time were delighted with some truly great food. The final homey touch came when I got up and went around the corner to the kitchen to ask for hot sauce, only to discover the entire family sitting around a table eating their own evening meal.

The next day we toured Carlsbad Caverns and ate a cold lunch of bologna on Wonder bread and bottled sodas deep underground in their cold, creepy, weird smelling and very dimly lit cafe-of-sorts deep underground. As soon as we got our blood sugar up to speed, we took the elevator to the sunshine level and headed the car straight north for the Rocky Mountains, then on to Taos, Denver, and Yellowstone Park. On July fourth, we went to a very fine restaurant in Denver, which could easily seat a hundred people. Thanks to the gasoline crisis, we were the only patrons in the room--ensuring excellent service!

From Yellowstone, it was Billings, Montana, where we visited my brother and his family. Bismarck was next and then across North Dakota and on to my parents place at Hackensack, Minnesota, where we fished, boated, reminisced, sang, ate and spent idyllic evenings sitting on the screened porch listening to the loons and watching the sunset as the mosquitoes fried themselves in the electric bug killer. Zap. Zap.

Author greeting his mother in Minnesota

It seemed my penchant for small agencies with long names might continue.

In the middle of this pleasant family retreat, I got a phone call from one of the senate staffers whom I had chaperoned around Alaska on my first senate tour. He had a job lead for me with a new outfit called the Office of the Federal Inspector for the Alaskan Natural Gas Pipeline and he asked me to call him when I got into town. How he found me in Minnesota, I will never know, but I am glad he did. We arrived in Falls Church, Virginia, on August 4, after traveling 5,493 miles in 31 days. I called my senate contact, got the job lead, and applied for the job of Public Information Director, a GS-14 position.

I was not selected. The job went to a woman who had a considerable amount of experience with the National Energy Regulatory Commission, a logical choice for a job that required knowledge of politics in the energy regulatory field, including natural gas. However, I had expertise in Alaska, something no one else had. The woman who got the top job interviewed me, and based on my Alaskan experience, hired me to be her deputy. All my benefits, currently in limbo, transferred to the new agency. I dropped a grade, from a 14 to a 13, but with no loss in pay.

The Federal Inspector for the Alaska Natural Gas Transportation System

I started work in D.C. on the first of October 1979, the beginning of the federal budget cycle. We rented a vacant condo in Fairfax, Virginia, and had our furniture delivered.

It was a relief to have a job. PJ enrolled in Falls Church High and discovered that their school system was almost a year behind Bartlett in Anchorage, so he breezed through his classes. Annette's parents were thrilled to have her daughter and her family back in Northern Virginia.

One week after I started work, the congressional committee responsible for overseeing the budget and the gas pipeline Inspector's office held a hearing. The congressman from Alaska, Don Young, was the committee chairman. I had met him, as well as both U.S. senators from Alaska several times while running the annual Alaskan summer congressional tours.

OFI logo design by author

The oversight hearing was held on Friday morning. I decided to attend, even though I was not a part of our senior staff. The new inspector in our office, the man in charge, was a retired colonel from the Army Corps of Engineers. He and several of our associate inspectors, including my boss, the new director of public information, went up to the Capitol in the company car, while I inconspicuously rode the subway.

The hearing was held in a large wood-paneled room with a semi-round dais at the front. It was standing room only, so I took a place along a sidewall with a bunch of other people. Attendance must have been over a hundred people. The inspector, along with my boss and the rest of his senior staff, moved up front and sat at a hearing table facing the dias, around which were about twenty leather swivel chairs and microphones for the congressional representatives. Don Young came out onto the dais from a door that obviously led to another small conference room in the back. He sat down, took a look at the standing room crowd, and said, "We have fifteen empty chairs up here on the dais that can be used by you folks who are standing. Please come up and sit." There was a pause and then the group I was in, closest to the dais, started to move toward the raised platform and the padded chairs. I paused, but decided that for me to become the sole exception from the exodus might cause more trouble than just going along with the group. So that is how I ended sitting on the dais-- fortunately on one far edge--looking at the front table where my boss and the inspector were sitting. They did not see me.

After about fifteen minutes of presentation, Congressman Young started asking questions, and leaning forward in his chair for emphasis, he asked how many Alaskans were employed by the inspector's office. The inspector glanced at his general counsel and then replied, "Two. We have two employees, Congressman. We have a civil engineer who recently worked for the Bureau of Land Management and is presently in route to this office, and we have Paul Steucke, who previously worked for the Joint Federal State Land Use Planning Commission in Alaska." It was both an odd and interesting moment for me. A few minutes later, the meeting ended, and I quickly returned to our office without being noticed.

That meeting took place on Friday. I thought about Don Young's question all weekend and on Monday morning I went to work extra early. I knew the inspector got to work ahead of everyone else and I was waiting outside his office when he arrived. Even his secretary was not yet in the office. I told him I had an idea I wanted to share with him, and he said, "Come in and sit down."

I told him I had been at the hearing and heard Don Young ask if we had anyone in Alaska yet. "This may seem brazen, I said, "but I am the man you need to help get things started in Alaska. I'm not your regional director, but I know Alaska and I have a good Alaskan resume." He said he would look into it. Three days later he walked briskly into my little office and said, "All right, you're on," and walked back out.

I was surprised, and my new boss was shocked--I hadn't told her about my brief conversation with the inspector--and she was not happy. She wanted me working for her in Washington, not in Alaska out of reach, but it was a done deal, and she dared not argue with the inspector, who in three days had researched my credentials and my contacts with all three congressional offices in Alaska. (By the way, they never backfilled my D.C. position.)

I told Annette and our son that night, and they were thrilled. Both would be able to go back to their respective schooling, Annette to finish her work towards a degree in social work and PJ back to his advanced high school.

A federal transfer is a valid lease breaker. We immediately told our rental manager we'd be leaving on the first of December and began sorting and packing; some boxes from the move to Virginia were still in the basement unopened. Having been through all this before, we knew that we could get paid lodging on either the Virginia or the Alaska side of the

move, but not both.   We still had the unsold condo in
Anchorage, so we opted to take a motel in Falls Church after
our household goods departed. We spent Christmas with
Annette's family, and then, like our first move to Alaska, drove
west in the winter. Fortunately, the only snow we encountered
was in the Cascade Mountains east of Seattle. The Ford rode
and functioned perfectly. At Seattle it went to the shipping
yard for the trip north by boat, and we flew to Anchorage.
Home again.

The condo was completely empty, although we had
electricity and water. We borrowed sleeping bags, a few
cooking and eating necessities, and camped in it for two weeks
while we waited for the furniture to catch up with us.

The day after we got back, we were still on the bedroom
floor in our sleeping bags when the telephone rang at four
o'clock in the morning. It was my previous boss lady in D.C
wanting to know what I had been able to get done since
arriving. Thus began a four-year political game of cat and
mouse between us--and more about that presently.

A moving company always tells you they will pack up
your stuff, load it on the van, ship it, *and also unload and
place it wherever you want it to go in the destination house.*
The reality at the destination end is that most of the time they
get the larger pieces of stuff in the right room, put the beds
together and quickly take their leave, since you, having just
moved in, don't yet know much about where you want things
to go. This time was different. I told the movers, "You may not
believe this, but I know exactly where everything goes--
because we moved out of this same house six months ago."
And thus we got a real bonanza of house-settling work out of
our unlucky crew! By the time they drove off, it was long after
sunset. Outside it was cold enough to put ice in the inside
windowsills and send frost creeping along the edge of the rug
by the sliding patio door. It was deep winter in Alaska, and we
all three had a lot of work to do, but we were happy, very
happy.

By the time I arrived in town, the inspector had hired a temporary regional manager, a former engineer for the Bureau of Land Management. He was a tall, honest, cowboy type, who used a lot of chewing tobacco, the kind you put under your lip and spit occasionally. Once during a car trip, he offered me some, but I politely declined, claiming I had enough bad habits already. He was not offended.

Our first office was in a privately owned building on Fourth Avenue, and as we rapidly added employees, we moved into the old Federal Building. But for a little while, I was a one-man band: handling all the incoming calls, helping interview people, and working with the media, the company that was going to build the gas line and the native corporations. My old boss in Washington kept calling, wanting to know what I was doing. I explained that I could hardly keep up with the telephone calls, much less do anything else. Again, she did not sound happy.

Things moved quickly. The Alaskan Northwest Natural Gas Pipeline Company located their main office in Fairbanks and within six months was doing preliminary fieldwork. The Federal Energy Regulatory Commission, FERC, was in the middle of a very convoluted legal and legislative process to give Northwest Pipeline permission to move forward with the project. The entire 48-inch pipeline was to go from Prudhoe Bay, Alaska, alongside the existing oil pipeline for a significant distance and then follow the Alaska Canadian Highway to the border, where it would split into two pipelines, one going to Chicago and the other to San Francisco. If built, it would be the world's largest pipeline. The Alaska segment would be 745 miles long and cost about 19 billion in 1980 dollars

My BLM cowboy friend gratefully dropped the temporary leader's role and became the chief engineer. The new regional inspector was a retired U.S. Army Corps of Engineer colonel, and the spitting image of a British officer; thin, six-feet-two, mustached and blessed with a classically dry sense of humor. The pipeline company had several professional public relations people on board, with whom I worked closely on a weekly basis.

A few months after we settled into our new office, our inspector sponsored an inspection trip for many of the staff working in the District office. Although this may have looked like a boondoggle, it really was a good way to give these people an idea of how spacious and varied Alaska is and how important the project would be to everyone in the United States. My assignment, of course, was to arrange all the details for 25 people to tour the state.

My first step in arranging a large tour was to suggest the sites or locations for stops. With an approved itinerary, I could begin making appropriate arrangements for lodging, food, and transportation. The latter involved chartered buses and aircraft, usually de Havilland Twin Otters, used worldwide and nicknamed the *workhorse of the north.* These twin-engine turbo props can fly at speeds as low as eighty knots and they can land and take off from very small, and even rough, landing areas.

On this particular trip, we used a twin-engine Fairchild F27, which holds forty passengers and has a high wing that allows a clear view of the ground. The Anchorage regional inspector saw one on the ground at the Fairbanks airport and inquired about it. The owner said they were currently refurbishing the inside with new carpet and seats, and would make it available for our tour.

They flew it down to Anchorage, picked up our party of thirty, and we cruised along the oil pipeline route to Fairbanks, where we visited the UAF permafrost tunnel, and the Pump House restaurant. The next morning we continued flying north along the pipeline over Atigun Pass to the ARCO landing strip for a tour of the oil field.

One of the beautiful and fun things about the F27 was watching out the windows as the wheels of the plane left the ground during takeoffs and during landings when the tires met the runway, kicking up a spurt of dust or dirt. The landing gear folded down out of the high wings like a long-legged stork,

OFI staff tour, in historic costume provided by the photo studio at Ester, Alaska, just south of Fairbanks. Author upper far right.

one pylon on each side with two large tires on the end of each pylon. That day as our plane made its approach to the ARCO strip at Prudhoe Bay, everyone watched as the pylons came down and the ground and tires got closer and closer until they met the gravel with a small puff of dust, and then... as we all watched...

....a tire came off the airplane, and with a great leap of new found freedom, bounced across the tundra at 100 miles per hour until it disappeared into infinity.

The plane taxied to the ARCO terminal, and all our passengers got off and loaded onto buses headed toward the main building. I walked forward to the cockpit and quietly asked the pilots if they knew they were now flying with one less tire. They were surprised. Gosh! Really?

As soon as I got into the ARCO building, I used their telephone to call the Office of Aircraft Services in Anchorage. The OAS was a part of the Department of Interior, but supplied, on a reimbursable basis, all the aircraft and aircraft services used by any federal agency in Alaska. They did outstanding work. I told them to immediately start looking for two Twin Otters to get us back to Fairbanks that day and fly us on the rest of our tour. The F27 owners, who did not want to lose the entire charter, assured us that their aircraft would be able to fly us back, but I knew enough about planes to realize that would be impossible.

A Twin Otter is not very fast, but it is very reliable

OAS called around to see if there were any Twin Otters already on the North Slope that could ferry us back to Fairbanks, but there were none, so they had two sent up from Fairbanks. I knew this was going to take quite a while. They had to get the flight crews from somewhere, get to the airport, get the planes ready, and fly three hours to the ARCO landing strip. Fortunately, we were in a wonderful location for recreation, rest and food. ARCO provided everything free of charge while we waited for the new aircraft that finally arrived about 11 PM. It was almost 3 AM when we arrived back at our hotel in Fairbanks. We'd had a very long day and the next day would start at 7 AM on schedule.

I flew around Alaska in a variety of aircraft, including helicopters, but this incident and the one in Juneau with the Grumman Goose were the closest I came to crashing. If the remaining tire on the F27 pylon had not held, the pylon would have dug into the earth, sending the aircraft flipping end over end, tearing it to pieces. I did not share this experience with anyone else, not even my family, for a very long time.

* * *

There were many groups of people in Alaska hoping the pipeline would provide them with employment. I talked to our Native staff person and we agreed that someone should travel around the state to let folks know that the much-anticipated employment was not going to occur in the near future. My prognosis was not something the Northwest Pipeline Company wanted everyone to know, so in order to be truthful to the native community, yet still retain my job, I had to keep my communication very low key. To this end, I wrote and prepared a slide presentation, explaining the scope of the project and including the fact that employment opportunities, if any, were a long way out. I sent the D.C. office a courtesy copy.

The Native affairs specialist and I flew around the state with our presentation, one location being Kodiak, where many Filipino families were working for the big fish canneries. We gave our talk in a large meeting hall to a standing room only crowd, who then invited us to eat with them at a local family's home.

Fortunately for me, as I will soon explain, the Native affairs man had invited our staff anthropologist to come along on this trip. Our director questioned his inclusion, but I supported the native affairs specialist, encouraged the anthropologist to come with us, and he did.

When we arrived at our host's home for the dinner, we found it packed with most of the 50 to 60 people who had been at our presentation. The hostess directed us into the kitchen, where a huge amount of prepared food was laid out. We were invited to sit in the four chairs drawn up to an old table, the kind with chrome legs and a chrome strip around the edge. The three of us and our host sat and ate and talked and ate and chatted some more. I paid little attention to the time and what else might be going on around us. Then my anthropologist friend whispered in my ear that everyone else was, as is customary, waiting to eat until all the guests had completed their meal. I was grateful for his courteous protocol advice.

We all immediately got up and moved to the living room, and as soon as we did, the hostess dished out food to everyone else. A short time later, we thanked our host, excused ourselves and flew back to Anchorage. I was later invited to give this presentation to a group of federal agency directors in Portland, Oregon. It seems that the truth, no matter how subtly conveyed, was in demand.

The Canadian government established their Office of Federal Inspector that mirrored our responsibilities. In the spirit of cooperation, I sent them a copy of my slides and presentation for their use in Canada. Much to my surprise, I received an invitation from them to visit Calgary and give the presentation to their staff. In thirty years of civil service, this was my only opportunity to travel to another country on official business. My old boss lady in D.C. got word of my invitation and invited herself to attend, so she was witness to my presentation--evidently I could not be trusted to deliver a speech that the Washington office already had read and seen.

While in Calgary, the Canadians invited us to fly a nearby portion of their pipeline route in a helicopter. I started to get in the back seat when everybody at once asked me to sit up front with the pilot. My former boss said, "I think they want you to take pictures of the pipeline from the front window." So I did, and gave them the exposed rolls of film when we got back on the ground.

The Canadians teased us about the lack of progress on the US part of the pipeline and gave each of us a cute little cloisonné lapel pin of a turtle crawling out of a pipe. The two connecting Canadian lines were built on schedule, and they are currently pumping gas from fields in Canada into the Midwest and Northwest United States. The US portion of the line was never built.

Canadian Pipeline Inspector's lapel pin turtle, teasing us about our slow, turtle like progress on the U.S. part of the pipeline

By 1983 the national need for the gas had substantially subsided. One Friday morning I got a call from my Northwest Pipeline public affairs colleague, who told me they were about to lay off a bunch of people in Anchorage, Fairbanks, Salt Lake City, Houston, Pasadena, Washington, D.C., and the headquarters in Irvine, California. This was a shock, but I figured it must be common knowledge if the staff at Northwest was telling me about it and so I had no concerns about responding to a reporter from the *Anchorage Times* who called me later that afternoon.

The next day the *Times'* article quoted me extensively about the employee layoffs. The reporter had also called the company and quoted them, but from that point on, the media considered me the primary source of information.

The Anchorage Times: Saturday, May 8, 1982,

NORTHWEST EMPLOYEES GET NOTICES
By Dave Carpenter.

The lead company on the proposed Alaska Highway natural gas pipeline laid off more than half its staff Friday, one week after announcing a minimum two-year delay for the floundering project. The cuts by Northwest Alaskan Pipeline Co., in addition to those of contractors associated with the project, brought unemployment for over 600 people – 100 of them in Alaska.

The staff cutbacks, disclosed to employees Friday morning, were effective immediately. They involved both staffers at Northwest's tiny Anchorage office and 23 of 51 employees in Fairbanks, including the firm's Alaska spokeswoman, Kathleen Kelly.

Northwest relayed first word of the dismissals through the office of federal inspector for the pipeline.

Paul Steucke, the office's external affairs representative in Anchorage, also said Fluor Northwest – the projects prime contractor, doing design work on the pipeline -- is closing its 72-employee Fairbanks office.

Elsewhere, Steucke said Fluor is laying off all but seven of 191 employees at its Irvine, Calif., headquarters; the Ralph M. Parsons Co., contracted to design the gas conditioning plant is trimming its Pasadena based staff from 200 to 20, and Project Management Contractors is releasing 107 of its 130 Houston employees.

The assistant to federal inspector Jack Rhett said his office will not be laying off employees, but will not replace those lost through attrition. Steucke said Rhett still believes the project will "eventually" be built by the private sector even if Northwest fails, hence the no-fire policy.

This caught our Washington, D.C. office off guard. Much to my surprise, Northwest had not informed our Washington office, and because I thought they were already aware of the news, neither did I. My previous boss told me they were not at all happy with me!

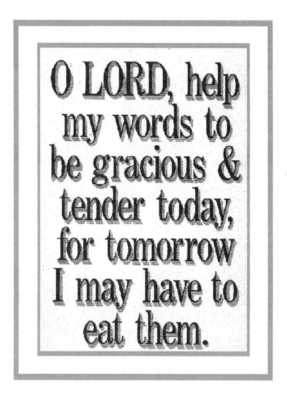

When I first came to Alaska, I found a plaque in a gift shop that reads, *O Lord, help my words to be gracious & tender today, for tomorrow I may have to eat them.* I thought that particularly apropos for a public information person and hung it on my office wall where I could look at it every day.

After that unfortunate mistake, I pasted the above article on the back of the plaque so I could easily remind myself to always, always, always coordinate the release of information.

Our federal budget cycle started on the first of October. By mid-summer of that year, fifty percent of our agency's employees in Anchorage were out of work--including me--through what is euphemistically called a Reduction In Force (RIF). The rest of the staff went on the first of October. For the second time in my career, I was let go from a federal civil service job. Yes, as I again discovered, even in the federal government you can lose your job. *

This time we did not move. Annette had her social work degree and was fully employed with the State of Alaska's child and family social service department as the supervisor of the adoption unit. PJ was a chemical engineering student at the University of Oregon in Corvallis--and this time the government provided me with a nine-month severance pay package. (I didn't receive any severance pay when the LUPC job closed--only because no one ever thought to apply.)

*The Alaskan portion of the project was resurrected again by the State of Alaska and different construction companies in 2007, but as of this writing has not yet been funded or started. The natural gas withdrawn during the extraction of oil must, by state law, be re-injected back into the ground.

* * *

The F27 and the Grumman goose aviation incidents allowed me to be of some help to a woman who had sustained a huge loss, when I was a potential juror for a suit seeking compensation for an accidental death on the North Slope during the oil pipeline construction. All sixty jury candidates sat in the courtroom as the judge and the lawyers slowly filled the jury by pulling a number out of a basket and calling out the corresponding name. By the time the fifth juror had been selected, it was obvious to me from the attorneys' questions that the husband of the woman who was bringing suit had died in an aviation accident while working on the oil pipeline project, and that the defendants did not want to pay her a fair sum for his death.

I was the next person selected. I sat in jury chair number six, and the judge told me to answer the ten questions on a large flip chart-- name, address, occupation, and so on. I worked my way down the list without incident until I got to the final question--*Do you know any reason why you should not serve on this jury?*

I answered yes, and the judge cleared the courtroom, leaving only the bailiff, court reporter, the widow's two lawyers and the twelve defense lawyers sitting on the other side of the room. Then the judge leaned forward, looked over the top of his reading glasses, and said slowly, "Please explain."

I told him as a part of my federal job, I had flown in many airplanes all over the state and that on two occasions I had come close to dying in a work-related aviation accident. I said, "I find I am biased in favor of the plaintiff, Your Honor. The one thing that makes me willing to do so much flying in Alaska on official business is the assumption that my family will be appropriately financially compensated should I die in an airplane accident." The judge said, "You are excused from jury duty."

As I left and walked up the aisle past the widow's attorney, he whispered to me, "Thank you." Two days later, they settled out of court.

* *

Paul Steucke Sr.

The Artist Returns

When we moved back to Anchorage in 1980, I was able to use one of the bedrooms as an art studio and start painting again after a hiatus of many years. A space, a room, dedicated to painting is needed if an artist is to succeed. I did a few paintings and sold them to people at the office, and then I gathered my courage and sought the advice of a successful local artist about showing my work.

He was at an art show of his own when I approached and asked if we could talk sometime soon about what I should do. "Call me in the morning," he said, "any morning. I always work in the morning." So I did. Byron was not only an outstanding, popular watercolor artist, but also a very friendly, gregarious and helpful fellow. I admired his work. One of his original watercolors has hung on our living room wall for 25 years. He advised me to call one of the owners at a local gallery that represented him and ask to show them my work. I had been visiting this gallery for years; it was the best gallery in the state.

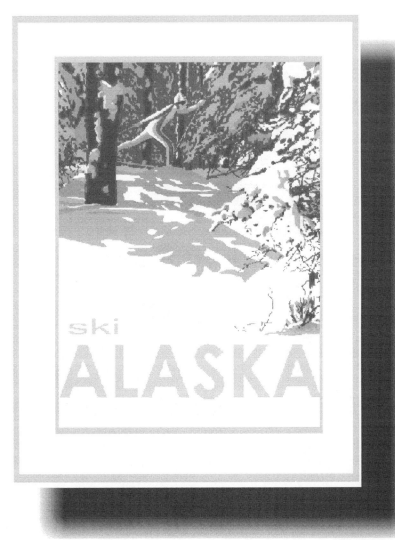

Commissioned silkscreen poster for the Alaska Cross Country Ski Club.
Edition of 1,000

I had hoped to do this in private, perhaps before they opened in the morning, but one of the co-owners said to just come in on Saturday, so I arranged to visit them the moment they opened, as I was very nervous about having other people look at my work. I parked my car at the curb in front of the store in an attempt to get my stuff into the gallery the moment they opened. My plan did not work. Jean, the co-owner and a successful artist herself, showed up thirty minutes late and told me to bring my paintings in and stack them around the gallery, leaning them up against the wall with the bottom edge of the frame on the floor, so she could see them.

Meanwhile, my greatest fear was being realized as customers began coming in the front door. I was so nervous I could barely stand still. I knew Annette would want to know exactly what was said and how it went, so I hid a little tape recorder in my breast pocket. After I had all ten paintings in place, Jean walked around the room accompanied with some customers, then came over to me and said, "We have an open space for the first two weeks of December. We could show them then and see what happens."

Two weeks later they hung the show; however, one piece, *hoping*, sold before it ever got on the wall. I had asked the gallery to help me price them. Most sold for about $400.00. (A gallery customarily gets 40 percent and the artist supplies the frames--New York City galleries get 50 percent!)

People would look at my paintings in a show and say," Your work is beautiful, why don't you quit your civil service job and paint full-time?" I would explain the difficulty of earning a living in the art world. When I have a show in an art gallery, it will usually hang for two weeks and then go into temporary storage in the basement, along with several hundred other paintings by other artists. Galleries usually have a room set aside for shows, and another room or rooms for a rotating mixture of many other artists' work. I may, at any one time, have, at most, two or three paintings on the gallery walls.

"Hoping," watercolor on art board
Edition of 500

Let's say one of my paintings is priced at $2,000. Someone has to walk through that gallery, see my painting, decide they cannot live without it, and have an extra $2,000 in the checkbook they are willing to part with. The gallery gets half, so I am down to $1,000. I already have paid at least $200 to pay to frame it, so I am down to $800. The IRS gets 10 percent, so I am now down to $720. My research time plus supplies cuts that figure down to about $650. To earn $50,000 per year I would have to sell approximately 77 of these paintings a year, or to put it another way, I must create three such saleable paintings every two weeks, with no time off for illness, holidays, vacations or family emergencies. My work currently sells for an average price of $10, 000, and has sold for as much as $24,000, depending on the artwork, but not even the top price will provide me with a steady living equal to a moderate civil service salary. The myth of the starving artist in the garret attic studio is not a myth. That is why I chose a BFA in graphic design and not fine art.

   That first show at Artique Art Gallery in Anchorage was a
success. All but one piece sold before Christmas and the last
one sold within the year. Considering the work involved in
producing them, they were a bargain, but at the time, I had
built no reputation as an artist. On the Saturday they hung the
show, I went to a local nursery to buy some plants, and when I
wrote out a check, the clerk looked at it and said, "Oh, you're
the artist advertised in the paper this morning." I told her I was
not aware of any advertisement, and she said, "It's a very
attractive painting you did." As soon as I got home, I looked in
the morning's paper--and could not believe my eyes.
   I also was very shy about having my work hanging in the
gallery. I could not bear to go into the gallery directly, so I
would walk back and forth on the sidewalk across the street
and look from a distance. When they closed the gallery for the
day, I would cross over and peek through the front window in
amazement.
   Several people came up to me after my first show and
volunteered to finance prints of my work. After talking to the
gallery owner, I turned them down, trusting the gallery would
know what to do. However, the gallery never did

independently print my work. I don't know why. (During the Renaissance, successful artists had a wealthy sponsor, like the Pope or the Medici. Today's art sponsor is the print market.)

I eventually found a sponsor for two of my Alaskan paintings in KAKM public television. They made 500 prints of each *Pioneer Barn* and *Heading Out* as a fundraiser. These sold out. I received fifty artist proofs, but no cash.

I convinced the gallery to print 500 copies each of two of my pieces, *Hoping* and *Heading Out,* by offering to share the printing costs 50/50 and giving them 60 percent of the profit. These prints quickly sold out, but even so, the gallery never invested in making any other prints of my work. However, my relationship with Artique Art Galley blossomed, and I had many one-man and group showings there.

Eventually the newness wore off and I became comfortable being known as an artist. But I was never comfortable with newspaper art critics, who more often than not can't create anything of merit themselves. They always seem more interested in pumping up their own egos in the press than in giving an unbiased evaluation of the art.

Arco-Alaska Airlines Art show, Prudhoe Bay, Alaska, 1977.
Clockwise: Left to right: Cecelia Jorgenson, Carolyn Strand, Paul Steucke,
Nancy Stonington, Byron Birdsall, Rie Munoz, Kate Boesser, Doug Hudson

"Kiana," Brooks Range, watercolor

KAKM fundraiser print, "Pioneer Barn," acrylic

One show stands out in my memory. Senator Ted Stevens of Alaska, along with my art gallery and the Alaska fishing industry, put on an all-Alaskan art show and spectacular seafood feed in the U.S. Capitol Building. Due to my unemployment, I had been painting full-time in my garage and had produced some very attractive pieces, four of which were included in the show. It was held in an immense wood paneled ballroom. The seafood table, piled high with king crab and other delicacies, was at least 30 feet long. The wine was free, served in stemmed wine glasses (and no plastic anything!), and the crowd was so thick that it was all but impossible to move through the room. Many senators, congressmen and staffers showed up (including Senator Ted Kennedy) and it was a gala affair. Two of my paintings sold, one of which, *Heading Home,* had three interested buyers at $1,500. The painting is now a part of the Rasmuson Art Museum collection in Anchorage and is valued at over $20,000.

KAKM Public Television
10th anniversary coffee mug,
designed by the author

"Heida Dancer", 30x40 inches, acrylic on canvas (sold at the D.C. show)

The day before the show, Annette and I attended a cocktail buffet at Alaska Senator Gravel's upscale home on Capitol Hill. I remember a service gentleman standing behind a linen-covered table out in the garden shucking Chesapeake oysters upon request--Annette found this beyond wonderful. Early in the evening, Senator Gravel invited the artists and their spouses on a private tour of the White House offices, and we loaded into a Secret Service bus for the short trip. I remember that after we pulled through the iron gates, the bus driver, trying to turn the bus around, backed into a hedge bordering the oval drive, thereby greatly annoying several newscasters trying to record their nightly news report.

Inside we were shown some of the better-known rooms and ended the tour looking across a yellow velvet rope into the Oval Office. Just a few feet down the hall were some staff work stations and two restrooms. Some of the gentlemen in our group could not pass up the chance to put their feet in the same place a president does, but I declined; I thought I'd had enough honor for one evening.

Senator Ted Stevens with the artist at the U.S. Capitol Alaskan Art Show.

"Heading Home," watercolor by the author, from an art review in
The Washington Times

The *Ski Alaska* poster I did for the national, cross-country ski race (page 174) brought me another offer to design a silkscreen poster extolling the wonders of Alaska. For years, KHAR radio printed and gave away Alaskan art prints, calendars and posters to publicize the radio station. They asked me to create a poster to commemorate the silver anniversary of Alaska statehood.

Silkscreen prints and posters differ from other printed art material in that they use opaque paint instead of translucent inks. My design included a printing technique in which the printer places a light paint color (like white) on one side of the print frame, and a dark paint on the other side, so the two will blend, creating a shading affect in the middle. It was not until the printer started printing my poster that he discovered the blending was not working. At this point, there was no choice but to keep on going, even though a subtle but significant part of the print design was lost forever. Fortunately, the printer and I were the only two people, out of the 5,000 who received the poster, who knew that it would have looked better if the printer had been able to produce it as originally designed.

The radio station increased their publicity by having me sign the prints at a giveaway in the JC Penney store downtown. I left my office at 9:50 AM on the advertised day and walked the short distance to the department store, only to discover a two-block line of people waiting in the cold to get into the store. It was not until the manager opened the door and let me in that I realized these people were waiting to get the poster. The manager put me at a signing table, along with an employee to move the prints across the table to me, so we could smoothly move people along. After three hours of signing, the print supply was exhausted, and I rose from the table--desperate to locate a restroom. Then I went upstairs to a private conference room and signed prints for the store employees.

The generous response to the KHAR poster prompted the Spenard Builders Supply to print a similar publicity poster for their Alaskan customers. Print signing in their stores, again with large numbers of people waiting in line, was held in Anchorage, Eagle River, Fairbanks and Kodiak.

During one of my many government management-training trips, I met an instructor who had worked in Europe teaching management skills to federal employees and military people on various posts. On her trips, she often came across the owner of

KHAR Silver Anniversary poster, edition of 6,000

a traveling art company out of Kalamazoo, Michigan, who sold art prints on the bases. She sent me the company literature, writing, "You can do better work than this. Why don't you contact them." So I did.

When I first started work for this publisher, civil war art was a big market item in the galleries. Realistic battle scene work was already being done by several outstanding artists, including Don Stivers, and I immediately decided against any effort to compete with their mastery in that subject. Instead, I focused on paintings depicting non-battle elements of the Civil War soldier. During research trips to the battlefields in Pennsylvania and Virginia, I learned that many realistic re-enactments are put on each year by people who want to experience the life of a civil war soldier. These are huge events, with horses, tents, cooking fires, and battle, complete with the firing of period cannon and rifles, all the participants clad in period costume. I was thrilled to have found so many models.

Being essentially uneducated about the various working issues of artist/publisher agreements, and too happy with the prospect of being published in general, I signed a ten-year contract with the Kalamazoo gallery without consulting a lawyer as to my best interests in the business relationship. My contract called for me to produce, and for them to print a minimum of two of my paintings per year for retail sale. Not necessarily specifically military artwork they wanted, just any two pieces. They never prepaid me for my artwork, but they had first right of refusal on any piece I produced. Over the next ten years, only two of my civil war pieces were accepted and reproduced. Since they never commissioned me to do a painting, with any given piece I could not know until after it was completed, whether or not they would publish and promote it. I took all the research and creation risk. Each print sold for $100 to $400 each, depending on the subject, for which my return was 7 percent of the retail sale. They sold three of my West Point originals on consignment, a pair for

$22,000 and a single for $24,000, for which I received 50 percent of the sale price.

As time went by, I gradually became more and more unhappy with their business practices, including their accounting methods. They kept written communication to a minimum, and I came to believe that was intentional. For example, I have no bills of sale showing what clients paid for the original paintings the gallery sold. Eventually things reached a point where I came to doubt that my royalty payments accurately reflected the sales of my work. I successfully sued for back unpaid royalties, and we parted company. The next chapter covers the happier aspects of our business relationship and my successful West Point works for the Kalamazoo gallery. But first, a few words about my second disappointing gallery experience.

"Drummer Boys", *CSA and USA*

Next I worked with a gallery/agent who kept trying to get me to invest in his company by donating a portion of the sale of my painting *Cadet Prayer* to his gallery, thereby making me an investor. I declined only to find out six months later via a telephone call from their potential client that they had already sold the painting to him for $11,000. They owed the same buyer money for printing and mailing services, and were planning on deducting $5,000 from the sale price in return for the printing services. This in effect made me an investor in the gallery, something I told had them I would not do. I told the client about this run around, and he backed out of the deal. The gallery soon went bankrupt, and I sold the painting to the same client for $9,000, discounted to $6,000 if he would donate the painting to West Point. It now hangs in the Cadet Chapel.

For a while I was able to retail my West Point work as 11 x14 posters via my website. I did this so people who could not afford a $250 lithographic limited edition signed and numbered print could obtain a $45.00 poster.

These were quite popular with parents whose children aspired to attend West Point. Unfortunately, a corporation in Atlanta has trademarked college and university logos and names and now makes a royalty profit from anyone who wants to use those names, including the name West Point or West Point Military Academy. I believe it is illegal to use names and logos created by the government with public money, but I do not have the resources to obtain a court opinion on the matter, so I accept the current situation.

"Flanking the Cavalry," acrylic on canvas

I can continue to sell my artwork but cannot use the West Point title. I discontinued the sale of West Point posters.

West Point Gallery

All artwork by the author

"...the Long Gray Line has never failed us. Were you to do so, a million ghosts in olive drab, in brown khaki, in blue and gray, would rise from their white crosses thundering those magic words, Duty, Honor, Country. General Douglas MacArthur, USMA, West Point 1962

"Duty- Honor-Country," General Douglas MacArthur
Acrylic on canvas, 1993

Print edition of 6,000

In 1993, my original publisher suggested that I produce a painting depicting General Douglas MacArthur's farewell address to the Corps at West Point, on May 12, 1962. While doing several different sketches of possible designs, my wife mentioned that I might want to consider using spirit images of famous West Point generals in the painting, a technique artist Norman Rockwell used in his Boy Scout paintings. This I did.

The publisher produced and sold 6,000 prints of the painting, which sold for $150 to $350 each, depending on the series edition chosen. The West Point Class of 1993 purchased 500 prints as a fundraiser and had them signed by, comedian Bob Hope, General Colin Powell, General William Westmoreland, General Norman Schwarzkopf, and General James Ellis. These sold for $800 and are now valued at over $4,000 each.

Creating a painting based on a historical moment presents two challenges to the artist. The painting must be as true to the event as possible, and it must be pleasing to the viewer. The first challenge requires a considerable amount of research; the second requires the ability to subtly modify certain aspects of the event so they will harmoniously fit into the boundaries of a canvas. Research required a trip to the Academy library at West Point, the MacArthur Foundation in Norfolk, Virginia, the National Archives, and the Library of Congress in Washington, D.C. There is very little visual documentation of the presentation of the Thayer Award to General MacArthur and his speech that took place in the large mess hall. There are a few professional black and white photographs, some personal family snapshots, and a dark, blurry black and white 16mm film clip of the event, but not much else.

The rostrum, large dual microphones, and MacArthur's posture and suit were documented in one front-view, professional close-up photograph. The family snapshots were used to identify the floral arrangements and some participants at the two head tables, particularly General Westmoreland, Superintendent of the Academy at the time, and General Leslie R. Groves, President of the Association of Graduates.

The cadets were seated at tables in the room. I moved them forward, closer to the rostrum, an artistic liberty I had to take, otherwise they would have become insignificant dots in the background. Another close shot of MacArthur includes Cadets Blumhardt* (far left foreground in painting), James Ellis (center forward view), Kirchenbauer* (forward, far right), and Grebe (middle rear, fourth from left).

The ghosted figures represent a historical cross section of soldiers, and are dedicated to the memory of all military who have served our country. From left to right they are: World War II officer, D-Day, a Vietnam advisor; a captain in Korean War; General John "Blackjack" Pershing; General Robert E. Lee; General George Patton; World War I doughboy; and General Ulysses S. Grant. I regret that, due to limited space, I was unable to represent all the various types of personnel who fought in defense of our country.

A few subtle things were done to balance the color of the painting and arrange various elements. For example, the ceiling light chandeliers are an accurate representation, but several were removed from the painting so they would not appear in awkward locations. Some pink color was added to the flowers, and cadet-jacket grey was placed throughout the ghost figures to distribute and balance the overall color of the painting. The microphones on the rostrum are accurate in design, but have been reduced in size so as not to dominate that part of the painting. The ceiling, walls and windows were based on research sketches and photographs I took at West Point.

In 2009 I received a request from the U.S. Military Academy Museum at West Point to repaint the damaged faces of Blumhardt and Kirchenbauer. While the painting hung at West Point, someone had used a cigarette lighter to burn the features off, two of them were burned to the point of creating a hole in the canvas.. After repair was completed, the painting was reframed with protective glass and again hung at the Academy.

Following are two letters, one from General Westmoreland and one from a woman who was present at the speech and admired my painting:

William Childs Westmoreland

General, United States Army, Retired
Box 1059
Charlestown, South Carolina 29402

July 16, 1993

Dear Lew:
Vladimir Arts USA

Your letters to me of June 17 and June 21 have been received.

Indeed Mr. Steucke's painting of General MacArthur addressing the USMA Corps of Cadets is superb. The individual to the left of the lectern is me, as you probably know. For many reasons I would like to purchase personally the print of the lithograph. Should I make the purchase from you or the MacArthur Memorial Foundation?

You note that one of the classes present during the address has purchased the original and donated it back to the Academy. Further you asked if "I would be interested in personally presenting that painting back to the Academy?" Indeed, I would be pleased to do so, except I consider that a decision of the Class that purchased the painting. If they wished me to do that, I trust they will contact me.

Best Wishes,

Sincerely,

W. C. WESTMORELAND

July 7, 1995

Dear Mr. Steucke:

Enclosed is a letter that I wrote to you a couple of short years ago at the end of my cadet's plebe year. (I never got around to sending it. Obviously.) Now when I saw "Cadet Prayer" I had to put my procrastinations aside. You did it again. This really looks like Tom did when he was a plebe. (Not so much anymore because he's older.) You must be tapped into my psyche somehow. Thank you so much for such lovely remembrances of Tom's life at the Academy. I know that more than once he has chosen the harder right. I also know that he will continue to do so. Thank you.

Beat Navy
Melinda Mc

Mr. Steucke:

When I received the advance information concerning the art work selection for this year, I knew I would be interested because my cadet has a great admiration for General MacArthur. However, I was totally unprepared for what I would see when I opened the envelope. It was as if you had painted this picture expressly - exclusively for me. Tears came to my eyes and goose flesh to my arms. (Literally.) You see, my son Tom, is president of the class of 1996. On march 20, 1993 I sat along side General Graves at the front table and watched my kid deliver one of the most important speeches of his life. There were very few dry-eyed adults in the hall that night. Thank you so much for what promises to be a very special and personal memento of Tom's years at the military academy.

Beat Navy
Melinda Mc

"Cadet Prayer," Acrylic, 1994

A portion of the Cadet Prayer, reads: "Make us choose the harder right instead of the easier wrong, and never to be content with a half truth when the whole can be won." My publisher suggested the theme of a cadet at prayer in the West Point Chapel for my next painting.

I liked the subject, but it presented a very difficult design problem. I needed to include the cadet, the altar, and the forty-foot high stained glass window above and behind the altar. However, if I painted a direct view of the window, only the back view of the cadet would be seen. While pondering this problem, I happened to look down at the sunshine coming through our living room window, casting light on the carpet. I immediately realized I could solve the problem by painting an elevated front view of the cadet at prayer, with the window's beautiful, stained glass pattern sun-projected on the chapel floor. The particular window sections shown in the painting represent Duty-Honor-Country. The words are reversed on the floor because light coming through the window would do just that, project the image backwards. The window, light pattern on the floor, the cadet (who modeled for me) and the environment are accurate. An edition of 6,000 prints was made. The painting was purchased by a West Point graduate and donated to the Chapel at West Point.

"Red Sash," acrylic, 1997
Print edition of 6,000

The inspiration for the *Red Sash* painting came from a book about West Point in which the author described the moment when a young student, fresh out of high school--reports, as directed by the West Point acceptance letter, "to the man in the red sash." The *man* part has changed. Women are now admitted to West Point until they comprise approximately 15 percent of the Corp. All members of the year's new senior class or firsties wear the red sash, as they are called.

Each June these new cadets, plebes, report for duty on Reception Day, or R day. It was amazing to watch these young men and women go through the transformative process of signing legal documents, receiving of medical checks, immunization shots, military haircuts, new clothing, discipline, training and much more--all of which begins by reporting to the man in the red sash.

They shape up quickly. At the end of the day, it was a very moving experience to sit in the grandstand as they marched in formation across the parade field, where in front of thousands of parents and relatives, they took the oath of allegiance. It was a very proud moment for all concerned. I am grateful that I had the opportunity to be there and to live in a time in our history when I could photograph and portray an African American plebe and a woman senior cadet in the red sash.

"Hidden Treasures", Acrylic 1977
Print edition of 5,000

    Hidden Treasures was suggested and supported by the Officer's Women's Club at West Point. I requested that they provide the props, two children to model for me, and the attic of an older house at West Point, which they did magnificently. The painting is based on several separate photographs I took on location. The background in the room was one photo, the children another, the chest and material on the right another, and the dog still another. Phillip seemed a bit uncomfortable, but Samantha was having a good time. I brought along some Hershey chocolate drops to sweeten the three-hour process. It worked; they did a great job for my cameras. The original painting, in my possession, is available for purchase.

"Crossing the Plain," Acrylic, 1999
Print Edition of 6,000

In March of 1998, I was at West Point to sign and endorse my *Red Sash* prints (similar to a book-signing event). While there, I noticed a weather report for snow the next day--a wonderful possibility that I hoped would happen, as it changes the way everything looks. I set my alarm, awoke before daylight, and looked out the window to find everything covered with ten inches of fresh snow. I put on two pair of pants, several shirts, my lightweight Caribbean-style jacket, and draped a hotel towel over my head to keep the wet and cold out of my neck. I crossed the deserted Thayer Hotel lobby in my weird garb and stepped out the front door into the new world of white. There was no noise, no people, no traffic--just the glow of streetlights and the quiet hiss of falling snow.

I had been to West Point many times and was aware of the superintendent's beautiful house that faces the marching plain, and that image was in my thoughts as I trudged through the fresh snow toward the barracks and the plain. The first two cadets I asked to pose as a model declined, saying they were late for an appointment. The third cadet agreed, and for that, I am grateful. I told her I was an artist, but I must have looked very strange in my Arabian-like costume. The photos I took of her became the *Crossing the Plain* painting.

"Pershing Sallyport," acrylic, 1999
Print edition of 6,000

My second opportunity for a snow scene painting came as I walked through the old barracks courtyard and saw the massive wrought iron lamps on each side of the Pershing Sallyport. The stone walls of the Pershing Barracks, completed in 1895, were dusted with the flakes blowing down in waves from above. There was no sound or activity except for one cadet passing through the tunnel; my photo became *Pershing Sallyport.*

The pair of snow paintings went into print, and the originals were purchased for $24,000 by a West Point graduate from Chicago. My return, as established by my contract with my publisher, was 50 percent, $12,000.

"Snowtime", Acrylic on canvas, 2002
"In the depth of winter, I finally learned that within me there lay an invincible summer,"
Albert Camus

That West Point trip resulted in a third winter painting, which depicts a cadet pushing through a snowstorm that has reduced visibility in the quadrangle to almost zero. The wind is drifting snow off the roof of the old original barracks, (now used as a museum and office). The immense, four-sided clock on top of the pillar shown in the background is the only one left of several that were used to provide accurate time to cadets prior to the use of pocket or wrist watches, hence the title, *Snowtime.*

Three months later, in stark contrast to the March snowstorm, I was at West Point to do research for several other possible paintings. It was mid-June, very hot, and the annual pilgrimage of high school students was about to descend on the Academy for R Day. My main purpose was to take photographs of the color guard that always leads the body of cadets onto the parade field, to use for a painting celebrating the 200th anniversary of the Academy (see page 204). I also captured some other possible subjects, including flowers in the garden at the superintendent's house--I thought it would be appropriate to illustrate the Academy slogan, "An Officer and a Gentleman." A hundred years ago, the Academy, in addition to academics, taught the cadets the art of civilized living thought to be appropriate to an officer--etiquette, drawing, sculpture, literature and music. The good manners remain, but the arts are no longer in the regular curriculum.

"Seize the Moment," acrylic, 2001

This painting was originally titled, *Take Time to ...* (as in the proverb, "*smell the roses*"). The concept, based on the "officer and a gentleman" phrase, was to emphasize that cadets should be taught to be gentlemen (and ladies) and not just battle-trained officers in the army. After the painting was completed, some people at West Point suggested that the title be changed to *Seize the Moment*. I heard from others at the Academy that the entire concept was being critiqued by a previous publisher of mine as being too soft, meaning, I guess, you'd better stick to battle stuff. After his derogatory comment became common knowledge, my sales of the piece dropped to zero. The original painting was later purchased by the family of the young woman cadet in the painting.

"Academy Rose", Acrylic on canvas, 2003
(Available for purchase.)

Paul Steucke Sr.

"Reservoir Reflections" (the Chapel tower is reflected in the water),
Lusk Reservoir, West Point, USMA
Acrylic, 2000, (available for purchase)

"Mr. Ferrar's Mirror," acrylic, 2009

The barbershop painting is based on the closely shaved haircuts given to each plebe on "R Day." The barber, Mr. Ferrar, cut hair at the West Point barbershop for over 30 years. The young man in the chair is looking with disbelief at the figures reflected in the mirror. They are, from left to right: A cadet at West Point (Patton), "Blackjack" Pershing, Patton, Lee, Bradley, Eisenhower, Davis, Ridgway, Westmoreland, Grant, MacArthur, Thayer, and a cadet in the upper right corner representing women cadets at the Academy.

This painting, in my possession, is available for purchase.

"Bicentennial, 1802 -2002," Acrylic on canvas
The original is available for purchase.

The present day Academy color guard marches toward us while the cadets of the past, in period uniforms, pass in review behind. All 200 years of the Corps are listed in the background. The various emblems of the Army's services are arrayed around the outside edge. The top says, "United States Army Military Academy – Bicentennial." West Point is always referred to as the United States Military Academy; however, I inserted the word Army, to distinguish it from the Air Force Academy in Colorado and the Naval Academy at Annapolis. The original is available for purchase.

Annette and Paul Steucke,
Kona Hawaii

Hawaii

People in Alaska like to go to Hawaii, sometimes several times a year. Hawaii is due south of Anchorage in the same time zone. It seemed like everybody we knew was an expert on Hawaii, so in 1983 we went to Maui to become experts too.

Landing at the airport was a low-key experience. The terminal and baggage area were mostly open-aired, full of wild sparrows swooping in and around the ceiling, contributing their little sparrow chirps. It was already a relaxing place to be. Our rental car took us across the island past the sugar cane fields to the little town of Lahaina (which is not so little anymore.)

Photo by Robert Mobley

Annette at the magic window in Lahaina

On the airplane, Annette saw an advertisement in the Hawaiian magazine, *Onion,* for a highly recommended casual restaurant along the waterfront. Never having been to Lahaina, we parked on the street at the north end of town and started walking south along the main road. After a half hour, we reached the restaurant, at the very end of south Lahaina. It was a very long walk, and by the time we arrived, Annette had a huge blister on her heel.

The beautiful warm weather, the swaying palm trees and singing birds were a different world from the frigid Anchorage we had left that morning. The restaurant had painted plywood walls and concrete floors, and it was doing a brisk luncheon business. We chose a windowed booth with only a strip of grass and some white sand between the ocean and us. After we ordered our hamburgers. I sat looking out the window. Then I looked more closely. Finally, I stood up and very slowly reached out to touch the glass, except, much to my surprise, my hand actually went through the window. It felt like something out of science fiction. Of course, there was no glass-

-we just had been in Alaska way too long to recognize an open-air restaurant.

I walked back to the other end of town to retrieve the car, and while Annette waited, she walked out on the beach grass, stripped off her nylon stockings and soaked her feet in the surf. That was the last time she ever wore stockings in Hawaii.

A short drive up the coast took us to the resort area of Kanapali and the Marriott Hotel that was everything we expected and more. I pulled the car up to the unloading area, and a smartly tailored young man opened our car door and pointed us toward the front desk. As I was waiting to register, I idly watched one of the parking valets get in the car. Our bags were still stacked on the sidewalk, and as the car backed up, the angle of the front wheels caught the corner of the largest piece of our new suede luggage and flipped it about six feet straight up into the air. It was an *aha* moment for everybody in the lobby--the busboys, the desk clerk, other people and me. Like the pause button on a movie, everything stopped for a few seconds. I turned and looked at the desk clerk, who said, in a flat monotone, "Excuse me for one moment," and headed for the car and the bags.

When he returned, he said the manager would be with us shortly and went back to registering. The manager appeared almost instantly through a door behind the desk and without even looking at the car, said, "I am very sorry; let's see what damage has been done." He waved to the busboy, who already had our luggage en route to the desk. "Perhaps we should go inside," he said, indicating the door he had just come through, "and see if anything is broken."

We opened the bag, and found everything intact, although the leather had a sizeable black tire mark on the outside. I was surprised that nothing had broken, considering the distance it travelled without the aid of anything but physics. The manager excused himself to talk with another employee standing nearby and quickly returned with $200 cash in his hand, a free room upgrade and another nice apology. The damage was minimal and the bonuses were a nice trade for a little cosmetic adjustment to the bag.

The Maui Marriot was a vacation dream. The restaurants, pools, courtyard, palm trees, breakfast and lunch by the pool, the beach, feral cats, geckos, sparrows, warm, soft air, flowers, the afternoon singers, mellow, mellow, mellow… a wonderful way to relax. In the next ten years, we went to Hawaii fifteen times for similar delicious getaways.

While walking the streets of Lahaina, we came upon a small, brand new restaurant. A double doorway and window facing the street allowed passersby to watch the chef and owner, Mr. Gerard, hard at work in his small kitchen. We read the bill of fare posted just outside the entrance, and Annette immediately wanted to try it. We enjoyed an extraordinary good lunch, (sautéed calamari steaks and lemon, butter lettuce and island greens in a light vinaigrette, freshly baked bread and cold, crisp wine), and made a reservation for that night's dinner. We came back many times on that and future trips to Maui. Over the years *Gerard's* prospered, eventually becoming one of the highest rated, and most favored establishments in the islands, but my fondest memories are the thrill of discovery and that first impromptu lunch in the little ten table cafe.

In Reston I had purchased and sailed a 14-foot sailboat that with a good breeze would fly across the surface of Lake Ann. The Marriot had two similar sailboats hauled out of the water at the beach. When I found out they were for rent I made arrangements and reserved one of the boats for a 10 AM sail. They gave me a life vest to wear. (Never go sailing without one, as the chance of capsizing a small sailboat in a good wind is about 75 percent guaranteed.) Both boats had a round bottom and were broad across the beam, not anything for a race, but good enough for some fun.

I assured the caretaker of the boats that I knew what I was doing (I did) and shoved off. They told me not to go out very far because the afternoon trade winds would soon come up.

While sailing around the anchored pleasure boats, I noticed that the extended steering stick on my little rental had broken off, but I didn't think of it as a problem since the water was vary calm. I soon discovered my error.

The extended steering stick is a small but very important part of the steering and turning mechanism. Attached to the front tip of the rudder, it allows the sailor to lean out over the edge of the boat and use the stick to push the rudder, which in turn steers the boat.

This sounds confusing, but stay with me. The rudder must be capable of being shoved hard all the way over when coming about (turning). This stick, about two feet long and the diameter of your finger, is attached with a pin to the top of the more solid two-foot stick that is part of the rudder (the rudder is a flat board at the back of the boat that swivels side-to-side allowing the boat to be steered). In a stiff wind the boat will blow over unless you counterbalance by leaning your body out over the edge of the boat--hiking out--that's part of the fun. The length of the extra-extended steering stick is needed when y

Paul Junior "hiking out" with extended steering stick in hand.

our body is out there over the edge of the boat and you need to shove the rudder fast and/or hard enough to get the boat to turn around. In a strong wind, this maneuver must be done quickly.

When the trade winds arrived, I tried to turn the boat toward shore, but the lack of the extended stick meant that the very moment the boat should turn and come about; it would stall with its nose pointing into the wind. It just would not complete the full turn. I tried unsuccessfully again and again to turn toward shore. My only option was to swing the boom the other direction for a jib (or boom) turn, which frequently will capsize the boat. In a jib turn there is little control of the boat and the power of the boom swinging from one side of the boat to the other is enormous. If it hit me in the head, it would knock me out. And now I was rapidly heading out to sea. I had no choice but to try it.

The boat capsized the moment the boom swung across, and I went into the ocean. The sail and mast, of course, were now pointing straight down into the water. I soon found out that the boat had another small but very significant problem.

Large sailboats have a heavily weighted fin that hangs permanently below the boat. The principle of speed with a sailboat is to transfer the energy created by the air pressure across the sail against the underwater fin. This drives the boat forward. Small boats accomplish this by hanging a flat board through a slot in the bottom of the boat. A narrow box, sticking up from the floor is used to keep water from squirting up into the boat. Pulled up, the dagger is in the sheath. Dropped down it is in the water, out of the sheath. This design allows the dagger board to be raised up into the boat for beaching on shore. A spring clip is used to keep it in place.

The usual technique for righting a small capsized sailboat is to grab the top of the dagger board (now sticking three feet straight up into the air) and using ones body weight, pull sideways on the board until the boat becomes upright.

As soon as I surfaced, I knew I was in trouble. The dagger board would not stay up. Instead, it slid down into the boat until it almost disappeared. There was nothing for me to apply leverage to, nothing to grab and pull over. Meanwhile, the waves were now deep enough to hide my sight of land, and froth was whipping over the tops of them. I dove under the boat and pushed the board up, only to have it slide down again. After several attempts, I was exhausted and crawled up on the overturned boat, a difficult feat due to the round, broad bottom. There I sat, cold and wet, watching the hotel get smaller and smaller as the ocean got bigger and bigger.

Then a rubber boat with an outboard engine came into view, carrying two hotel employees who evidently had been watching me through binoculars. I hollered to them across the wind that I was grateful to see them. (I don't think they could have known just how grateful I was.) My sailboat had a yellow, fifty-foot cord tied to the chrome cleat bolted in the snout of the boat. The guy running the small outboard motor came up beside the sailboat and told me to get in the rubber boat, which I did with some difficulty. He told his partner to take over the motor, and jumped into the water to save the boat.

While he tried to get the dagger board to stay up, we circled down wind and I tried to grab hold of the trailing yellow lead line, but without success because our rubber boat was two feet higher than the water surface. Then the outboard motor got swamped by an incoming wave and died. *God,* I thought, *this is not good!*

My rescuer kept trying to start the engine, as we drifted further and further away from the sailboat. It was a case of pull the start rope, nothing, pull the rope, nothing, pull the rope, nothing. We silently rode up one wave and down the other side, but I decided the last thing he needed to hear from me was panic, so I encouraged him to remain calm and keep trying, "Take your time," I said, "It will start, just go steady." Meanwhile, I was beginning to wonder if the Coast Guard would ever find us, as the wind howled and threw froth off the tops of the waves. I could see the headline, *Alaska tourist and hotel crew lost at sea.*

But eventually the motor started, and I raised my eyes to the heavens with a sincere thank you. We caught up with the sailboat and I grabbed the lead line out of the water just as the first man righted the boat, and we took off at an angle for the hotel. The sailboat zigged and zagged behind us, so I hollered back to drop the dagger board to control the boat, but either the guy did not hear me or he thought to himself, *I am not about to accept advice from him!*

When we pulled up onto the beach, I explained to the hotel guys how important that missing stick was and why it is needed, and I also told them that the dagger board clip needed fixing. Then we noticed that the frail clip that holds the boom to the mast had broken when I did the jib turn. Even if I had been able to right the boat, I would not have been able to sail it. They refunded my deposit and declined to charge me for the rent.

A telephone call several hours later gave me a chance to tell the hotel manager about the defective boat and praise the employees who came out to get me.

* * *

An Anchorage neighbor told us about a great experience he had sailing in a traditional sailboat to snorkel in Molokini Crater off the shore of Maui. The water there is so clear that you see beautiful fish 100 feet below. Most of the tour boats to Molokini are steady catamarans that can carry thirty to forty people in comfort, but I thought it would be more sporting to feel the thrill of the wind in a real sailboat. I should have known better.

I found Captain Jack (his real name) in the phone book, and the next day we arrived at the appointed dock at 9 AM. The older, wood boat was about twenty-eight feet long, with a single mast and two standard sails, one in front and the other on a boom that extended over the enclosed cabin. A small outboard motor was attached to the back area. Another man and his twelve-year-old son were also paying to visit the crater via a real sailboat. We cast off with Captain Jack (no crew) and sailed out toward the crater.

The sun was bright, the air salty. The boat sliced through the water, heeling to one side in a pleasant, wet-wind manner. Jack cast an eye toward Annette in her bikini as he told us that a few weeks earlier he had taken a group of women schoolteachers out and that they had all taken off their upper swimsuit parts and went topless. He emphasized that it had not bothered him a bit. Annette did not take her top off.

Being on an older, slower boat, we arrived at the crater after all the other tour boats had anchored and their patrons were splashing around having a good time. Captain Jack threw out the anchor and let it drift to the bottom of the state-protected reef, where it immediately started to drag across the coral bottom. Several tour boat operators hollered out that what Jack was doing was illegal. Our brave captain gave them the universal third finger and went inside the little covered cockpit to drink beer while we snorkeled and swam.

Before long, some tour boats began to leave, but we, having arrived late, hung in until we had the Crater all to ourselves. For some reason, I didn't feel altogether comfortable with being alone out there any longer. I poked my head into the cabin and found our captain reclined all the way up front with a beer in his hand. I said I was ready to leave, and he slowly got up, pulled anchor and set sail. We moved out of the protected, lagoon side of the crater and headed slowly into the trade winds and the four-foot swells that were kicking up an uncomfortable bow spray.

By now the tourist boats were far off in the distance, hugging the shore, while we true explorers braved the open trades. Captain Jack tied the sail directly over the center of the boat and directed the boy's father to keep it pointed to a specific landmark on the far shore. Then he disappeared down into the cabin.

After an hour of this pounding, I studied the distant boats and realized that we were barely going forward at all--I could have walked faster than we were moving! Because the sail was lashed directly amidships, we were slicing right into the wind, a condition that threw large amounts of water over the boat with each wave plunge. Once again I went below, this time to suggest that we might move a little faster if we used the outboard motor. Jack cranked it up, and immediately our speed doubled to about four knots--not great, but at least we were now gaining distance! Unfortunately, it also doubled the pounding that we were taking as we went up and down into each wave.

I went down to the cabin to escape the drenching froth in the back open area, only to confront a new problem; the young boy caught my eye and silently pointed to the water seeping into and above the cabin floor. Now I knew that there was a space under the floor, so that seepage meant we had taken on at least a foot of water. I quietly located the Coast Guard required life jackets stowed inside the cabin, mentally calculated that the trades would eventually blow us to shore, and then hollered to Jack that we were taking on water.

He gave the tiller to our other brave tourist and put his head inside, saw the rising water, and went forward, lifted some boards, pulled out two electrical wires, tied them together, and the bilge pump started working. I was relieved, but not feeling very well. Being in the cramped cockpit without being able to see the horizon made me suddenly sick and I raced to the back of the boat and projectile vomited over the side. Once was all it took; after that I was fine.

Hour by hour we crept slowly along. Finally, I could see the bay, and our captain soon motored us in with the outboard. Our finale was fitting; Jack, misjudging both speed and distance, crashed the front of the boat into the dock so hard it smashed the wood. Several boat captains sitting on a nearby dock cheered loudly. My prayers answered, I was grateful to put my feet on land. It was a real adventure, but one I neither recommend nor wish to try again.

"#12," acrylic on canvas

The Partner

She came into my life at the age of twelve when her parents moved into a small brick rambler down the street. She was smart, cute and lots of fun to be around. No one had air conditioning then, and when the 95-degree heat of the day cooled off and the cicadas began to sing, I would ride my bicycle down the block to her house in the evening air to play Kick the Can and Sardines--group games that have all but vanished, replaced by individuals playing computer games.

A few years later, we went to high school together, riding the school bus for the hour-long trip to Fairfax High. We shared the lab table in biology. I remember that in spite of her straight A class grades, the teacher failed her for the course because her bug phobia kept her from catching and mounting an insect collection—a strange pass-fail requirement. Although we often hung out, playing badminton and riding bikes in the summers, we never dated.

Home from college in my sophomore year for the Christmas holiday, I got a phone call from her inviting me to go to a party. I never hesitated for a moment, even though I was dating another girl. In the middle of the party, we got in my Buick and drove down the almost empty Route 7 highway from west Falls Church to Leesburg and back. She snuggled up to me on the cracked, red leather bench seat of the Buick. We barely even talked, didn't need to. It felt so right to be together. I went back to school and began writing her every day and seeing her as often as I could get home.

That June I went with my parents to my brother's home in Montana for his college graduation. My family's gentle teasing about the letter waiting for me when we arrived showed they were beginning to realize that something serious was developing between us. A year and a half later our partnership was formalized with a wedding—a union that has lasted over fifty years. We now have four children and seven grandchildren

My partner has taught me about life, love, women, philosophy, writing, and good food. Living in an intimate relationship with another person, like life itself, requires flexibility, personal introspection, and a willingness to keep on changing and growing. "For richer or poorer, in sickness and in health." Those words mean so much more to me now than they did when I said them at the altar in 1960. Over time, we have gone from very poor to quite comfortable, and have nursed each other back to health numerous times.

I was half-way through my junior year in college when we got married. The country was in a recession and jobs were scarce. The previous year I had received a significant fellowship from the Virginia Art Museum in Richmond, but the year we married the fellowship went to my college roommate, so things for us were financially difficult.

Annette has worked on and off throughout our married life to help us get through the hard times. In Richmond she found a job processing claims with a small life insurance company located a few blocks from our campus apartment. A few days before completing her first year, her supervisor called her in at closing time on a Friday and let her go, citing too many days off (unpaid) because of illness (a severe kidney infection) although under my subsequent questioning, the supervisor admitted that Annette's work had been excellent. We knew the real reason was that after one year they were required to give sick leave, vacation and health benefits. Annette got a job clerking at JC Penney, and later she went to work for a brokerage firm that hired young women to walk back and forth on an elevated runway, hand posting the minute-to-minute stock price changes on a big chalkboard.

Summer came, and while Annette continued to work for the stock company, I looked for a job, any job. I had applied for and been awarded the Museum fellowship again, but that would not begin until September. The paper advertised a position with the city driving a street cleaning machine, so I took the required exam. During my interview, the man behind the desk kept referring to the many family men who were trying to get this job during a recession. He asked me if I had allergy problems, since this was a dusty job. I told him no. He told me I was the number one scorer in the exam. Nevertheless, I was not offered the job. He knew, of course that I was a student, soon to be off to a different kind of work.

Annette's work, my National Guard check, and my part-time artwork managed to get us through the summer until the fellowship award kicked in at the start of my senior year. In the late winter, Annette noticed that she wanted to sleep a lot, and the stock market job, which required her to stand on her feet all day, was so tiring she took naps on the ladies restroom sofa during her lunch, rest breaks and while she waited for me to pick her up after work. In March, poor as we were, we were thrilled to find that Annette was pregnant.

I graduated in June and was very fortunate to find work with the Virginia Extension Service in Blacksburg, Virginia, for an annual salary of $4,000. Annette's three young daughters, who had been staying with her grandmother and three aunts in Rochester, Minnesota, while I was in school, joined us in Blacksburg. Our son, Paul, Jr. (PJ) was born November 22, 1962.

Annette did all the things a wife and mother does to make and keep a home and raise children, while I went to "work." A man gets credit for his work, but until recently, the multitudes of work that women do to keep a home and care for children has not been sufficiently valued. When we moved to

Waukesha, Wisconsin, Annette helped out with our expenses by working nights and weekends in a dry cleaning and laundry business. I took care of the kids during her work hours, but she still continued to do all the food preparation and house work. She was a busy partner.

After several promotions and transfers within the government, we ended up in Anchorage, Alaska, where Annette went to work part-time as census taker for the monthly employment census and the 1980 national population census. At this time, the 800-mile pipeline to get the oil from Prudhoe Bay to an ice-free port in Valdez was under construction and everything in Alaska was in a boomtown mode. The Census Bureau did not have an Alaskan office. Everything was directed by Seattle people, most of whom were unfamiliar with Alaskan culture, conditions and challenges. In the "Last Frontier," the idea of an individual providing information to the government on a variety of subjects (employment, crime, health, income and others) every month for six months, did not find favor with many, and the job required superb people skills from the interviewers.

To establish a foundation for surveys, census workers made hand-drawn maps of roads and dwellings. Seattle then randomly selected a percentage--such as every fifth address-- for current occupant interviews. In the chaotic and overcrowded conditions of the pipeline era, Annette went 360 miles north of Anchorage to Fairbanks to plot out the houses and rudimentary, thrown-together shacks. A month later when she went back to re-interview, she often found that some of the shacks had vanished and others had sprung up in new locations.

The rental apartments and houses in Fairbanks often contained as many as fifteen or twenty (mostly male) pipeline workers identifying the premises as their home base. Although the situation was potentially dangerous, she never experienced any problematic behavior from the men she interviewed. The biggest problem she had was catching the occupants when they were "home" between work shifts at Prudhoe Bay and the pipeline.

One week the Bureau asked Annette to map seven remote and widely scattered villages within five days time. When I looked at what they were asking her to do, I was shocked and did not think it could be done. However, she made a lot of phone calls, chartered some bush pilots, and to my amazement, managed to complete the assignment on time.

Annette at the controls of a Cessna air taxi flying to King Salmon. Photo taken by the pilot from the back seat.

Another month she flew 800 miles out to the very end of the Aleutian Chain to determine if any new housing had been built in Dutch Harbor. The mayor of the tiny village happened to be on the same flight heading for home, so she asked him to look over the current map for any necessary corrections. When he verified that there had been no changes in the village, she was able to save a days work, ride the same plane back to Anchorage and get home in time for dinner.

As I mentioned, it was not easy for management in Seattle to understand the difficult conditions that Alaska presented to census work. One winter month, Annette was sent to map houses on the north side of Eagle River valley, a decidedly rural location that never got any direct sunshine due to the shadow of the mountain and the low angle of the winter sun. Cold, dark, and sans telephone lines, there was only one single-lane dirt road, holding about ten houses over the five mile run. On the day she and I set out in the Ford Bronco to map, everything was frozen solid in minus 40-degree temperature.

I remember that at one point I stopped the vehicle and looked across fifty feet of foot-thick ice that had come off the hillside as water during freeze up. Of course, it was not flat but had a downhill slope to it, and that made me feel very uncomfortable. I thought to myself, *Seattle does not know what they are asking us to do.* I put the vehicle in four-wheel drive, got a running start, and we got safely across, but it had been scary, and I dreaded our return trip.

We slowly wove our way up the valley until the road ended at a fenced property featuring several hand-made signs: *Keep Out! This Means You! Danger! Do Not Enter! Trespassers Will Be Shot!* As if that was not enough, three or four large, angry dogs barked and snarled at us from inside the fence. We got the message. I was convinced that we should not enter that property for the purpose of conducting a federal government interview, or any other purpose. We mapped and went home, and when it came time to interview, Annette marked the file *unable to complete,* and left it to braver souls.

Eventually it was the numerous fierce dogs that finished her. She told her supervisor she was resigning because she no longer wanted to deal with dangerous situations--such as the big pair of malamutes who were so fierce that they tried to bite her through the windows of the car, while their owner cursed at her to get off the property. No more Last Frontier!

The nursing profession seemed a possibility, so she enrolled in a program at the University of Alaska, where she excelled in class work, but when she began hospital training, her empathy with patients and desire to spend more time with them brought the realization that nursing really was not quite what she wanted. Her advisor said, "You are really very good talking with patients; maybe you should consider being a social worker. And so that is what she became. My partner graduated from UAA with a BSW degree, worked for a year, and then eighteen months later earned a MA in child and family therapy and psychology from Saybrook Institute in San Francisco. She truly enjoyed her work with children, women, and families at several non-profit agencies during the remaining years we lived in Alaska.

The Federal Aviation Administration, Alaska Region

While being unemployed was great for my art career, it was not going to pay the mortgage. Fortunately, Annette was employed with the State of Alaska Social Services office, and her salary and my severance pay carried us financially for a year.

Most federal agencies had a regional office in Anchorage, and I was actively seeking employment with any of them. I had gotten my pay scale rating back up to a GS-14 prior to the demise of the Inspector's office and was looking for something similar, when I heard that the public affairs officer for the Federal Aviation Administration regional office was planning to retire within the year. So I applied for the job.

In the middle of a Hawaii trip, I got a phone call from the regional administrator telling me the FAA public affairs job was mine. This was a very pleasant surprise--the job interview had taken place months earlier. Now all I had to do was learn the job, along with the usual variety of words, titles and descriptions that were a part of FAA but totally new to me. I had rapidly educated myself to an agency's parameters and culture several times before and knew I could do it again.

In my years with FAA, I had the pleasure of working with many outstanding people, and especially the two employees who worked with me in my division. The three of us became a smooth operating team that assisted each other countless times.

KAL-Soviet Shoot Down

My transition into the new FAA job, effective the first of October, was not without excitement. On September 1, 1983, a Korean Air Lines Boeing 747 civilian airliner was shot down by a Soviet military jet fighter over the Kamchatka Peninsula after the Korean plane crossed Soviet airspace due to a navigational error. All 299 passengers and crew were killed. Most accidents are the result of at least three or more factors that line up to create it. This one was the result of many converging causes, including errors on the part of the flight crew, the Soviet Union and the United States.

The first factor was the constant border air games conducted by both the United States and the Soviet Union. In the far north above Alaska, the Soviet Union constantly sent out its Bear bombers and fighter escorts to test the US air defenses over the polar region. Whenever our northern radar systems picked up their incoming aircraft, we would send our fighter aircraft from King Salmon, Fairbanks, and Anchorage to greet them. The United States also did this type of testing by sending out silent US military radar surveillance aircraft, the RC-135, along the border to obtain information about the Soviets.   But unfortunately for the Korean aircraft, the nighttime profile of the RC-135 is very similar to a Boeing 747. There are five air routes established by the FAA to carry aircraft from Anchorage to the Orient. These invisible paths or routes in the sky abut each other at fifty-mile intervals. The most northern one, used by the KAL flight, comes quite close to the Soviet border.

Another factor was that in April of 1983, five months prior to the KAL incident, the United States held a large naval fleet exercise in the North Pacific in which United States Naval aircraft had repeatedly penetrated Soviet airspace, and this had resulted in the dismissal or reprimand of the Soviet military officials who had been unable to shoot them down. Even further compounding the KAL situation was a Soviet missile test on the Kamchatka Peninsula scheduled for the very next day.

And finally, a very significant factor contributing to the KAL shoot down was that of a pilot error combined with FAA equipment that was down for maintenance. This was first explained to me by Murray Sayle, an international correspondent and investigative reporter who was working on the KAL story. Murray, in addition to being an outstanding writer for the *New York Times* and the *New Yorker Magazine*, is an experienced sailor and trained navigator. This knowledge convinced him that the pilot had flown the aircraft by magnetic compass rather than by using the onboard inertial navigation system. Murray's theory did not fit what many people wanted to hear. It was not a dramatic conspiracy theory that would help sell books; it only explained a plausible truth. Murray could not get anyone in the media or book business to take him seriously.

We met several times while he did research in Anchorage. During one of our lunches, he unfolded a large diagram of the cockpit instrument panel and explained to me that the instrument that showed the captain of the aircraft that he was on magnetic autopilot had been, according to KAL maintenance records, stuck in the on position. This meant that he would not have been able to rely on the instrument to tell him if he was on or off the magnetic course out of Anchorage airport. Murray said that if one plots the location of the downed airliner back to Anchorage, it fits the magnetic compass theory perfectly. This was later backed up by the KAL flight data recorders, the black boxes, when they were finally released by the Soviets ten years after the incident.

Murray first published his simple, but unappreciated theory, in "*The New York Times Review of Books*," April 25, 1985.

Thirty days after the shoot down, I became the public affairs officer for the FAA Alaskan Region and assumed the responsibility of answering any and all news media or public inquiries regarding the incident. My responsibility was short-lived. Due to litigation, the United States District Court for the District of Columbia issued on December 22, 1983, a gag order to all parties, including me, to not "divulge any information or documents obtained in the course of the litigation proceedings," and that included the news media.

In the meantime, we had a visit by the FAA's Assistant Administrator for Public Affairs out of Washington, D.C.. He wanted to visit our Airway Facilities equipment building at King Salmon to determine if the FAA could have known (as alleged by some popular conspiracy theories) that the KAL flight was off course, by utilizing a radar scope specifically designed to allow FAA technicians to be sure the King Salmon radar was working properly.

The scope was still in operation. We went to the building and an examination showed that the equipment was useless for determining the location of any commercial aircraft because: (1) there was no one ever on duty to watch the scope (to be useful this would have to be monitored 24 hours a day, 7 days a week, week in and week out), and (2) the equipment was not designed, nor was it capable at the time, of identifying any of the little moving light blobs as any one particular aircraft. (In air traffic control centers, these lights have a written tag identifying the aircraft that moves along with the light blob.) So the conspiracy books were wrong about FAA being able to identify that the flight was off course, and would have been able to warn the pilot.

* * *

KAL-DC 10 Navaho Accident

Anchorage International airport, like many winter environments in Alaska, gets *ice fog,* a weather condition in which the ground level humidity freezes, filling the air with opaque crystals and blanketing all low-lying areas with white frost. Sometimes the only view from the airport control tower would be the tips of the B-747 tails rising above the fog layer like shark fins slicing through flat, white water.

On December 30th, three months after my arrival on the job, a KAL DC-10 carrying a cargo of Christmas material and a crew of three, started a takeoff in the ice fog at the Anchorage airport. At the same time a Piper aircraft, South Central Airlines commuter flight with seven passengers and a crew of two was waiting at the other end of the same runway to take off. The pilot of the DC-10, taxiing in the fog, missed his approved runway turn off and instead, started to take off on the same runway that the Piper was sitting on. A few seconds later, the Piper, parked on the same runway, appeared out of the fog in front of him.

The KAL pilot made an instant decision that saved everyone's life. Since he was moving at takeoff speed on a frozen runway, he realized that trying to stop would guarantee a collision, so instead, he immediately raised the nose of the DC-10, and his front landing gear bounced off the top of the Piper just above the cockpit, putting a dent right where the DC-10 wheel hit. The rest of the DC-10, being taller, cleared the little airplane. The big KAL aircraft then overran the runway and crashed in a large ditch area and burned. (Actually, the big plane would never have made complete lift off because the particular runway it was on was too short.)

The accident occurred at 2:05 in the afternoon. At 2:20 I received a telephone call from the Alaska bureau of the Associated Press asking for confirmation about an accident at the airport. I was totally unaware of any information, but told them I would check and get back to them.

Each region in the FAA has a sophisticated radio system that ties all the airports and facilities together. For a state the size of Alaska, it is quite a large system. I had a pager and an FAA radio with me at all times; this equipment was tied into a central emergency center in the regional office, the Regional Operations Center. The ROC was staffed 24 hours a day, seven days a week, with three people. I immediately went down the hall to the center, but they had no information. At 2:30 I received word that an accident had occurred, but did not know anything else.

I immediately called the AP and gave them what little information we had. By now all our telephone lines were lit up with incoming media calls. You could not lift a telephone receiver to call out; as soon as you cut off a potential caller to get an outside line, the phone would ring with another incoming call. Our best source of information was now the Air Traffic Division located at the other end of the building, so I ran to their office to find out what was happening. At 3:30 we forwarded the telephones in our office to the air traffic office, and using the most current information, I drafted the first of several news releases for staff people to read over the phone to reporters. By this time all the major media outlets, including *Time Magazine*, UPI, Reuters, NBC, CBS, and ABC New York were on line waiting for us to read the announcement to them. Once they found out we were the source, they would not hang up, but waited on line for over fifteen minutes while I drafted the first statement. We had four people reading the one page statement to media on the telephone without a break for over four hours. At 4:30 I drafted a second statement, and then another at 5:30 with new information. At 8:00 PM I left the building and in response to local television stations, gave live interviews at KTVA, KTUU, and KIMO television.

Fortunately, no one was even hurt in the accident. The crew of the DC-10 climbed out the emergency cockpit exit window, and the passengers and crew of the Piper walked down the runway and back to the terminal. As soon as the networks found out there were no fatalities, the story dropped from crisis to normal.

A few hours later, I accompanied the Alaskan regional manager of the National Transportation Safety Board, while he surveyed the burning DC-10 wreckage and the Piper, which was sitting on the runway with its doors open, briefcases still inside, a visible dent over the cockpit. The ground around the DC-10 was littered with Christmas toys and little greeting cards that sang a song when opened. Everywhere I walked, I could hear Christmas carols from the cards that were flapping in the gentle breeze. It was an eerie experience, listening to all those wee voices singing in the white fog.

* * *

Ten days prior to this accident, a Boeing-747 making a night landing at Anchorage airport hit an airport maintenance truck that was near the end of the runway. The driver opened the door of the truck and dove to the ground, but he was beat up so badly that the doctors did not think he was going to live. I saw the remains of the truck, and it was not pretty. The landing gear of the airplane landed in the bed of the pickup (you could not do that intentionally if you tried) and the only thing left from the cab back was the frame. The back of the cab was pushed all the way forward to the engine. The area the driver was sitting in was flat, mashed up to the dash, which was mashed up to the motor. This accident occurred because of an error by an air traffic controller in the tower who forgot the maintenance driver was on the runway. This particular controller was, at his request, subsequently moved to an administration position--with no loss in pay.

Author under KAL Boeing 747 engine, where the four wheels (missing)
used to be, prior to landing in the bed of an airport maintenance
pickup truck in 1983, Anchorage, Alaska

I frequently received telephone calls from the news media wanting to know who the controller was that had caused an accident, and I would, as calmly as possible, tell them to go to hell, because there is no way we would dump additional pressure on a controller who is already grieving a mistake. Their job is hard enough without that added pressure. I discovered over the years that the news media seemed to be willing to spare no time or expense in their quest to obtain the name of a controller who made a mistake.

The FAA's Air Traffic Control Systems

The Federal Aviation Administration, like many federal agencies, has changed to keep pace with the industry that it regulates. Starting in 1926 with the Air Commerce Act, the technology initially consisted of guiding aircraft with bonfires and it has now progressed to the modern use of radar to guide aircraft across the nation.

Air traffic control tower, Anchorage, Alaska

The agency is responsible for ensuring that any object flying in the nation's airspace does so safely. FAA inspects and regulates the entire aviation industry, including the design and construction of all aircraft, the operation of aviation airlines, pilot training and proficiency, and the guidance of aircraft to prevent collisions. This responsibility requires a very large workforce that includes inspectors, pilots, electronic technicians, and air traffic controllers. The most recognizable of these employees are the air traffic controllers, an unusual and much sought after breed. The FAA recruits and selects controllers using a variety of specialized tests, and trains them vigorously at a facility in Oklahoma City. The dropout rate at the academy is between two and four percent.

There are two types of jobs for air traffic controllers. Some controllers work at airports getting aircraft to land, park, taxi and depart without hitting each another. Other controllers work in one of the FAA's Air Route Traffic Control Centers, (ARTCC). All pilots and aircraft--a single engine piper, a commercial airline jet, or a military aircraft--are handled in exactly the same way.

Air traffic controllers have a difficult, indispensable job and they definitely earn their money. (Starting annual salary is $50,000 and rises to as much as $198,000 in 2009 money for the most difficult locations.) They must be able to transform the two-dimensional information on a radar screen into a three-dimensional scenario in their mind, in order to safely control an assortment of aircraft flying in different directions at different altitudes. They also must have a temperament that can take an eight-hour shift of the inevitable stress of being responsible for the protection and safety of many people's lives. The controllers take great pride in their work and tend to think of themselves as "special." In truth, they are special, although everyone who works with them tries to play that down in order to keep them reasonable.*

Control of air traffic is a step-by-step handoff system. A commercial jet, for example, loads passengers on board the aircraft and the pilot requests permission from the controller in the tower to pull back from the gate. Then he requests permission to taxi to the end of the takeoff runway. A passenger might now look out the window and see fifteen jets lined up in a row waiting to work their way to the end of the runway.

* *In 1979, prior to my employment with the agency, air traffic controllers, in violation of their hiring contract, went on strike for higher wages. This blatant attempt to cripple the nation by shutting down the air traffic system was done after many attempts by the agency to meet their demands. President Reagan gave them a brief grace period to come back or else be forever banned from working for the FAA. Some thought about it and returned to work, but 11,400 others never came back. The president refused to capitulate to blackmail. Instead, a small cadre of air traffic managers, military controllers, and retires who were willing to come to work on a temporary basis, operated the system. They gave up vacations, sick leave, transfer, and promotions for years, while the FAA hired and trained new controllers.*

The ability of an airport to get aircraft on and off the ground in a speedy manner is based on the number of runways and taxiways available. Aircraft must be kept two minutes apart in order to take off and land safely, thus at night you can usually see five or six approaching planes in the air, their landing lights lined up in the distance like pearls on a necklace. Naturally, a second runway moves traffic faster, as does a third and a fourth. Chicago O'Hare, which has seven active runways, handles an average of 2,500 flights per day! This airport, which is not the only airport in Chicago, uses 70 controllers a day, 24 hours a day, 7 days a week, 365 days a year, to operate the system. The airline companies could not possibly provide or operate this system on their own.*

There are several controllers in the tower and each one is assigned a segment of the flight. As the aircraft moves, the flight information and contact with the pilot is transferred from one controller to another. The tower system uses pre-printed information strips for each flight that are inserted into plastic sleeves and passed from one controller to the next. The strips go in at the top of a slanted rack and slide down slowly, one sleeve on top of another, to the bottom. This seems overly simplistic in today's computer world, but it works--reliably-- even during a power failure. The departure controller makes sure the runway is clear and then releases the pilot to takeoff. This seems simple, but at an airport like Chicago, you can have two aircraft taking off from separate runways while two other aircraft are landing on two other separate runways (That's a lot of responsibility--we are talking about the safety of a possible 1200 passengers, plus flight crews.)

---

* The FAA does not regulate airline schedules. For awhile, the airline companies, being in competition with each other, scheduled more and more flights into the prime landing times--so much so that it was impossible for the airport system (number of available gates and runways) and the controllers to handle the aircraft without delays. The airlines blamed the delays on the FAA. Eventually the FAA had to sit the various airline senior staff down in one room and tell them they would have to stop the massive over-scheduling. They agreed and the problem was solved. The media wrote many times about the epidemic of delayed flights, but never informed the public about the true causes and solutions to the problem.

The departing aircraft is then handed off to a different group of controllers, who are housed in a dark room at the base of the tower and have no visual contact with the plane. These controllers work from the radar screen, with an identity tag that follows the little green blurred dot as the plane leaves the runway. They use a separate radio frequency to tell the pilots what to do and when to do it.

Radar, invented by the British at the beginning of World War II, is an electronic beam of energy sent out from the rotating contraptions you may have seen on top of an airport tower or building, usually located at the corner of the airport property. This beam goes out into the air, hits an airplane and bounces back to the radar system, where the signal is sent to a large, greenish phosphorescent screen that has a bright green line rotating around the screen from a center post (dot). Scattered around the screen are little green blobs or blurs (they have a short tail) that hop forward a tad each time the green line sweeps past. There might be a dozen of these little blobs advancing across the screen at any one time, going in different directions. Accompanying each green blob as it moves across the screen, is a little word tag that identifies it as to airline, flight number, and elevation.

The controller watching this display has to keep track of each blob and make sure they do not hit each other. Remember, they are flying at different elevations and at different speeds, so to the casual eye, one blob might look like it is going to hit another, but actually the planes indicated by the two blobs are on different altitudes, with one flying safely above the other. The monotony of the rotating green line against the overall green screen in a semi-dark room would be enough to put most of us to sleep.

Back to our departing flight, the controller in the base of the tower, who can talk to any of the pilots in his/her sector, keeps track of the aircraft until it reaches a few miles out and has gained enough altitude and distance to make it easier for everyone to relax. The controller then tells the pilot to change radio frequencies and report to the Air Route Traffic Control Center (ARTCC).

There are twenty-one ARTCC located across the country, each one staffed with controllers who are doing the same thing, moving the aircraft on to its destination, one controller at a time, from one ARTCC to another, until the takeoff process eventually becomes a landing process at the destination airport. Remember, whether the aircraft is a Boeing 737 with 300 passengers, a military jet fighter, or a Cessna with two people on board, the same FAA procedure applies to them all. "Have a safe trip," is more than a polite expression.

The FAA is also responsible for designing, installing and maintaining all the equipment that allows the controllers to facilitate the aircraft's flight: runway lighting, airport approach radar beacons, ARTCC radar, navigation aids, emergency generators, FAA facilities and more. Without these unseen electronic heroes of communication, there would be no system, no way to know who was flying where or when. Unscheduled downtime or failure of this equipment is not tolerated.

FAA Air Route Traffic Control Center (ARTCC), Alaska

The construction and maintenance of the aircraft is just as important, so the FAA regulates that too. Anyone who builds an aircraft, from a home built experimental category to a Boeing 747, must have numerous FAA inspections and approvals during construction and thereafter for the useful life of the aircraft.

Pilots must pass regular FAA tests, including a physical exam. Mechanics, who keep the aircraft operating, must pass stringent tests (just think of what it must take to keep these oversize jet engines in perfect running condition.) Unlike an automobile that might simply sputter to the side of the road when something ceases to work, an airplane must function properly or it will fall out of the sky. All the parts in an airplane must work every time, with no exceptions. The airplane mechanics do the work, but it is the FAA that specifies that all parts on an airplane must be replaced with new parts on a scheduled basis, even if that part is not broken.

Flight standard regulations are kept up-to-date and enforced by a large cadre of FAA employees, who inspect the aircraft, look into the company records, and if necessary, along with FAA lawyers force a pilot, air taxi operator or airline company to cease operations until they comply with the regulations.

Not to be forgotten are the private pilots of small aircraft across the country, classed as general aviation. They also must abide by all the FAA regulations and standards. The FAA has fifty-eight Flight Service Stations across the country to coordinate and provide advice to these air taxi and personal travelers. A general aviation pilot can file his intended flight plan with an FSS and they will keep track of where and when he will land. If the aircraft does not return as scheduled, FAA will mount a search and rescue effort.

This agency is a typical example of our nation's civil servants who quietly provide outstanding service on a daily basis. These are the sometimes maligned *bureaucrats* who keep our many government services functioning, be it food inspection, land management, justice, housing, security, military defense, fish and wildlife management, transportation, coast guard, the weather service border patrol, agriculture or research, and many more.

While the political leadership changes, political priorities shift, and the budget goes up and down, these worker-bees keep the gears of our society moving steadily along. Most of us never bother to think about them unless we hear some reporter or media personality bashing the government, and even then we forget about the millions of civil servants who daily do their very best to make sure the system works for everyone.

I never, in thirty years of civil service work within six different agencies, met a GS employee who was lazy or shirked their duty. I am also proud to say that I have never known a federal civil servant accept a bribe for doing his or her job. Of course it probably happens, but I never saw or heard of it on my watch. (Remember, the terms *civil servant* and *political appointee* are not interchangeable.)

This routine refusal for tips or other back door payment is consistent with work in the federal government in the GS levels, and it is something that amazes many foreign visitors to the U.S.

The next time you get on a commercial airplane flight, remember that the FAA, the federal government, and the civil servants of America, in addition to the airlines and crew, are getting you there safely.

Wien Air Alaska, formed in 1927 by Noel Wien in Nome, Alaska, was one of the first airlines in the United States. It closed in 1984. Like many outstanding airline companies, it closed due to the de-regulation of the U.S. airline system. Large airline companies bought out the smaller ones.

However, accidents do happen. When I started work for the FAA, I quickly realized that a significant part of my new job was going to be working with the news media. Alaska is a large rural state with vast amounts of uninhabited land and very few roads. The steady Alaskan joke during the construction of the oil pipeline was that *if you Texans don't stop bragging, we'll cut Alaska in two and make Texas the third largest state in the union.*

Aviation, especially in small private aircraft, is a major part of the Alaska transportation system. There are more pilots per capita in Alaska than there are in any other state--about 10,000 aircraft and 9,000 pilots. Accidents in the state, about 220 per year, are sometimes very dramatic, so the news media loves to report about them. In comparison, there are approximately 50,000 deaths nationally each year due to automobile accidents, a fact you seldom hear the news media mention. During the summer, we might get several aviation accidents a week in Alaska, but during the winter, we usually would not get one for months. Of course, the media never said, *Good news again today; it has been thirty-six days since there was any kind of aviation accident in Alaska.*

Also, the air taxi business is big in Alaska, and hunting season always brought a rash of accidents. Aircraft taking off from a beach full of tree stumps or from a lake, overloaded with meat and gear, were prime accident potentialities. Floatplanes taking off from a lake were sometimes so heavy from all the meat packed in the back that they just went vertical before crashing backward into the water. There are many mountain passes in the state that are littered with the wreckage of small private and air taxi planes, most of these accidents occurring due to a passenger's *I've got to get back to the office* syndrome. A pilot must be specially trained and certified to fly in clouds. To fly without being able to see the ground requires a human being who can refrain from relying on his or her senses and instead trust the various instruments in the cockpit. This is more difficult to do than one would expect, and many pilots have died because they tried to fly in the dark or in bad weather without proper training.

Another danger complicates lack of instrument training when a pilot starts out flying by sight, and then tries to cross a mountain pass (Alaska is full of them), only to find that the rising level of the ground under him as he climbs up into the pass is forcing him into the cloud layer he had been flying under. By the time he realizes the situation, he is trapped. He does not know how to fly in the clouds, the ground is rapidly coming up under him, and the sides of the mountain pass have now become too narrow for him to make a safe turn around without hitting the ground or flying blind into the clouds. The pilot invariably makes the attempt to turn, but unfortunately, a wing very often clips the side of the mountain. The resulting death by trauma or fire is usually instantaneous.

I assisted the NTSB on one such investigation. In 1985, a single-engine de Havilland Beaver on floats crashed while coming back to Anchorage from a hunting trip with two clients, both under thirty-three years of age. The pilot was twenty-seven. The Alaska Army National Guard provided a HH-60 Pave Hawk helicopter for the regional director of NTSB and me to travel to the site. The weather was cold and overcast, and Merrill pass had snow on the ground. We flew over many old aircraft wreckage sites, the result of similar accidents in the past, and finally located the wreckage mashed against the side of the mountain, the tail and one wing clearly visible. A black bear was sniffing around the wreckage.

The helicopter could not find a level place to land because the area was full of large rocks, so it hovered over a frozen creek while we jumped to the ground with our gear and worked our way through the rocks to the crash site. Two of the helicopter crewmembers, one with a radio, came with us. He also brought a flare gun that was used to force the bear to retreat. We waved our arms up and down, hollered, and threw rocks at it until, head down, it slunk up into the pass.

We could tell that the aircraft had tried to turn, clipped the right wing and crashed into the rocks, severing the lower

wing at the base and catching fire. Fuel stored in the upper
wing had drained straight into the seating area. I backed away
and took a few photographs of the wreckage, while the others
wrestled the two passengers into body bags and started hauling
them down toward the frozen creek. I joined them, making
four of us trying to slide the heavy, slick bags along the snow.
It was tough going. The snow, not yet hard-frozen, would not
support our weight, and the path crossed hundreds of rocks,
some the size of small cars, all with a crevasse under the snow
waiting to trap our feet as we made our slow way across the
landscape. The helicopter was not where we had deplaned.
Hovering a machine that size consumes large amounts of fuel,
so they had moved it about a half-mile up the creek bed to a
small frozen pond and shut off the engine.

The bodies weighed approximately 200 pounds each, and
dragging them was exhausting. Every step was a torment as my
foot and leg went down up to my crotch in the snow. First me,
then the man in back, then me again, and so on.
Eventually, the crew on the helicopter saw us and came to
help. I was so tired, I could barely walk to the helicopter.
When I got there, I sat in the doorway, took off my shoes, and
literally wrung the water out of my socks. Wet and cold socks I
could stand, but squishy with cold water was unacceptable.

De Havilland Beaver, 1985

The pilots cranked up the
rotors and we flew back to
Anchorage, where a funeral
home hearse was waiting for us
on the tarmac. It was the end of
the day and the experience for me. The NTSB guys went back
the next day for the pilot.

In August 25, 1985, *The Anchorage Times* (no longer in
business) interviewed me at length to determine why the
aviation accident rate in Alaska had increased by 83 percent

between 1983 and 1985. As everyone understands, but at times seems to ignore or forget, accidents are not created by the FAA or the NTSB. Many times, they are created by pilots and air taxi outfits trying too hard to make it in a competitive market. Tom Westall, manager of the FAA's Flight Standards Division, said in response to a question about FAA's push to reduce accidents, "We're looking at a typical peak accident situation beginning in the middle of August –right about now. It reaches a peak in late September and then keeps going down until by December we have very few accidents." Mr. Westall and his inspection staff of forty-five were successful in highlighting safety issues that brought the accident level back to 1983 levels.

The NTSB badge that the author carried for on-site investigations

The relationship I had with the director of the Alaskan Bureau of the National Transportation Safety Board was very unusual. Having already worked for six agencies, my philosophy was why make a little agency try to solve media problems with such a small staff (four in this case). I told them they could use our media mailing list and any other help they needed. The NTSB director was quite helpful in explaining to me the causes of accidents in Alaska. However, there was an intra-agency relationship issue that had nothing to do with the regional NTSB director or me.

The NTSB's is charged with investigating transportation accidents and based on their investigation, inform Congress and the controlling agencies, such as FAA, what changes should be made in the regulations to prevent future accidents.

The NTSB always gets to be the good guys in this scenario, whereas the agencies that have to live with administrative, congressional and corporate world politics are seen as the bad guys--it is not always easy to fight the real world in behalf of the small personal world of death due to accidents. As a result, most employees in the FAA, especially the inspectors, did not care much for the NTSB in general. They didn't like being caught between fewer inspections (pressure brought on by corporate complaints) and the need to protect the public. An example of this situation is the aviation rule that allows a parent to hold a child under two years of age in their lap while flying in a commercial aircraft. This rule saves the parent from having to purchase a separate seat for the infant; however, from the NTSB point of view it will guarantee the death of the infant in the event of an accident. Scientific testing has shown that it is impossible to hold an infant in one's lap during a collision, be it an airplane or a car. NTSB wants the practice abolished, but FAA still allows it.

Whenever the aviation accident rate went up in Alaska, NTSB was more than willing to tell the news media what FAA should do to fix the problem. The news media would come to me for answers--answers that sometimes were difficult to find. Then our inspectors would increase their inspections and reduce the accident rate, only to be restrained by a variety of measures, mostly political. This up-down cycle would repeat year after year.

During the 1985 cycle, the NTSB regional director in Alaska was making all kinds of noises about the accident rate. Eventually his actions resulted in CBS News sending a film crew and correspondent Richard Wagner to report on the "disastrous" aviation accident rate in Alaska. I was interviewed for forty-five minutes on camera, a long time for a continuous interview that for me, held the possibility of saying the wrong thing in answer to one of their many questions The segment aired on August 30, and the only piece they used out of my entire interview was a ten second end segment in which I said, "If the FAA does not have enough inspector staff, then

Washington should look into that and give us more people, if it is determined that we need more."

I had been interviewed for the FAA job by the regional administrator, the top FAA man in Alaska. However, a few months after reporting for work, he told me to report to his deputy, a change I did not like, but could not complain about. I quickly realized that the deputy wanted me and my two-person staff to do far more projects than it would ever be possible to complete, so I devised a written weekly report that I sent to him and all the senior staff directors telling them what we were working on, including the number of media calls we got that week (one year I was interviewed on Alaskan TV ninety times). Once my boss realized the extent of our workload, the suggestions all but disappeared. After I started my reports, the regional administrator asked all the division managers to provide one too. These were grouped as a package and circulated among senior staff, and turned out to be a very useful management tool.

The author at one of many media and television interviews

Occasionally I received a request from the newspapers that allowed me to have some fun. This one came from the *Anchorage Times* while I was reading *The Tao of Pooh,* by Benjamin Hoff:

Anchorage Times, January 5, 1989

Which way do wind(s) blow?

Dear Bud:

How many winds are there? Weather reports in the newspapers and forecasts on TV sometimes say "wind" in Kenai and Talkeetna and other times "winds" in Ketchikan and Valdez. When the Federal Aviation Administration gives the wind direction to a pilot for airport information, it is always spoken in the singular. My dictionary also considers the word singular for most usages. Sincerely, J.B.

Dear J.B.:

Cottleston, Cottleston, Cottleston Pie
A quote from Pooh, and a little of I.
Ask me a riddle and I reply,
Cottleston, Cottleston, Cottleston Pie

Cottleston, Cottleston, Cottleston Pie
Wind a clock, and clock the wind, why?
Ask me a riddle and I reply,
Cottleston, Cottleston, Cottleston Pie.

Cottleston, Cottleston, Cottleston Pie
Is it wind or winds, or a breeze going by?
Ask me a riddle, and I reply,
Cottleston, Cottleston, Cottleston Pie.

Once again, J.B. your familiar letter arrives in the mail. Thanks for your continued questions of interest for the Bud column. But even Winnie the Pooh (as modified by Steucke) was confused by this question.

Paul Steucke Sr., FAA public affairs officer, sent this riddle. He also said that both the singular and plural forms of "wind" are used by the FAA and the national Weather Service.

"One brief puff might be called a wind or many individual puffs travelling in a group might be called a wind or winds. It appears to be a matter of personal preference whether to use the singular or plural form. The dictionary lists "wind" as a natural movement of air. It does not address what a group of wind(s) or wind(s) that follow each other are called (perhaps a hurricane). Looks like confusion with English profusion," wrote Steucke'

Yours truly, Bud.

* * *

Flying Jump Seat

My credentials with the National Transportation Safety Board and the FAA provided me with an unusual training opportunity while vacationing in Hawaii.

Annette, as a professional social worker, had an opportunity to attend a week long training class on the island of Maui in Hawaii, conducted by Dr. Elizabeth Kubler Ross. We decided it would be a good opportunity for us to meet for a short vacation. This also meant that, on this rare occasion, I would be flying alone to and from the islands.

I was using a Frequent Flyer first class upgrade on Western Airlines* which placed me upfront, close to the area used by the pilots to fly the large McDonnell Douglas L1011 Tri Star aircraft. This airplane, which seats 400 passengers, was unusual in that it not only had one large engine on each wing, but also had a very large engine molded into the top rear of the aircraft by the tail.

While enroute to Anchorage, via Honolulu, I stopped the cabin attendant as she walked past, and asked her to show the pilot my NTSB badge and my FAA identification. After we landed in Honolulu the pilot (the one with four gold stripes on his sleeve) came out of the cockpit area and stopped by my seat and introduced himself. We talked briefly and then I asked him if it

* Western Airlines, born 1925, ceased to exist in 1986 when Delta Airlines purchased the airline. Numerous airlines have disappeared as larger airlines, with more financial resources, bought them and then dissolved their identity into the larger airline. This was made possible by the deregulation of the airline industry in 1978 by President Carter and congress. Some airlines, like Alaska Airlines, managed to sidestep this corporate maneuver by transferring the controlling stock of the airline to the employees, thereby preventing the corporate board from selling the airline for their own profit.

might be possible, as a part of my aviation training, to sit in the jump seat, located directly behind the pilots seat, for the remainder of the flight. He took out my ID, looked at it, and taking the ID with him, said he would check with headquarters. I waited.

A short time later he reappeared, handed me back my credentials, and invited me to move up front into the cockpit jump seat. The jump seat is an FAA requirement that provides a place for an FAA flight inspector to ride and make a formal check/review of the pilots ability to fly the aircraft while in flight. Fortunately for me there was no jump seat inspection on this flight.

I sat in the jump seat and was astounded at the view that was provided by the most unusual airplane window I had ever seen. Unlike windows in the passenger cabins this window was made for viewing. Rectangular, about two feet wide by three feet high, it was without a doubt the best window on the airplane, any airplane. The pilot sat directly in front of me, the co-pilot on the right side, and a flight engineer sat with his back to me facing an array of dials and lighted switches. The shoulder harness was heavy duty, the kind that comes up between your legs and across your mid section before disappearing over each shoulder to a steel clamp behind your seat. I knew from previous discussions with some of my FAA flight standards friends not to talk or interrupt the crews concentration until the captain addressed me.

We pulled back from the gate. The weather in Honolulu was bright and beautiful The captain explained to me that we were taxing very slowly because the aircraft was heavy with a full load of passengers and fuel, which in turn put stress on the hot tires. The FAA airport Ground Control designated that we use the runway furthest from the terminal. This forced us to lumber a distance before we got there. As we went I slowly became aware, mostly through the seat of my pants, that something behind me was very, very heavy. It felt like I was sitting on the end of a diving board as we bounced along, the presence of the weight behind us like a hug wave, with only the nose wheel keeping us afloat.

The take off was exciting as I watched downtown Honolulu appear along with Diamond Head, and Hanauma Bay. We rose to 39,000 feet in elevation, cruising north toward Alaska. The flight crew was interested in what FAA had in mind with regard to lifting the mandatory retirement age, something that worried the flight crew. I told them I had heard that the retirement age might be lifted in five years. (I was wrong.)

After a few hours the cabin attendant brought our meal to us on trays. The aircraft was essentially flying itself on auto-pilot. The Captain watched what the computer was doing but left the controls to the computer. The sun set in a beautiful glow and we move north in the dark.

As we approached Anchorage the Captain took control of the aircraft. There was some radio conversation with the Anchorage FAA tower and then the Captain informed us that strong winds were forcing us to detour from the standard southern approach so that we were going to go around 180 degrees and approach from the other end, forgoing the fancy foolproof FAA landing system that allowed airplanes to land easily even in poor weather conditions. The co-pilot informed the passenger and flight attendants to buckle up.

As we went over the foothills and looked down on the twinkling lights of Anchorage I began to realize the importance of pilot training. Although we were in a very large aircraft the wind was buffeting us enough to make flying tricky. As I looked over the shoulders of the pilot I could see the lighted runway as he aligned the plane to the lights. It looked very small in the distance, like putting a band aid on the floor and saying to yourself I will land safely on that little strip of land.

The Captain said something terse into the microphone to the FAA Tower controller and continued to fly the aircraft down to that little band aid in the dark. He put it down right on target. I was impressed and told him so after we parked the plane. It was training beyond anything I expected.

The JAL UFO

Annual leave for a Federal civil servant is increased incrementally based on length of time in service. A new hire gets about two weeks a year of paid annual leave (sick leave is separate) at a rate of four hours per bi-weekly pay period. Someone who has fifteen or twenty years of service collects leave at twice that rate, but it is often difficult for a person in management to take the time off. I was fortunate in having great employees who were willing to be the public affairs officer when I was on leave. Like many civil servants, they did not receive anything in return for this extra effort except experience, a sentence in their resume and an outstanding annual performance appraisal.

Filling in for me was no little chore. The person on duty had to carry a pager and an FAA radio with them at all times so the Regional Operations Center could reach them to respond to media requests in an emergency. My wife has often said that when we flew out of state on vacation, once the baggage was released to the airline and I was no longer available by pager or FAA radio, the relief was decidedly evident on my face. In addition to filling in for me at vacation time, my staff and I took turns working the Christmas to New Year holiday week, so each of us only had to be on call every third year.

In 1986, it was my turn to take the holidays, which began quietly. In the middle of the week, I got a telephone call from Jeff Berliner of United Press International. He said a colleague had overheard a conversation in a Japanese bar between several Japan Air Lines (JAL) crewmembers about an Unidentified Flying Object (UFO) recently seen by Captain Kenjyu Terauchi while piloting a Japan Air Lines Boeing 747 cargo plane from France to Japan. The aircraft was using the shorter polar route via Anchorage to get to Japan and was near Fairbanks at the time of the sighting.

I told him I would check it out and call him back. After a few telephone calls, I was surprised to learn that our security office had in fact interviewed the flight crew of a JAL cargo flight about seven weeks prior to Jeff's call. It seemed the flight crew reported to our air traffic controllers that an unidentified aircraft was flying along with them as they crossed the Alaskan airspace on their way to Anchorage. Jim Derry of our security office had interviewed the captain extensively and realized that he was describing a UFO. The captain made drawings of it in detail and talked about how it followed them for about fifty minutes, and he also said that compared to the JAL Boeing 747, it was huge. I got the material from Jim together and gave it to Jeff, thinking nothing more of it.

Jim's report states that flight 1628, a Boeing 747, left Iceland bound for Anchorage on the afternoon of November 17, flying above 35,000 feet and under a full moon. It was the middle leg of a Paris to Tokyo cargo delivery of Beaujolais wine. The flight took the North Pole route to save fuel and as a result came directly from Canada into Alaska on a direct southern course toward Fairbanks and on to Anchorage. When they crossed the Canadian/U.S border, the FAA air traffic controllers (ATC) in Anchorage picked up the flight for routine tracking. FAA air traffic control followed the flight on radar and directed them to continue flying south across the Arctic Circle and over the small town of Talkeetna, a standard procedure for that flight route. As the crew turned the aircraft to comply with the instructions, they noticed a couple of lights in the distance. At first they ignored them, but knowing they should probably be alone in the night sky, they radioed the air traffic controller to find out if anyone else was up there with them. When told there were no other planes in the area, the captain replied in heavily accented English, "Ah, we in sight two traffic in front of us, one mile about."

Flights normally do not fly that close to each other, particularly at night. Air traffic asked the crew if it was military or civilian aircraft, and the captain said he could not tell. Asked if the other aircraft had navigation or strobe lights and if so, what color they were, the captain said they were "White and yellow, I think." Red, the international color for aircraft beacons, was missing.

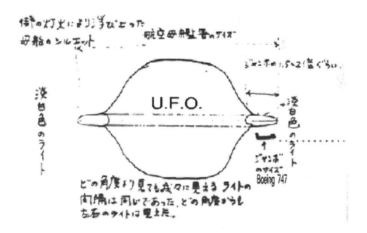

Drawing by Captain Terauchi

Captain Terauchi said the two lights began maneuvering "like two bear cubs playing with each other." The flight engineer handed him his camera bag, but the camera refused to auto focus on the glass surface of the cockpit. When he tried the manual focus, the camera shutter would not activate. Then the unknown source of the lights suddenly came directly at them, and "stopped in front of our face, shooting off lights so bright it lit up the inside of the cockpit with light and heat," causing the captain to fear he might be flying up the rear end of some super aircraft engine. The mystery ship appeared to hover in front of them for a while and then flew about 1,000 feet above them, matching their speed. The pilot could see what looked like exhaust pipes, and rotating rows of amber and white lights in the middle of those flying nozzles. He realized that no man-made machine could perform these rapid maneuvers and change of positions, especially at 550 miles per hour. This sort of thing continued for three to five minutes.

Meanwhile, FAA ground radar had not registered anything near the flight, but the aircraft's X-band weather radar, with the range set at 20 miles, did show a large green object about seven or eight miles away in the direction of the mystery flight. The FAA ground controller asked the captain if he had visual contact with the other aircraft. Terauchi said that he did, and then ATC said they also had radar return about eight miles from flight 1628. Becoming concerned, they radioed Elmendorf Air Force Base near Anchorage, and they, too, thought they might have something about eight miles from the JAL flight. By this time, the flight was reaching the city lights of Fairbanks, and the glow of the rising sun was making a red and orange stripe on the horizon. Using this natural light, the captain and crew checked to see if the other aircraft was still there, and what they saw was a "gigantic spaceship." The captain requested permission to drop his altitude to 30,000 feet.

Air traffic said "Okay," and requested they make a right 360 degree turn--a complete circle and an expensive fuel maneuver for an aircraft this large. When the turn was complete, the other object seemed to have disappeared. "We were relieved," said the captain, "but when we checked to our rear, the object was still there, in exactly the same place."

Then the Elmendorf military radar folks thought they might have a second image near flight 1628. Air traffic control asked if the captain wanted military help. "Negative, negative," he replied. One of the controllers speculated that perhaps a lost aircraft was following the Japanese flight, and he alerted the

Anchorage Regional Operations Center. That prompted the concern that the ghost flight might be foreign, so the US Border patrol was notified, and that, in turn, is how Jim Derry got involved. The incident was now officially logged into the system, so someone had to interview the crew when they landed at Anchorage.

United Airlines Flight 69 was just taking off from Anchorage airport, and the air traffic controller asked the pilot to take a look around the Japanese aircraft as they flew past it. A military C-130 (a large freighter-type aircraft) that was in the near area was also asked to take a look. Neither pilot saw anything other than the JAL aircraft. But Captain Terauchi said, "We were flying the east side of Mt. McKinley; we knew that

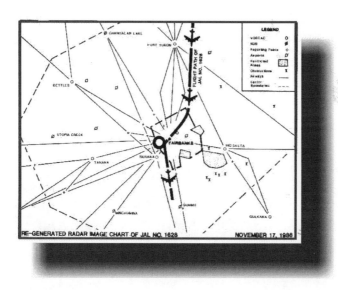

FAA reconstructed radar path of JAL 1628; Fairbanks radar site

they were watching us. When the United plane came by our side, the spaceship disappeared suddenly, and there was nothing but the light of the moon." As soon as they landed in Anchorage, the captain and crew were interviewed by Mr.

Derry, who obtained a very detailed report, including diagrams and drawings from the captain in both Japanese and English. Jim filed his report and presumed that was the end of it, Then Jeff Berliner called me right after Christmas.

Later, I was asked by the media why I did not announce this incident at the time it happened, and I explained, "You wouldn't have announced it either. For us to shout from the mountain top that we had a significant UFO incident would have made us look crazy; plus, as an agency we had no proof of anything except Captain Terauchi's words.

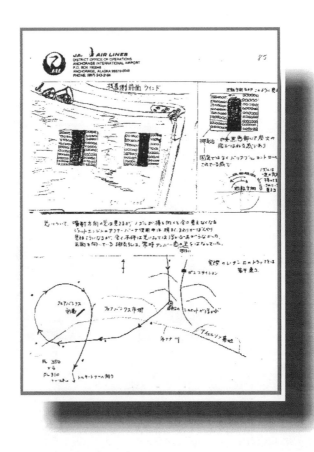

Drawings by Captain Kenju Terauchi on JAL letterhead

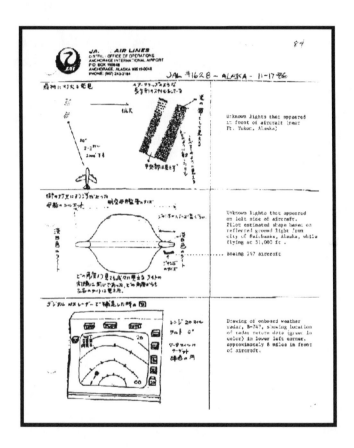

Drawing by Captain Kenju Terauchi on JAL letterhead

The FAA has a reputation as the very best air traffic management system in the world, and I am not about to put the agency into a UFO controversy based on the information we have."

This summed up the situation and the position that I took from then on. I had no reason to contradict the captain and certainly did not want to make him and the Japanese people look foolish. I had no evidence of anything other than the air traffic controller record, and for us to endorse anything, one way or the other, would drag the FAA into a UFO cover-up controversy that, even so, has been going on for years. As it was, we barely escaped the controversy. Quite frankly, we never
did form an opinion; we just shared all the data we had and let everyone draw their own conclusion.

But as soon as the story broke, things started to go crazy for us; the media, worldwide, wanted to interview us on television, radio, and in
print. The telephones rang for weeks. A Japanese film crew and reporter flew to Anchorage to interview me (it ran on Japanese television the next week along with new interviews of the crew). *The Washington Post, New York Times,* and all the major networks asked for interviews and aired the story.

On January 3, I announced that the FAA was reopening its inquiry into the incident. I really did not have much choice, as the media and public interest required me to do something. *The Washington Post* story quoted me as saying; "The reason we are exploring it is that it was a possible violation of airspace. This may sound strange, but that's what it was." The news media wanted a UFO story, ideally a confirmed UFO story, which I would not and could not do since we were not sure what we might have other than the captain's report. Backing that up, I said, "The object of the inquiry--collecting all the data and interviewing people--is to identify the object, if possible." I then flip-flopped to make sure that sentence was not misconstrued, saying, "However, considering the type of data we have available, no one considers it realistic that we can identify the object." Both statements were true.

We were getting more and more requests for interviews. Noah Adams, host of the *National Public Radio* show, *All Things Considered*, interviewed me and ended his questioning with, "Well, Paul…tell me; what do you personally think really happened?" This is a question that can reach around and bite you real hard from behind. I told him, "Noah, I can't really answer that question because the moment I do, my answer will become the agency answer, and the agency does not have an answer." Radio personality Paul Harvey ran the story two days in a row, producing yet another increase in media requests.

Under the Freedom of Information Act, we were deluged with requests from the general public for the Derry interviews and related information, so finally I asked my assistant, Ivy Moore, to create a comprehensive list of all the available materials that we could provide to the public.

On February 21, we issued a news release informing the public that they could get a complete list of all items that we had about the JAL incident. The release said, "Some persons may find the cost of purchasing the entire inquiry package of materials to be expensive and that it contains items they might not want. Hence, we have listed and describe each item, with the cost, so that your order can be tailored to fit your needs and budget. Please note that an order which totals $5.00 or less will be provided free of charge."

Hundreds of people ordered everything from small, free items to the total package (for $194.30), which included all written interviews, radar data, black and white photographs of the re-constructed radar screen image, cassette tapes of the interviews, and more.

(The material can be still be obtained by ordering from the National Technical Information Service ((NTIS)), 5285 Port Royal Road, Springfield, VA 22161, 703-487-4600, NTIS accession number: PB87-184206). Eventually a full set of materials was sent to the National Archives in Washington, D.C., at their request

In the midst of all this, I was surprised by one member of our senior staff who said in a staff meeting that he thought our effort to respond to the public's request for information was a joke. His office had previously loaned us a tape duplication machine that made three duplicate cassette recordings at a time, something we were doing on a daily basis. Without warning, he withdrew our use of the machine. I went into his office to discuss it and got into a shouting match, with me telling him he had no right to second-guess what I did with my program and that if he had a problem, he should complain to our boss, the regional administrator. I immediately went out and, with the permission of our administrative budget officer, purchased our own machine--which, by the way, the same guy later asked to borrow.

I held a press conference March 6 at the FAA office in Anchorage to release all the information we had about the incident. This included copies of the various interviews, the radar data from the ARTCC, cassette tapes of the interviews, and black and white photos of the radar screen showing flight 1628 on the radar, that was reconstructed from computer data that is routinely kept on a daily basis by the FAA. The reconstruction from the data tapes was done by the FAA's research facility in New Jersey, the only facility capable of doing this.

I made a drawing on the chalkboard of the B-747 and the ground radar sending a signal up to it, and the signals that come back to our radar--the transponder signal that comes back and is put on the controller's radar screen. Using the drawing I explained to the reporters at the conference; "Sometimes a double signal occurs when the radar energy that is sent up toward the aircraft (the primary signal) returns off the surface of the aircraft at a slightly different moment than the beacon (secondary) transponder signal, so the two do not match up as being at the same place at the exact same time." The secondary signal comes from a device inside the aircraft.

This sounds like government doubletalk, but what it means is that the radar received two signals from the same aircraft, not separate signals from two aircraft. That explained the double blips on the controllers radar screen, but it did not explain, nor

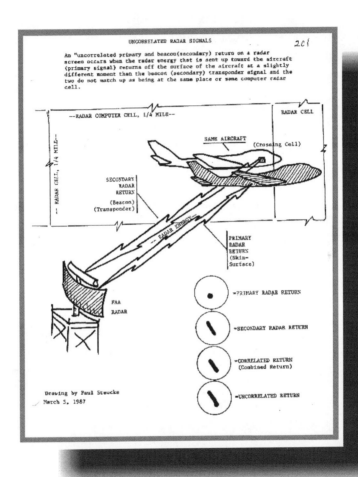

Secondary radar beacon drawing by the author, used at the press conference.

did it try to explain, what the captain said he saw. I was not about to touch that one.

The captain's comments, Jim Derry's interview and all the other assorted material collected in response to the media stories, fueled controversial opinions from both the UFO advocates and the UFO debunkers that, as I mentioned, are still ongoing today. On March 5, 1987, I washed my hands of it with the following announcement:

News Release, March 5, 1987

The Federal Aviation Administration has a number of employees who do scientific research with regard to aircraft, aviation, and related electronic equipment. The FAA does not have the resources or the Congressional mandate to investigate sightings of unidentified flying objects.

We have not tried to determine what the crew of Japan Air Lines flight 1628 saw based on scientific analysis of the stars, planets, magnetic fields, angle of view, etc. We have received letters from several persons suggesting that we ask the crew and others a variety of detailed questions from a scientific viewpoint. This we have not done and do not intend to do. We reviewed the data that was created by our systems, the interviews that were done by FAA to determine the status of the crew and the aircraft, and have provided that information to the public.

The FAA has completed its investigation of JAL Flight 1628, and does not intend to pursue it any further.

Paul Steucke, Public Affairs Officer, FAA, Alaska"

Press conference, release of UFO materials by author

The best and most comprehensive analysis and description of the UFO incident was provided by Marguerite Del Giudice, a reporter for the *Philadelphia Inquirer* newspaper, printed in the May 24, 1987 Sunday magazine issue. She attended the final press conference and after interviewing me, proceeded to locate all the other FAA employees who were a part of the story, (something I, as the public affairs officer, did not provide). She did an outstanding job, and I later sent her a letter of congratulations on her story, telling her I hoped a letter of praise from a government PR man was not the *kiss of death* for a reporter.

Soldotna II

Our regional leaders hired a full-time management consultant with a doctorate in psychology. Dr. Rob, as I will call him, was a very nice older fellow, a father figure, much like a priest or rabbi; he was someone you could talk to, laugh with, and weep with. Everybody loved him. He seemed to know what he was doing and he had our confidence.

The agency planned a five-day work session at a motel with a large conference room and restaurant in Soldotna, a tiny, remote town on the Kenai Peninsula. The retreat was called Soldotna II because we had used this location for the same sort of management workshop once before, utilizing a different consultant. Obviously, we thought, top-level management did not find the results following Soldotna I satisfactory, because here we were back again with our very own in-house management guru. Dr. Rob wanted to be sure this session produced the desired results, so for weeks before the seminar date, he spent a lot of time interviewing each of us on the senior staff to determine what we thought needed fixing.

We all knew what needed fixing: the top boss needed to tell his deputy and some of his senior staff to back off and do their job, but we were not about to say that. Talk like that just might get a person in trouble. But Dr. Rob convinced us all that dropping our honest complaints in the "old bitch bucket," as he called it, would be very helpful in identifying issues that needed to be addressed.

Soldotna II commenced, and after several days of preliminary management games, we got around to the old bitch bucket. We were gathered in the conference room, sitting in a big circle of chairs, when Dr. Rob said he wanted to pull some of the problem topics mentioned by the staff, out of the bucket and address them.

He called for any questions before we started. Yes, there was one big question raised by the manager of our regional civil rights office. How appropriate. This man, let's call him

Ben, had won many awards in his line of work and was trusted by the thousand or so Alaskan employees for his counsel and help with regard to fairness in the work environment. The first thing Ben did was ask the regional administrator and his deputy to leave the room, so everyone could talk freely about the bitch bucket process. They left, and before Dr. Rob could raise a question, Ben asked if everyone was comfortable with what we were about to do; that is, tell the boss and his deputy what they were doing wrong (and expect no repercussions??!). Everyone nodded their head and mumbled sure, et cetera, but wisely, that did not satisfy our civil rights man. He said, "Well, let's put our cards on the table. I want each person in this circle to agree that this is what we want to do and that we are in total agreement. We need a unanimous vote that we will tell the boss what we think." And he proceeded to ask each person, one by one, if he or she agreed. Everyone agreed.

Dr. Rob called the boss and deputy back in, and the first comment out of the bitch bucket was critical of the deputy and his management style. Our good civil rights man bravely shared his thoughts, as did several others. The prime offenders remained silent, even when asked directly what their opinions were. They sided with the boss and the deputy, and immediately it was beyond obvious that our PhD management consultant had allowed half the senior staff to hang themselves. What was worse--well, let's say almost as bad--I don't think Dr. Rob ever realized what was happening. I don't think he knew that everything had changed. You could smell the distrust in the room, strong as a truckload of sour garbage. From that point on, no one ventured to say much of anything about anything, no matter what came out of that bucket.

This was the third day of the management seminar and we knew it was also the last of Dr. Rob, since he had previously announced his retirement. It didn't seem to be a good time to tell him what was really going on, so no one mentioned the disaster, and he seemed oblivious to it all. We provided him with cake, humorous good luck cards, and lots of praise and then everyone *got the hell out of Dodge* as fast as possible. That was the last guru session for a long, long time.

Meanwhile things at work kept getting worse. The accident rate was climbing again, the media was hounding us for answers, and the agency was getting pressure from someone to back off on our inspections. Our legal counsel retired early, after he got racked by the media for not cooperating with some air taxi whistle blowers.* Thanks to the media attention, our regional problems were finally getting the attention of our headquarters staff. Most of the staff were surprised when, unannounced, the FAA top administrator flew out from Washington, just to have a closed-door talk with our regional administrator and our very new legal counsel. This caused quite a stir, considering he had to fly ten hours one-way in order have that little chat. Obviously, this meeting had to be some kind of rubber meets the road scenario.

After the top boss left, the informal feedback was that someone high up was pressuring our regional office to back off on the inspections because they were getting pressure from unknown sources that in turn were getting pressure from other unknown sources. We heard that at one point in the meeting, the new legal counsel was moved to interrupt and point-by-point lay out the history, when he realized that counsel, as well as the inspectors, were going to get the blame for the higher accident rate. (Within the year following this meeting, the system moved both the new counsel and the chief of inspections out of their jobs.)

Meanwhile, the news media continued to criticize the agency and the management for a lousy job, article after article. It made my position a nightmare. Finally, the D.C. office sent out its best management consultant and mediator to set the entire senior staff down in a location outside the office and find out why the routine inspection system, used successfully nationwide ,was not working in our region.

*Congress and most states have passed laws to protect whistle blowers, that is, people who speak up about problematic and/or illegal things being done by a corporation or agency. But even Congress has not been totally able to protect the federal whistle blowers from all the various forms of retribution.

I had seen this consultant (let us call her Cindy) work before, and I had great respect for her ability to find out what was going on and fix it. She came by my office before the group meetings commenced to see if I knew what was going on. I told her about Soldotna II, which no one else had mentioned to her. She said, "Thanks, that explains a lot," and left.

In the afternoon session of the first meeting, Cindy kept probing, trying to get people to open up. I had gained a reputation for not saying much, mostly because I usually think before I speak, and the time required to do that frequently allows other people to move the conversation to a different subject. However, Cindy finally had the group talking about the inspections and the accident rate, when I thought--and immediately said, "This reminds me of the *Godfather* movie, where the son interrupts the father at a meeting with the enemy mafia group, and the enemy group takes this as a weakness and tries to exploit it." As usual, no one paid much attention to me, but the mediator cut off the next person to speak in midsentence, "Did anyone hear what Paul just said?" No, they did not, but she did, and she repeated what I said word for word. There was dead silence as everyone realized the dreadful truth, that someone in management had been undercutting the efforts of the inspectors.

The very next morning the regional administrator told us he had been thinking things over and had decided he was going to retire. No one knew this was coming--his secretary, God bless her, wept--and it was a shock to all of us. He never said why he was retiring.

Several years later I talked with a high-level manager in D.C. who had also attended the *cut to the chase* meeting between the regional administrator, the regional counsel and the top administrator from D.C. Referring to our Alaskan boss and his retirement, my friend made a single, succinct comment, "He forgot who he worked for." Civil servants work for the public good, and when that goal is manipulated to someone's private advantage, the system fails.

The unknown, unexpected, interview

Once a year the headquarters director of public affairs held a five-day conference for all the regional public affairs officers at the FAA training facility at Palm Coast, Florida. It was a great way to get to know one another and trade ideas for improving the operations. On one of these trips, I happened to be riding in the car with the GS-15 manager of the headquarters communication office. There were no GS-15 positions in the field; GS-14 was tops, and like the other Washington, D.C. managers, Ray had been there for a good number of years. No one could even remember the last time anyone retired or transferred from one of the five GS-15 jobs in D.C. While we chatted, Ray mentioned that he was thinking of retiring. I don't believe he had told anyone else. We went on chatting amicably, and I did not think anything more about it.

Each week the Washington director held a telephone conference call with all the regions. We all looked forward to it because it provided information about what was happening both in D.C. and in the other regions. Several weeks after my initial conversation with Ray, he announced during the conference call that he was going to retire, that the open position would be announced soon, and that people within the agency as well as people from outside FAA could apply for the job.

A year before these events, I had been asked by two FAA guys I worked with in Alaska to apply for a GS-15 management spot with the Agency's International Affairs, Asian Division. My coworkers were hoping to change the political culture of the agency based on certain qualities of the person in that position. They wanted me for the job because they were familiar with and very much liked my management style. They helped me prepare an outstanding job application package, however, I was not selected for the job. That did not surprise me; the International Division was a pretty closed group, and I spoke only one language. However, I was able, with very little modification, to submit this same application for the D.C. public affairs job. The selection and filling of most civil service positions is a very slow process, and candidates speculate endlessly about what could possibly be taking so long. This selection was no different, although as weeks went by, I began to wonder whether they were ever going to fill the position.

Several months after the job opening was announced, the D.C. director held our annual meeting in Florida. There was some talk about the vacant GS-15, but not much. One of the five top guys in the D.C. office briefly mentioned to me, while we were in a lunch line, that my resume and application was impressive. He added that several of my regional colleagues had also applied for the job. Then late that Wednesday afternoon, the director pulled me aside and handed me a brief written description of a significant public relations problem that might occur for the agency, saying, "I would like to know what you recommend we do about this." Using one of his favorite expressions, he continued, "I would like an answer *tout suite,* meaning (in French) as soon as possible.

Everyone else in our group planned to have dinner and party at a nearby Mexican restaurant. I begged off, claiming an upset stomach, and headed straight to my room. Several hours later, I completed my hand-written public relations plan. After some snacks from a machine, I located a facility computer *and converted my notes into a formal plan. It was about midnight when I put it in an envelope and slid it under the director's door. The next day he quietly thanked me for the material, and that was that, nothing more. The scenario for which he requested my suggestions was so realistic that to this day I don't know whether it was an actual one or not, but I felt good about what I gave him. No one ever discussed it with me, and I don't know if he asked other applicants to comment on the same issue. If he did, I am sure my response was the fastest of the lot.

* *Portable laptop computers did not exist yet.*

Author in Minnesota enroute to Alaska
Photo by Boynton Hagaman

Jaguar XK-120

Soon after I got home from Florida, I happened to leaf through an automobile magazine at the local drug store and discovered therein a full-page advertisement for a Jaguar XK-120, the car of my boyhood dreams. Jaguar began building this two-seat roadster right after WW II. It was designed to be a racecar and was, for a long time, the best and fastest one a person could buy. A few years later, after a multitude of requests, Jaguar decided to manufacture and sell it to the general public, not just professional racers. Before long, everyone who was anyone in Hollywood owned one.

However, the car had a few significant design features that naturally limited general public sales. Because it was a racecar, it lacked a top and roll up windows. In fact, other than the windshield, it had no windows at all. In addition, heat from the engine got so intense in the cockpit that Jaguar eventually had to install air scoops on each side to bring fresh air into the foot area. This helped, but it created another problem by allowing water to leak into the cockpit.

Jaguar addressed the no-top problem with a removable canvas top and metal support system that could be stored behind the seats. This system was anything but perfect. It had to be bolted on, snapped in several places to the body, and the front end had to be bolted down into screw holes along the top of the windshield frame. Then, after all this effort, invariably the top leaked.

The side windows were made of Plexiglas and slid down into slot holders. These also had to be stored behind the seats or in the trunk, not a handy solution. Nevertheless, with the top down and the windows stored, it was a truly beautiful car with its swooping curves and Jaguar grille.

When I was fourteen, I became infatuated with it and kept a small metal model in my bedroom. Now at the age of fifty, I saw a chance to consummate my childhood longings by purchasing the replica I saw in the magazine advertisement. As the word *replica* explains, the car was a technologically non-identical but equally beautiful reproduction of the original (which at that time was selling for over $100,000). The body was formed of a hard, baked plastic material similar to fiberglass; it could be forcefully struck with a hammer without incurring damage.

Like the original, there was a canvas top that stored behind the seats along with the removable side windows, but also, as I was soon to discover, getting a good seal along the top edge of the windshield was very difficult. The water might not actually squirt in, but the car would usually leak a bit, nonetheless. One advantage the replica had over the original was the inclusion of a clamp-on hardtop that looked just like the canvas top, but was more comfortable in some ways. Of course, it had to be stored in the summer, and once in place it was awkward to remove and reinstall, so it usually stayed on all winter. Unfortunately, this top also leaked along the windshield seal. All the other parts of the car, the engine, wheels, shocks, electric system, and so on, were advertised as modern and easy to maintain.

I sold my 1980 Porsche 924 Turbo, cashed in some savings bonds, got a small bank loan, and Annette and I flew to Buffalo NY to pick it up. The next morning we paid $30,000 for the replica and drove away, little suspecting that we were at the beginning of a mighty poor experience with an automobile.

As we left Buffalo on the turnpike in a pouring rain, water immediately began to leak and wick across the inside of the hardtop roof, enough water to threaten my driving visibility. A second real problem immediately became evident. I kept our luggage to a minimum because the trunk was small and the luggage rack on the rear trunk was even smaller. Even so, our body weight and our bags in the back made the front of the car rise up several inches up, enough to make the rear appear to drag a little. Actually more than a little. We soon discovered that highway bridges have a break in the concrete where the bridge begins and another break where it ends. When the replica, with its nose in the air, hit these concrete road breaks, the out of balance suspension drove the twin tailpipes near the rear axle up into the frame with a thump-bump and an ear-piercing bang all of which was very unnerving indeed. It was just plain terrible. We soon started bracing ourselves for the sound and vibration every time we approached yet another break in the concrete. After thirty miles of driving rain and innumerable bridges, we turned around and got a room for the night. We were both pretty upset, but I think Annette was even more distressed than I was to see me beginning to have my childhood dreams dashed by poor workmanship.

We called the builder, who immediately came out in the rain and took the car to his home garage about ten miles away. The next day he pulled the entire rear axle out and installed another, trying to fix the problem. At my suggestion, he also bolted a pair of 12" x 2" x 4' steel plates, each weighing 100 pounds, onto the frame at the very front of the car. This did help. I also suggested larger shock absorbers for the back suspension, but he could not find any, so I left it at that and had some installed later.

We took off the next morning. Our goal was to drive to Seattle, with an intermediate stop at a family vacation resort in northern Minnesota, 1,175 miles away from Buffalo. When we reached Chicago, we passed a billboard with a temperature sign registering 90 degrees, and we knew that inside our car, even without the heater on, it was a lot hotter than the outside air temperature. Getting outside air into the car was very difficult because our replica didn't include the side vents built into the later models and removing the side windows while traveling was impossible. The eighteen-wheel truckers sounded their air horns at us and waved as we drove past them, while we eyeballed the center of their tires that were taller than our car. The rear axle was still double pounding the tail pipes and frame every time we crossed every bridge. It was enough to wear a person out!

However, we made it to our Minnesota resort, without further mishap, to relax with family and catch and eat walleye from the un-crowded lake. We had vacationed there with family quite a few times over the past fifteen years. One of the best features for our extended family was that the fishing cabins were all two or three bedroom houses (solidly built in the 1950's) so we could spread out into several different cabins. Everyone could visit and eat most of their meals as a group, but also have rest and privacy when desired.

We had been at the resort a few days when my wife told me she believed we should not drive the remaining 1,427 miles to Seattle in the Jaguar. She was adamant about not being willing to risk it in a car that might have serious safety issues. Neither would she agree to fly home alone and let me drive it to Seattle. Our marital discussion went back and forth without settling anything--until she startled me by asking about our life insurance policies and how to notify civil service in case of my demise. When I realized she was serious, I dropped my plan to drive it myself. Instead, I paid a visit to the used car lot in the nearby town of Perham to find out how and where to ship the Jag and rent a car for the drive to Seattle. A salesman said that a business in Fargo that made Shelby Cobra brand replica cars could probably help me. A telephone call brought the good news that not only could I could get some additional work done on the car, but when the work was done, they would ship it to Seattle and on to Alaska for me. I had found a wonderful solution to our problems.

Two days later, we drove the Jaguar to Fargo. I told them to put air shocks on the back and install a new steering wheel, as the type my man in Buffalo had put on pushed so far forward toward the driver that I had to steer the car with my elbows tucked back. We rented a Lincoln Town Car at the Fargo airport and after two weeks of fishing, drove in luxury to my brother's home in southern Washington, where my parent's lived next door. We had a wonderful reunion.

And we had a wonderful surprise while we were there. I got a telephone call from the FAA assistant administrator for public affairs in Washington, D.C. He asked me if I still wanted the GS-15 manager job, and I said that I did. As it turned out, that was the only such GS-15 job to come available for years. He asked me not to tell anyone except my family since he had not yet announced it. He also said he would have to go to the top administrator for approval, because although I was the best-qualified candidate, I was also a man. As the song says, *The times they are a changing,* and the beginning of a women-for-women's club at work was becoming evident. Men had preferentially hired men for years; now it was their turn.

Two weeks later, he told everyone on the weekly conference call that I had been selected for the job. Once again we were departing for Northern Virginia, our old hometown, only this time we knew we would not be back. We listed the condo and sold it to an FAA friend for just about what we paid for it fifteen years earlier--no profit, just our initial investment, thanks to the Alaska recession, but we considered ourselves lucky to have a buyer.

Our many FAA friends threw a big going away party for us with lots of presents, thank you plaques, speeches and good cheer. When I realized they were going to give me a farewell shindig, I asked that they invite John Hall, my old Forest

Service friend, and Esther Wunnicke, the federal co-chair of the Land Use Planning Commission. This was our third time moving out of the state, and I knew it would be the last. At least I did not have to spend the entire night before we left doing artwork on an annual report.

As for the Jaguar, we shipped it to Virginia, where I drove it for the next six years. Once I got the problems worked out, it was a lot of fun, but I don't recommend buying a replica unless you enjoy working on cars.

* * *

Moving day, the last time out

The Last Time Out... (to FAA D.C.)

The morning after our farewell party, we left the Anchorage Holiday Inn and headed down the Alaskan-Canadian highway in our reliable Subaru station wagon. When we stopped at Tok for the evening, I posted the following letter to the editor of both Anchorage newspapers. They were printed three days later.

> To the Editor;
> *Anchorage Times*
> *Anchorage Daily News*
> "Dear friends:
>> I would like to share three thoughts with you as we pass through Tok on our way out of Alaska.
>> First, it has been a wonderful experience knowing you and being a part of Alaska for 17 years. Thank you for everything.

Second, if you want Anchorage to be a two-newspaper town, start buying both newspapers; otherwise you will soon be a one-newspaper town.

Third: remember that the vote to move the state capitol from Juneau to Willow was decided by one person with one bullet. This was not a democratic decision, and the vote should be held again.

Paul Steucke

Although we had moved into and out of the state three times, we had never driven the Alcan Highway. Since it was built by the US Army Corps of Engineers during WW II, the road has been generally improved and the Alaska portion has been paved, which at least eliminated the dust, but the permafrost heaving still makes the drive about as exciting as a carnival ride. One becomes expert at analyzing the upcoming pavement in time to slow down over the worst of the ups and downs.

We planned to drive down the Alcan to Skagway and then ride the state ferry *Columbia* to Seattle. We brought along our copy of the indispensable Alaskan guidebook, *The Milepost.* With its mile-by-mile detailed description of all the Alaskan highways, one can plan a trip or find out where one is anywhere along the route.

The Subaru had two gas tanks. When the main tank gauge hovered around zero, I could switch to the reserve, but the small reserve tank didn't have a gauge, so judging how far I could travel on it was a guessing game. Of course this would vary depending on road conditions and what gas mileage the car was getting. On June 25 we left Tok with two full tanks of gas for the 400-mile drive to Whitehorse. As the day went on, the gas gauge eventually read half-full, then one quarter, one eighth--and then it read zero. I switched to the reserve tank and we drove on.....and on....and on. I wasn't very concerned because I had carefully planned the trip and knew I could soon get gas at a station shown in the *Milepost,* but when we arrived, we found a deserted station and a *Gone Out of Business* sign.

Now I became concerned. We drove on and I began to coast down every hill in neutral gear. After miles and miles of gas station free wilderness, I was ready to stop somewhere, anywhere there was the slightest sign of civilization. A few miles later, we came upon a combination restaurant/bar and gas station displaying a big *Closed* sign in two-foot tall letters. However, there were two cars parked around to one side, so I decided this was it, closed or not, and rolled off the highway.

I went inside and explained my situation to the two people sitting at the darkened bar, who I'm sure could sense my panic. They smiled and said Whitehorse was literally just over the next hill. It was, and we gratefully coasted into the first gas station we came across, problem solved.

The state of Alaska operates ten ferries between the major cities, towns and villages in the many salt waterways of the state. The 418-foot *Columbia* is the largest in the fleet, capable of carrying 931 passengers, 134 vehicles, with 103 private cabins and a restaurant. It's an impressive ship, but not a cruise ship in any sense of the word. Rather, it's a safe, solid, dependable, very large workhorse that gets people and vehicles between distant destinations safely. It does not cater to the customer.

The number of available cabins was severely limited on this particular run because all the college students who had worked in Alaska for the summer were returning to school, and the ferry was the cheapest way home. The maximum number of occupants for the cabins was 294 and the boat would hold a total of 931 passengers. That means that about 637 non-cabined passengers were spread around on the ferry.

We boarded just after midnight. After we checked into our cabin, we toured the ship and were amazed to find people, mostly students, camped everywhere. They were under the stairwells and all over the decks, some with pitched tents duct-taped down to the flooring. A partially open-air solarium on the top deck was packed wall to wall with chaise lounges. People stood in line for hours to lay claim to one of these reclining chairs in this prized location by filling it up with their sleeping bag, backpack and other stuff. I now realized how lucky we were to have our cabin, no matter how practical and spare it was. The stainless steel toilet was actually *inside* the stainless steel shower, so when we bathed, we were also washing everything in the little room, including the toilet.

The Alaska State Ferry Columbia, *the chaise lounge area with students, and some of the tents that were taped to the rear deck of the ship*

The next morning, as we glided down the inside passage, we went to the restaurant on the back of the ship for breakfast. I had French toast and Annette had bacon and eggs. That turned out to be the only meal she ate on the whole boat ride. Three hours later, she began to feel sick to her stomach and shortly thereafter was racked by violent vomiting and severe illness. It took her a good month to get over what we think was food poisoning, probably from the eggs.

Annette was incapacitated for the rest of the voyage. After seeing to her needs, I occasionally put on my parka and went out to the deck to get some fresh air and study the somewhat monotonous view of Douglas fir trees and cloudy fog. There were no distant, snow-covered mountain peaks or glorious sunrise/sunsets; it was nothing but dreary and drearier all the way. The outside temperature was cold, made even colder by the constant 17 knots we were travelling. Even with a parka on, it was uncomfortable enough to drive me back indoors after a short time, although the interior was always stuffy and overcrowded with people.

Our first stop after our departure was nearby Haines, then Juneau, followed by Sitka, Petersburg, Wrangell, and Ketchikan, over three days time. At each stop the same announcement was broadcast over the public address system, "This is a warning. If you do not have a paid ticket, get off the ship now. Anyone caught on board without a ticket will be arrested upon arrival at our final destination in Bremerton, Washington." (Bremerton is 100 miles north of Seattle.) True to the promised consequences, when we docked in Bremerton, we watched the police handcuff and escort several young men off the boat. I suppose they figured an arrest was better than living through an Alaskan winter with no money.

I had originally tried to reserve a cabin in advance all the way to Bremerton but was thwarted by the inability of the ferry system to know exactly what would happen when we arrived at Juneau. So after the first day, all the cabin passengers were asked to return their keys to the purser, who held them until he could figure how many new people were coming on board with cabin reservations. We all gathered in the small lounge by his desk and waited and waited. I was particularly concerned because Annette was still very sick in our cabin and the thought of having to find a space for us in the lounge for the next two days was a dreadful prospect. I was greatly relieved, and Annette even more so, when the purser finally handed back the keys to our very own humble space.

I can't say the trip was uninteresting, but I was very glad when it was over and we were in our car heading south on Interstate 5 to our son's family and home in Olympia, Washington. A few days later we visited my brother and parents in Woodland, Washington, east to Yellowstone Park, southeast to St. Joseph, Missouri, and at last, east to Falls Church, Virginia, and Annette's parents' home.

When I reported for work in the Washington office, I entered a working climate that felt less than ideal, though I didn't quite know why. It wasn't until a year later that I discovered the number two man in my division, a GS-14, had applied for and expected to get my job, but because of me, had not been selected. Although he always behaved professionally, he was never warm and friendly, and neither were two others on my staff who had wanted him to get the job. This made management difficult at times. I held a weekly meeting with my staff of twenty, but the old school group never supported me very much.

The second week into the job, I was hit more directly with a management problem from one of the women I supervised. Six of the twelve staff in our Media and Employee Communications Division were responsible for all press activities and the other six were responsible for producing a monthly employee news magazine that went out to all 45,000 employees, and also a weekly four-page newsletter that went to all Washington, D.C. employees. The weekly newsletter had a staff of two men and one woman.

Now, after working under my supervision for only two weeks, the woman came into my office on a Monday morning and handed me a letter of resignation, complaining that I had not given due recognition for her work on the newsletter. This gave me quite a shock. One reason I had been hired was for my track record and reputation for personal, friendly management skills. I immediately moved out from behind my desk and led us to the coffee table arrangement that was half my office and asked her to sit down and talk to me about it. After a few minutes, I began to understand that she thought I had demoted her in preference to one of the other employees. I had not done so; all three of them were the same grade and there was no designated manager among them, a situation I corrected immediately by asking her to be the recognized leader (with no increase in pay). The two guys did not mind, so everything went smoothly after that. A few years later, I reorganized the division by creating two equal branches, giving each branch a GS-14 manager. This upgrade for the newsletter folks allowed the manager to move up to my GS-15 position when I retired.

As part of my Washington job, I responded to media requests for accident information, set up press conferences to announce our agency actions and travelled around on the company jet with the administrator and deputy for special occasions.

In 1990, the citizens of Westchester, New York, and nearby New Jersey, being very upset over the noise created by large passenger jets passing over their homes, demanded and received via their congressional representatives, a multi-million dollar environmental impact study on the effect of aviation routes in their area. The five-year study involved a massive collection and analysis of data.

Over 35 public hearings were held in the N.J. and N.Y. area. The people were active, organized and angry. The hearings were packed with irate citizens, holding big signs, placards and handouts, who booed us and anyone who tried to justify the need for aircraft in our society. Our relationship with the media, New York City included, was strained because the citizens always briefed the reporters prior to our arrival and urged them to report our efforts as heavy-handed and bureaucratic. This was something the media seemed happy to do; we did not buy their papers, the New York public did.

My media strategy was to always repeat the facts, the need for aviation services, and the scope of the problem, over and over consistently until the media had to report the factual part of the problem as well as the emotional side of the story. After several years, the media tired of the story and printed short, balanced articles, including such little known information as, for example, the fact that over 4,500 planes a *day* travel in and over the immediate New York City area in the course of landing at three international airports. These aircraft do a daily choreographed fly in and out pattern that carries them on FAA controlled flight paths--and all without hitting each other in the air or on the ground. Trying to adjust this dance in the sky to accommodate all or even some of the people who live under a flight path is difficult, if not impossible.

As the FAA public affairs coordinator, I attended every hearing and provided interviews and information to the media and the public. Constant tact and diplomacy was required, although I did lose my temper on one occasion. We were holding a hearing in a high school auditorium, and the speakers were talking from a rostrum set forward on an empty, open stage.

While I was in the hallway talking to a reporter, a newspaper photographer hauled a ten-foot folding wood stepladder from the back of the stage and placed it directly behind the dais so he could get some good shots looking down on the speaker and audience. This creative photo strategy was discourteous and unkind to the speaker because the audience became far more interested in whether or not the photographer would fall, than in paying attention to the presenter. Someone found me in the hall and asked me to get the guy down.

I went onto the stage, where the speaker was still trying to give a presentation, and grabbing the ladder, told the photographer to get down. He said, "No." And I said, "I will give you two minutes to get the photo and then I will shake you down if necessary." He ignored me and continued to take photos. After another four minutes, I asked the speaker to step aside and I shook the ladder. The photographer screamed, the ladder leaned, and he finally got down. The audience cheered!

A few minutes later, I was called to the public telephone down the hall by the reporter accompanying the photographer

(No such thing as cell phones yet). The editor of the newspaper railed on for a while about how I had mistreated his photographer, and then I interrupted and let him have it in both ears. I explained what had happened and told him that whenever his people behaved so unprofessionally, I would throw them out, and he could write about that if he liked. I gave the phone back to the reporter, and that was the last I ever heard about it.

The hearings ended, and the agency, through massive and costly changes, was able to reduce the noise for about ten percent of the population. The media printed and aired our effort as wonderful and then dropped the subject.

Politics, I discovered, wears a particularly heavy hand at the Washington level. We had several employees in the office who were there primarily as a result of political arrangements. They were nice enough, but you always knew they had a string to someone, who knew someone, who knew someone in the White House. Civil service employees who had spent years working their way up the career ladder resented this violation of the system. My boss, the assistant administrator for public affairs, was a political appointee himself, but I always sensed that, even so, he resented these political implants in his kingdom.

When President Clinton came into office, there was the usual massive turnover of political people from Republicans to Democrats, and this included our boss, the assistant administrator for public affairs. When he resigned, the position went vacant for almost a year, leaving the deputy to do both jobs with no increase in pay or recognition. This happened so frequently--and sometimes on purpose--that the civil service rules eventually specified that an employee performing the job on an "acting as" basis for three months or more would receive the pay commensurate with the assignment.

The new political machinery eventually filled the position with woman who had been a vice president at one of the national auto rental companies. She never did move to Washington, but commuted every Friday and Monday from

Chicago via airplane. Before long it became obvious that she was going to change more than just policy and do it mighty fast. When she took over, we had five GS-15 managers--all men, I admit. One year later only one remained, and six months later, he too was gone. All the vacated positions were filled with women. She also forced several women middle managers to leave. She took control over the regional public affairs offices and their budget, closed half of them, which sent fifty people into the unemployment line. A year later she was gone, back in Chicago, job done. In the end, what she accomplished had no effect whatsoever on the agency's budget, but it hurt a lot of people and significantly reduced the agency's ability to communicate with the public.

President Clinton, shortly after he took office, appointed Vice President Gore to reduce government spending. The effort actually changed the national debt to a national surplus, something no one had done for years before, and certainly not after George W. Bush took over. Part of the reduction program included an early-out option with a handsome cash incentive bonus for any civil service employee who would be eligible to retire in six months or less.

I went, just as soon as I could. The thirty years between a twenty-five year old GS-7 employee and a fifty-five year old GS-15 employee might seem like forever, but if you're lucky to live long enough, the day will surely come when you find yourself qualified to retire. And as my father said, "You won't get rich, but you won't be poor." For thirty years, I contributed a portion of my paycheck into my retirement fund and now I was going to use it. I gave two weeks' notice, told my staff I did not want any sort of retirement party, cleaned out my office desk, finally threw away my old Soldotna II files and set up several new files for my replacement to ease the transition.

It was a relief to know I was escaping the deadly push of our Chicago commuting administrator. I am sure she would have made work life for me a daily hell. There are many tricks that can be used by a supervisor to make a great employee look incompetent, and she knew them all.

My last day at work included a mid-morning doughnut and coffee send off, at which I advised the young crew facing me to remember that their retirement date would eventually come, and to make sure that what they did in that thirty-year period was always honorable, so that when the moment did arrive, they could leave with their head held high. I then went back to my office and wrote a letter to each of my twenty employees, giving them a positive recommendation for their resume, and left.

* * *

"Sunshine Lily," acrylic on canvas

Kailua, Kona

The rental lease on our house in Reston and the retirement coincided perfectly; we took the cash bonus and moved to the Big Island of Hawaii, Kailua-Kona, a longtime dream come true. Our many previous vacation visits, about six months total time, had given us a pretty good knowledge of each major island. We chose to settle in Kailua, Kona, because it's less frequented by tourists and also because it is the largest and most diverse island ecologically. The first time landed at the Kona airport and drove the 12 miles into Kailua, I was shocked by the immense and arid expanse of black lava flows, and amazed to see snow on the top of Mauna Kea. It takes about five hours to drive completely around the perimeter of the island. The Big Island's original and official name is Hawaii, but after statehood, it became better known as the Big Island, to avoid a lot of confusion.

We made a house-hunting trip to Kona and found a beautiful place at the five hundred foot elevation on Sunset Drive just above the Keahoe subdivision. The first floor of the two-story home was rented by a single woman. Our top floor home had a great wrap-around lanai and a kitchen window that looked out over the ocean, a living room, two bedrooms and baths, vaulted beamed ceilings, and a garage. It was almost square-shaped, with an open-air circulation cupola in the center.

We planned our departure from Reston carefully. I spent weeks cleaning out stuff and throwing it away. In fact, we hauled seven full trashcans out on the street for collection every Monday for a couple of months. One third of what we owned went to Goodwill or the dump, one third went into storage, and the remaining third we shipped to Hawaii. I sold the Jaguar for $10,000 (after driving it for six years) and we drove our 1997 Chevrolet Lumina van to the West Coast for shipping.

The moving company sent a young man out to advise us, quote a price estimate, and sign the paper work. The day of the move, the van pulled up with a huge, full-size shipping container that I estimated was twice the size needed for our goods. I was right; at completion, the container was only half-full. After the van drove off, I called the company and told them I was not going to pay for a full-size container when one-half that size would have been adequate. They first suggested we could put our car in the empty half, and I said that was not acceptable. The next day they called again, and after some discussion, agreed to reload our goods into a half-size container. I told them to take the inexpensive bookcases apart if necessary, or even just trash them if they did not fit into the container (they fit).

We left Reston for the last time and headed west to Seattle and Hawaii, stopping enroute at the Minnesota lake resort for two-week vacation with Annette's parents and family, always a pleasant experience. Annette's brother John met us in Rochester

"Koi Lilies," acrylic on canvas

so we all could visit with their Aunt Rene, who was in a retirement home there. At dinner that night, every once in a while I thought I saw a mouse run across the floor. Upon closer attention, I realized that it was not a mouse, but something else, some odd phenomena that I was experiencing in my left eye. I passed it off as incidental, foolish as that now seems, and the next day the three of us drove to Minneapolis, where we met Annette's parents and continued the six-hour drive northwest to the resort sixty miles east of Fargo, North Dakota. It was Saturday, two days before the Labor Day holiday, and we had been on the road for three days.

We checked into our bungalows, relaxed, went fishing and enjoyed the warm spring weather. Sunday we did more of the same. The weather was beautiful. Monday was a holiday. By now I was beginning to wonder what was happening to my left eye, but not knowing for sure, I said nothing to anyone. On Tuesday, seven days after we left Virginia, I made an excuse to drive thirty-five minutes into the nearest town, where I looked for an eye doctor. None there, but the local pharmacist told me there was an eyeglass place in the next town.

> Unfortunately
>
> I said nothing
>
> to anyone

It was getting close to noon when the druggist called the optician, who said he would wait for me rather than go out to lunch. I drove down the interstate at eighty-plus miles per hour and got there in twenty minutes. He examined me right away and told me I had a detached retina in my left eye and would need immediate surgery to repair it, or else I would go blind in that eye. Then he called a retinal specialist in Fargo and got me an appointment for the next day. It was now hours past noon, and I had a long drive back to the resort. When I got back around

5PM, everybody was wondering where I had been for so long, and Annette, who already had guessed that something was very wrong, was sick with worry.

The next day at Fargo, the eye surgeon confirmed the detached retina and gave us two options. His first recommendation was that we have surgery immediately in Fargo, which would require a post-surgery two-week stay in town. The second option was for us to drive to Seattle as planned and get the surgery done there. We learned that there is a two-week window for saving a retina. It is best to do the surgery immediately, but after the first couple of days, the damage doesn't get much worse for the next ten days or so. I decided it would be best overall for us to quickly get to Seattle and have it done there. We could stay in our son's home, an hour's drive south of Seattle, during the recovery period. We had reservations about three weeks away to barge freight the car to Honolulu and then go on to Kona, and our airline tickets out of Seattle were "frequent flyer" prepaid.

Much as we hated to miss our vacation with family, we left the resort at 5AM the next morning for the three-day trip, with Annette at the wheel and me reclining in the passenger seat. She drove the entire trip, as fast as she dared, while we listened to books on tape and worried.

Before we left Fargo, Annette called my brother in Woodland, Washington to tell him about my detached retina. Wally immediately got in touch with a friend who'd had the same eye problem. When we stopped the first day, I called him from our motel, and was very surprised and very grateful to hear that he had me all lined up with one of the preeminent eye surgeons in Seattle. We arrived in the eye surgeon's office just before closing time on Friday. After examining me, he said there was no longer a reason to perform emergency surgery, so he would do it the following Monday afternoon.

After a weekend at my son's home, we checked into Swedish Hospital. I woke up late that night with a huge patch on my left eye. My doctor said, "I have to see you everyday for the next three days to make sure the surgery works." Works!

Yes, sometimes they have to do it twice. That gave me a sinking feeling.

The retina is a thin membrane on the back inside wall of the eyeball. Most of us learned in high school biology that we have rods and cones in our eyes that collect the light images and transmit this data in electrical form through a nerve to the brain, where it is somehow transformed again, into what we call *sight*. Like most body functions that we take for granted, it is an amazing process.

The retina can develop a tear or hole in it that allows the clear gel in the eye to slowly seep behind the retina and push it away from the blood supply in the back wall of the eye. Unless the retina is reconnected to that blood supply, it will peel away in total until there is no retina left. Many years ago, the only way to encourage the repair was to have the patient lay with the torn side down, immobilizing sand bags on each side of the head, and not move for three months, so that gravity would pull the retina back into place.

Torture can come in many subtle and mentally outrageous ways; being forced to keep one's muscles in the same position for hours, days or weeks is one of them. Fortunately, a surgical solution for a detached retina is now performed by doctors (some of whom are angels). The surgeon first repairs the tear by working through the front of the eyeball with a laser light to fuse the torn tissue together. Then he sews a curved silicone strip onto the backside of the eyeball to reduce its circumference and pull the eyeball onto the retina, so it can reattach and heal.

Saving someone's eyesight must be one of the most significant things one person can do for another. How anyone learns to do this, much less has the courage to do it, is beyond my comprehension. I am truly and forever grateful for the medical care I received,

After the surgery, the patient must lie in bed, head tilted to an angle for two weeks, so gravity can help the repaired retina stay in place until fully healed. The doctor must look into the eye routinely during this fourteen-day period to make sure the retina is getting a good blood supply and is healing well. I never cared to check my eye in a mirror while I was recovering, but everyone told me it was totally blood red.

My brother generously came up from Woodland and with Annette's assistance got our car to the shipping dock in Seattle. After two weeks, the doctor said we could keep our flight to Kona, but insisted that I see a retina specialist in Honolulu on a regular basis for checkups. A cataract did develop in that eye, a common result of the surgery, and two years later, a surgeon removed my cloudy lens and installed a prescription plastic lens that has worked just fine.

So we flew to Hawaii. Before long our household goods and our car arrived, and we settled into a daily routine day of shopping at the local market, hanging out at the beach and playing house. But after a while, we spotted a few flaws in Paradise. First, we noticed the nocturnal lizards showing up in the house. Four to six inches long and so translucent that their innards could be seen, these geckos gave us the creeps as they wiggled across the walls, the ceilings--they went anywhere and they were not pretty or cute or respectful of others. Every day we found little gecko presents on the kitchen counters, and one morning there a gift on Annette's bed pillow when she woke up, motivating us to immediately buy white mosquito netting and drape it from the ceiling over the entire bed

I searched for entry points and discovered that the beautiful overhead beams coming into the house from the four-foot overhang had never been caulked, and thus provided a gecko interstate highway into the house. I caulked, and caulked some more, and the creature count dropped. Then I discovered that the four-foot square cupola in the center peak of the roof had a two-inch gap in the screening--where the builders must have just said to heck with it, who needs screening. I closed that gap too, and after that, the visitors dropped down to a minimum.

Warm climates are notorious for bugs, and Hawaii certainly has its share, many of which were imported by ships from far-off locations. At one time, there were no mosquitoes on the island. Nor were there any cardinals, sparrows, cats, rats, just to name a few imports. In 1883 sugar plantation owners brought in mongoose to eat the rats, forgetting that rats are nocturnal and mongoose sleep at night. The state now has an active program in place around all Hawaii airports to prevent the introduction of the Brown Tree Snake that was introduced to Guam by military aircraft during WW II. The snake has just about eliminated the bird population on that island. They are not poisonous, but they do sometimes bite, and any snake that is six feet long and climbs trees is scary.

Our elevation and location on the mountainside was home to giant red centipedes the diameter of a large man's forefinger and six to ten inches long. Oh, they were really creepy and their bite was dangerous. We also had ants, big ones that came out at night. One evening Annette opened the bathroom door to find scores of them scurrying rapidly in radial lines from the toilet water tank (!?) The insect guy came the next day, took the lid off the tank and pointed to a small hole in the ceramic cover (which is left over from the molding process of the hollow lid). He took it out to the lawn, sprayed the inside and out they came. Wow!

After we got well settled in our new environment, I looked around for art opportunities. My search led me to a beautiful gallery in Waimea (since renamed Kamuela) near the Parker Ranch. *Upcountry Connection* carried paintings and drawings, sculpture, jewelry and other art items. The owner liked my portfolio and invited me to write something about art for the *West Hawaii Magazine.*

The Art of Creation by Paul Steucke
The West Hawaii Magazine, June 1995

It might be a new recipe for *Spam*, a new tool for repairing a car or a mathematical formula for plastic. It could also be a photograph, a painting, piece of sculpture or furniture. If it is new, it is the result of someone creating something that did not exist before.

For thousands of years artists have been thought of as magicians because they create something that talks to us, something that expresses feelings. They create music that has a profound effect on how we feel, sculpture so enticing that you want to touch it and visuals so powerful that you want to look at them over and over again. That is the magic.

The many ways we express ourselves is impressive: from opera to rock, graffiti to the Sistine Chapel, chilidogs to Chinese honey duck, from the bunny-hop to the waltz, and everything in-between. Some are the expressions and talent of one person, and others involve hundreds of artists working together on one project.

Artists express their feelings by creating something that allows them to share those feelings with others. They conceive an idea--a new way of being, thinking, seeing, feeling or hearing--and then convert that idea into something tangible that will communicate to another person. Sometimes the idea and the creation happen at the same time, or the ideas and feelings expressed can change numerous times while the artist is actually working on a painting or other art object.

It is not enough to just have an idea or feeling. The artist must have the necessary skills to convert an idea into a work of art. A musician must know the harmonics of sound, just as a sculptor must know the fracture qualities of marble. Rollo May in his book, *The Courage to Create*, has provided some interesting insight into the process of creating. He says, "The first thing we notice in a creative act is that it is an encounter." That is why it is difficult to write the first musical note, brush the paint on the blank canvas or write the first word on a page.

"The second thing we notice is the intensity of the encounter the absorption of being caught up in it and being wholly involved." May says, "All artists at some time have had the experience at the end of the day of feeling tired, spent, and so certain they can never express their vision that they vow to forget it and start all over again on something else. The struggle to create can at times be overpowering, but it is also very rewarding."

Into the Barn,"
(Randy) acrylic on canvas

The process of creating has also intrigued me. Over the years, while painting, I have written down some brief thoughts about the process. Here are a few:

* A good painting will consume the room and everything in it. It will scream for attention, no matter how bold or how subtle the painting is.
* It is so easy to forget – when I look at a finished painting – how much hard, hard work it took to create. The pain of creating it is lost in the joy of its being.

* Sometimes a 30-minute painting session is so intense that I will have to lie down on the floor to rest.
* One brush stroke, one line, one dash – no matter how small will change everything in the painting.
* A successful painting leaves me on a high, so I celebrate with a dish of chocolate chip mint ice cream. An unsuccessful painting leaves me feeling low, so I eat a dish of chocolate chip mint ice cream.

Most of us have heard the phrase, "Beauty is in the eye of the beholder." Fortunately, this is a true statement. We are all individuals and we differ in what we like, Otherwise we would all be wearing the same clothes for every function and purpose. And that would be pretty dull.

Listen to your heart and find out what is beautiful to you. Then purchase what appeals to you. And don't be afraid to change styles or mediums. We all change as we go through life.

"Stay Put,", (Parker Ranch) acrylic on canvas

If you cannot buy original art, buy prints. And don't listen to art critics; frequently they do not know what they are talking about. The objective is for you to enjoy the experiences provided by art.

Creating something is a dynamic process that is emotional, personal, challenging, and a lot of fun. As Thomas Edison said, "One who is afraid to make mistakes is afraid to succeed." That goes for the patron as well as the artist.

I talked to the owner of the gallery about doing some paintings of the cowboys on the nearby Parker Ranch. She said, "Well, here comes your opportunity," as a cowboy from the ranch walked into the store. She introduced us, and when I expressed a desire to visit the ranch, Randy said, "We'll be training horses at the horse barn starting Monday at 6 AM. You're welcome to come and visit." That was good enough for me!

The Parker Ranch, located in the high meadowlands of the Big Island of Hawaii, is now the largest privately owned cattle ranch in the United States. In 1809, a single generation after Captain Cook first came to the island, a nineteen-year-old sailor named John Parker, tired of eating salt beef and pork, jumped ship for the good life of Hawaii. King Kamehameha I, the monarch who united all the islands, already had an increasingly large herd of cattle that had started with a small gift from British explorer Captain George Vancouver. At the time, they were roaming the entire island, so the king hired John to round them up and manage the herd. Over time, this became a profitable private business, run by the Parker family until very recently, when the last surviving Parker created a trust to manage the ranch.

On Monday I rose at 5 AM, ate a light breakfast, grabbed my photo gear, and in the glorious sunny morning, headed for the ranch thirty minutes away. When I arrived, two cowboys were rounding up some horses. Randy, the one I had met at the gallery, introduced me to Lester, the manager, who leaned across the front fender of his pickup truck and looked through my three ring binder portfolio with interest. When he got to the last page, he closed the binder and said, "Welcome to Parker Ranch. You will need to fill out and sign a legal disclaimer, so the ranch is not held libel for anything you might do foolish enough to get hurt. You are welcome to ride up with us later in the morning."

Lester gained his extensive horse experience growing up on a family ranch in Colorado, and Randy was the professional horse trainer the Parkers hired to break all their horses. The two men had known each other for some time. The word *breaking* is a misnomer where Randy is concerned; his techniques were always gentle and non-frightening to the horses. The training

Randy, Lester and Chris: Parker Ranch cowboys, pastel portraits

barn had several arenas, some of them circular, in which Randy stood in the middle while a horse trotted around the outside edge on a lead. Each cowboy, or *paniolo* as they are called in Hawaii, was assigned about eight horses and used several of them each day since, unlike the mighty steeds in Hollywood westerns, real horses cannot gallop all day and they tire quickly at working speed.

For several weeks, Lester and Randy let me ride in their heavy-duty truck which pulled a two-horse trailer. Slowly, in low gear, the truck and trailer went up and down the hills and gullies until we reached the lower half of the higher meadows. Then the saddled horses were unloaded, and Chris and Lester rode up into the hills, leaving me behind to enjoy the view. (I have ridden horses on a couple of occasions, but Lester, wisely, never invited me to ride a horse on the ranch, and I never asked.) They would show up an hour or so later, along with fifty horses in a bunch, bringing them down to a corral to be examined. Colts of varying ages were intentionally handled and checked.

"Chris and Dog," acrylic

The horses were curious about me and would walk over and stick their noses across the fence rail to check me out.

Lester had hired Chris, a young man who lived on the ranch, to help work the horses with him. Chris had a black dog he found wandering around lost-like up in the hills. The ranch allowed local people to come in with dog packs and hunt the wild pigs that inhabit the backcountry. Randy and Chris figured their foundling had gotten lost from one of the packs. One of Chris's friends offered to adopt the pup, so Chris just called him *dog* instead of giving him a proper name but the guy never came for him, so Chris officially named him Dog. Dog was very sweet natured and loved to jump up on the back of the truck and ride with them every day, all day. He was a very happy dog.

After several weeks of Randy's and Lester's friendship and generous hospitality, I had collected more than enough photographic material. Eventually I completed many paintings based on those photos, some of which were shown in the Upcountry Gallery and other places, most of which have been sold.

* * *

And then it happened again. One morning about 9 AM, when Annette and I were getting our stuff together to go to the beach, I noticed something funny about my right eye. My main symptom with the detached retina in my left eye was a brown, window-shade-like area that slowly came down the line of vision. I could still see through it, but it was like looking through a very dirty yellow window. However, this was a bit different; the window shade was coming in from the side. This time I did not wait so much as one minute to find out what it was.

The telephone book listed several eye doctors, but when I called, none of them answered. Finally, about noon I found one in Kailua that was open. The receptionist asked if I had an appointment. I told her this was an emergency. She told me I still needed an appointment. I asked her if the doctor was in. She said yes, and that was all I needed to hear. I told Annette what was going on and drove to the doctor's office, about five minutes away. On the medical and insurance forms the receptionist gave me, I wrote at the bottom in all capital letters, underlined, *Emergency, Possible Detached Retina!* (In hindsight, I don't think she had a clue as to what this meant.) After a long wait, I got to see the young woman doctor, who confirmed that I did indeed have a detaching retina in my right eye. She also told me that I was unusual, in that most retina tears are the result of a sports injury. There is a fifteen percent chance of getting a detached retina without a sports injury and a two percent chance of getting one in the other eye after the initial one. I hit both percentages.

When we moved to Kona, I contacted and had already visited a retinal specialist in Honolulu several times, taking a commuter flight to Oahu and back each time. I told the Kona doctor about my previous experience with the left eye retina, and she immediately called my Honolulu doctor, who told me to get my body to Honolulu as fast as possible. I called Annette, and by the time I got home, she had packed a small bag and arranged for a friend to care for our houseplants. We hurried to the airport.

Unlike some of the more popular tourist islands such as Maui, at that time you could not get a commercial flight off the Big Island after 7:30 in the evening. Our arrival at the Kona airport was just in time to catch the very last flight of the day to Honolulu. We landed, grabbed a cab and were in Dr. Drouilhet's office by 8:15 that evening. He was standing by, along with a colleague who did the routine exam work, and as soon as that was completed, we went to Queen's Hospital for surgery. I remember being wheeled down the hospital corridor on a gurney with the doctor walking beside me as we went to the surgical suite. I looked up at him and said, "Please tell your wife how much I appreciate your being with me right now."

I woke up in the morning, staring with my fuzzy left eye at a white wall barely six feet away from my bed, and started to feel quite panicky because I was essentially blind. Due to the long healing process, I had not yet gotten glasses for my left eye, and now my doctor had ordered me to stay on my right side. All I could see was that flat, white fuzzy wall. I begged Annette, who had spent a very anxious and sleepless night in the hospital's spartan guest rooms, to get me out of the hospital. She did her best. I was discharged about noon, and we checked into the nearby Pagoda hotel. After Annette got me settled, she walked to the shopping district and brought back a portable cassette player and headphones. I began the first of many, many days of listening to a New Age healing tape, whose repetitive choral chants helped to put me into a healing meditative state. However, I listened to that tape so many times that I can no longer stand to hear it because it makes me feel like I am back in that bed again. We ate all our meals downstairs at the Pagoda's restaurant (the only one for blocks around), and of course I couldn't begin to read the menu. I even had to put my hand on Annette's shoulder and let her lead me through the halls and lobby to a table. It was a sobering, depressing, disheartening experience.

Five days later, the doctor let us fly home to Kona, and I began the required recovery regime. I had to lay on my right side for fourteen days, interrupted only by meals and trips to the bathroom. Next to my bed, we set up a small television (laid on its side) and a video tape player. I watched movies, one after another, for most of every day. As time went on, it became increasingly unpleasant to stay in one position. Annette would help me stick to doctor's orders by jabbing her elbow into me at night and yelling "Get back on your side," and I would say "I am on my side," and she would holler," You are not; now get back on your side--doctor's orders!"

At one point, still unable to see clearly in my left eye, I became despondent and asked Annette to see if the doctor would prescribe a tranquilizer to keep my thoughts quieted down. He told Annette he didn't think I needed it and to give me a couple of Excedrin instead, but when I called him five minutes later, he must have heard the anxiety in my voice because he agreed to prescribe a small amount of Valium. I took it for two or three days and it settled me down. Day-by-day things got easier. After two weeks, we went back to Honolulu for a checkup, and after that, it was monthly visits.

Dr. Drouilhet is a great doctor who saved my eyesight. I sent him a thank you card every year for the next ten years.

I did not tell Dr. Drouilhet about the slow service I got from the eye doctor on Kona until they sent me a bill for $3.48, the part not covered by my health insurance. Then I sent a blistering letter to their office and a copy to Dr. Drouilhet, who later suggested we consider moving to a location with more medical specialists and a sophisticated hospital. The only thing on Kona was a six-bed clinic. Hawaii was beautiful but no longer the place for us.

"Morning Prayer", Acrylic on canvas. Lester and Randy, Parker Ranch

Our rental lease was coming up for renewal. We analyzed our overall situation and decided to move to Olympia, Washington, to be near our son, his wonderful wife and their four young daughters. We bought a house, complete with an art studio, five doors down the street from the family. It was a wise decision. My spouse was a terrific grandmother to those girls, and I think I was a good grandparent too. It has been an honor and a great pleasure to be with them throughout their childhood, and it is a great blessing to still be a part of their lives now that they are delightful adults. Wally and Joan live sixty miles south of us in Woodland, Washington, and we enjoy getting together with them about once a month. Overall, Annette and I are content and happy here, and life is very good.

* * *

Annette reading a bedtime story to grandchildren Kerianne and Taylor, in Olympia, Washington, 1996. As of this writing, Kerianne is attending the University of Minnesota to obtain her PhD in bioengineering, and Taylor is in her third year at Pratt Institute in New York, working on a degree in architecture.

This is a very small portion of the night sky showing the Sagittarius
constellation, courtesy of the US taxpayers and the NASA Hubble space
telescope. What is actually *out there* is so overwhelming that it is beyond
anyone's comprehension.

"The Earth does
not belong to Man.
Man belongs to the earth"
Chief Seattle, Suquamish Tribe, 1854

◆

Light traveling at a constant speed of *186,000 miles per second*
takes just over one second to travel between the earth and the
moon.

◆

Light, at 186,000 miles per second, takes about *eight minutes*
to go from the sun to earth.

◆

Light from a star called Proxima Centauri, the sun that is
closest to our sun, travels *4.5 light year*s before it reaches
earth.

◆

Light from the Andromeda Galaxy, the closest to our own, at
186,000 miles per second, takes *2.4 million light years* to
reach us.

◆

"We only have to look at ourselves to see how intelligent
life in the universe might develop into something
we wouldn't want to meet."
British Astrophysicist
Stephen Hawking
2010

Remember,
The past is nothing more
than a memory.
The future is nothing more than a thought.
Everything is always
in the now.

Wherever you go, whatever you do,
that is where you are.
.
What is... is.
now

The author at
8 years,   18 years,   30 years,   45 years,   72
years

All Forms are Unstable

Day by day, night by night, each of us slowly reaches and crosses the meridian of our life span until we are eventually closer to the end than we are to the beginning. It is a sobering realization. Life is a trip from birth to death. From point A to point B. It is bracketed by two mysteries. We really do not know why we come and we do not know what is behind the curtain we call death.

Human ingenuity, based on intuitive curiosity to build and improve, has created social and technological changes that have allowed us to change the way we live and work. This process has been building century by century, one creative idea built upon another. New developments in science and engineering have provided us with wondrous material, scientific and medical advancements.

Things we not only thought impossible, but also things we never dreamed about are now a reality. Everyone knows a list: television, cell telephones, putting man on the moon, antibiotics, and the electric toothbrush. I am sure George Washington was impressed with the changes that occurred in his lifetime. I certainly am impressed with what I have seen. It does not seem possible that things will be invented and discoveries made that we haven't even considered, but they will.

Social behavior, changing people rather than things, has been slow compared to technological changes. Fortunately,

"Heavier than air flying machines are impossible". Lord Kelvin President, Royal Society 1895

there has been some improvement. Not as much as most of us would like, but there has been progress. We have a global attempt at social regulation in the United Nations. Racial and sexual equality are slowly becoming accepted. Women in business have a far better chance of success than their mothers did.

Time is a word, a concept. It is all the conscious moments of our life, sunrise to sunset, that are important. We remember the past, try to plan for the future and are alive in the present. Fast cars, roller coasters, vacations, sports, live theater, cooking, dinner with friends, caring for babies, creating art, and riding in a convertible with the top down are all moments of the present. We love them because they provide us with the opportunity to be alive in the present moment, in the now.

Sometimes we are deluded into thinking that we are in control of our body, our life and everything else. We are not. Can you tell your heart to stop beating even for ten seconds? No. Fortunately, everything in your body is operating separately, independently from your ego-thinking mind. Something is keeping your body functioning, and mostly it is not the ego-you. The coordination and cooperation needed to keep us alive is impressive but we seldom think about it. The thinking part of us likes to believe it is in control, so it can build upon itself and obtain more and more power, more control. And for most of us it does just that, as in I am wiser than you, smarter, know the answers, can make recommendations to others, have been there, done that, etc. My ego and thoughts are easily offended. You don't believe me? Then you are wrong, because I know all the right answers. I will collect others who think like me and we will cross the mountains and the oceans with armies, and force you to believe as we do. The examples abound.

We live in the now, not the past nor the future; even the moments in which we are thinking of the past or future are always taking place now. Learning from the past and planning for the future are parts of everyday life, but they are not who you are.

> # *The body is not who we are; the body is what we live in.*

There are times when I've been able to be totally aware in the now. It is a delicious experience--I feel in tune with everything around me. I can even sense the rotation of the planet. The next time you see a sunset on the horizon, realize that what you are looking at is not the sun sinking, but the earth rotating at approximately 1,000 miles per hour. The thought could put you into the now.

Eckhart Tolle in his book *The Power of Now* says that all forms are unstable. Even the pyramids of Egypt, in relation to the universe, will crumble. Our individual form, the body, is very unstable, with a lifespan that is very short in comparison to the age and predicted lifespan of the planet. Tolle compares life to a wave in the ocean, the ocean being the universe and the waves being all of us. We are individual, as a wave, but every wave put together makes the ocean. Everything on the planet is unstable. All it takes is one unpredictable asteroid to hit our planet and all life, as we know it will be over.

As I mentioned earlier, some kind of force or forces operate your body. You can open and close your hand, but you cannot keep it alive by thinking every second of every day, "I must pump oxygenated blood all the way to my fingertips and back." Something else is doing that, and it is not your conscious thinking process. You might be able to take an aspirin to help sooth a pain, but you are not in command of your body, something else is.

I am 72 years old as I write this. Historian, author, and philosopher Joseph Campbell said, shortly before he died, "I don't feel like an old man; I feel like a young man who has something wrong with him." How true. As a volunteer art teacher at a local retirement home, I discovered that if you want some perspective on your age and ageing, spend some time with people who are eighty and ninety plus years old. .

Don't believe everything you think.

When a person dies, we miss their interaction with us, our relationship. However, it is very obvious in looking at a dead body that what we see is no longer that person, that spirit. The body was a carrier for the spirit, which has moved on.

The universe is so large that it is impossible for us to comprehend. Our bodies cannot in this form travel 186,000 miles per second for two and a half million years just to reach the closest neighbor galaxy. However, it might be possible for the soul, the spirit, that part which is really us, to upon our death, travel into another dimension of the universe. Perhaps that is why we are here; to recognize our spirit, and via this spirit, travel to the far reaches of our world and beyond. Having someone you know well, a beloved person or pet, die is a sobering and painful experience, but it may not be as sad a transition as we think, it may be the doorway to even more life.

Paul

Appendix One: Acknowledgements

My editors, Chichi (Chihuahua) and Annette, hard at work.

* One of the last opportunities to edit or change the text in a book is when the printer sends a bound copy, called a Galley Proof. As Annette started reading it for the very first time, she picked up a red pen and automatically started editing. She was well into the second chapter when she said, "This is a wonderful stuff," and resumed reading and editing. Four months later, she set the red pen down and proclaimed, "it's finished!" I am truly grateful for what she did. I am also grateful for the many times she had to carry my part of the family workload so that I could find the time to write and design this book.

* Several people reviewed the galley proof and provided helpful comments and praise, which was very encouraging. I wish to thank Eileen Fisher, and my poet friend, Ivy Moore, for catching errors in my early drafts. My friend and FAA collogue Ken Smith made sure my FAA stories were not fiction, and George Fisher, of FBI fame, gave me a wonderful quote for the back cover.

*Page 93, selected at random from the galley
proof, as edited by Annette*

* The Internet site, Wikipedia, was very useful to check facts.
* The Federal Aviation Administration, Office of Public Affairs
  provided the detailed FAA employment, salary, and aviation
  data.
* Toastmasters International granted me permission to use their
  logo.
* Thank you, The Virginia Museum of Fine Arts, for the fellowship
  funds that allowed me to complete my college education.
* I wish to express my appreciation to Erich Marohombsar from the
  Microsoft Customer Service department for the free counsel that
  allowed me to learn and set a Table of Contents and install page
  numbers in the book. He was wonderful.
* Last, I want to thank the many supervisors and friends who took
  the time to mentor, teach, and guide me through 30 years of
  federal civil service. I hope I have been as successful in
  passing that gift on to others as they were in passing it on to me.
    Paul

Appendix two: NASA News Release, Kepler

NEWS RELEASE

Houston, Texas, NASA Space Center, March 7, 2009

The National Air and Space Administration announced today the launch of a $600,000 telescope named after German astronomer, Johannes Kepler, to see if there are other planets in space that are similar to earth.

Jon Morse, NASA's top astrophysicist said, "I believe this attempt will revolutionize what we know about the universe. What excites me is that for the first time we are going to have a mission that can take a full census of the kind of planets that exist around other stars."

"These planets are too small and too difficult to be seen with past telescopes, but they are precisely the kinds of planets on which life could exist." Morse said.

During the mission, Kepler will measure changes in the brightness of more than 100,000 stars, every 30 minutes, searching for "winks" in light that happen when a planet passes in front of its star. That is how Kepler will know when it has found another Earth.

The search will concentrate on a small part of the universe located in the Milky Way Galaxy. It is estimated that it will take at least three years to find another earth-like planet.

(Footnote: Kepler already has discovered numerous unknown planets within a very small area of search.)

###

Appendix three: Cost of living chart

Inflation Sample: The cost of living in The United States

Year	New House	Yearly Income	New Car
1957	$ 12,220	$ 4,594	$2,157
1962	$ 12,550	$ 5,556	$2,924
1994	$ 119,043	$ 37,070	$12,371
2006	$ 305,900	$ 48,201	$25,000

"From here on out the mountains don't get any higher.
From here on out the mountains don't get any higher.
From here on out the mountains don't get any higher.
But the valleys get deeper and deeper.
(Folk song)

Appendix four: Artist Exhibitions

2009 Olympia West Annual show, Olympia, Washington
2007 Ocean Shores 38th Annual juried show
      Recipient: Best in Northwest Award
2006 Ocean Shores 37th Annual juried show
2006 Marjuli Gallery, Ocean Shores, Washington
2003 The Brick house Gallery, Puyallup, Washington
2001Washington State Arts Council, Lt. Governor's Office
1999Clymer Museum of Western Art, Ellensburg, Washington
1999Washington State Arts Council,, Lt. Governor's Office
1998Celebration of Western Art, group show, Puyallup, Washington
1997"Art Walk", group show, City of Olympia, Washington
1996Potomac Art Gallery, Leesburg, Virginia
1995UpCountry Connections Gallery, Kamuela, Hawaii
1993Reston Art League, USGS Annual Show, Reston, Virginia
1992Reston Art Gallery, Juried group show, Reston, Virginia
1992Images Gallery, Martinsburg, West Virginia
1989Alaska Audubon Society show, Juried, Anchorage, Alaska
1988Alaska Museum Statewide Juried Show, Anchorage, Alaska
1988New Horizons Gallery, Fairbanks, Alaska
1986Artique Ltd. Gallery, Anchorage, Alaska
1985Artique Ltd. Gallery, group show, Anchorage, Alaska
1984New Horizons Art Gallery, Fairbanks, Alaska
1984Artique Ltd. Gallery, Anchorage, Alaska
1983Invitational Group Show, U.S. Senate, Washington, D.C.
1983New Horizons Gallery, Fairbanks, Alaska
1983Artique Ltd. Gallery, Anchorage, Alaska
1983Alaska Juried Watercolor Society Show, Anchorage, Alaska
1982Alaska Statewide Invitational, Washington, D.C.
1982Alaska Museum Statewide Juried Show, Anchorage, Alaska
1981Artique Ltd. Gallery, Anchorage, Alaska
1980Artique Ltd. Gallery, Anchorage, Alaska
1976Eastman Kodak National Traveling Exhibit (Photo art)
1968Society of Federal Artists, Washington, D.C. (Photo art)
1967Society of Federal Artists, Washington, D.C. (Graphics)
1961 Richmond Museum, Juried group show, Richmond, Virginia
1960 Richmond Art Director's Club Juried Show, Richmond, VA
1959 Texaco Oil Co. Juried art competition, 2nd prize, Richmond,
      Virginia

Appendix five: General Services Pay Scale

General Services Pay Scale, 2009

General Services (GS) Pay Schedule for 2009 in US Dollars

Step	1	5	10
Grade 1	17,540	19,873	21,944
2	19,721	21,695	28,815
3	21,517	24,385	27,970
4	24,156	27,376	31,401
5	27,026	50630	35,135
6	30,125	34,141	39,161
7	33,477	39,057	43,521
8	37,075	43,225	48,199
9	40,949	47,774	53,234
10	45,095	52,610	58,622
11	49,544	57,799	64,403
12	59,383	69,278	77,194
13	70,615	82,385	91,801
14	83,445	97,355	108,483
15	98,156	114,516	127,604

Steps 2 -4, and 6- 9 exist but are not shown. Steps 1 to 3 are one year apart automatic pay raises, and steps 4 – 6 are two years apart, the remainder three years apart. For example, it takes 21 years to go from Step 1 to Step 10 within the same grade. Promotions never go down in pay. A GS 12, step 10 would be promoted to a GS-13, step 4.

Appendix six: About the Author

 Paul Steucke, author, graphic designer and fine artist for over 40 years, has lived and painted in Anchorage, Alaska; Reston, Virginia; Olympia, Washington; and Kailua-Kona, Hawaii.

He has a fine arts degree from the Virginia Commonwealth University, College of William and Mary, and has received two competitive art fellowships from the Virginia Museum. His work has been exhibited in Richmond, Leesburg, and Reston Virginia: the U.S. Capitol, Washington, D.C.; Anchorage, Fairbanks, and Prudhoe Bay, Alaska; Martinsburg, West Virginia; Honolulu and Kamuela, Hawaii and Olympia, Seattle, and Ellensburg, Washington.

As an artist, he has designed publications and symbols, and provided illustrations and photographs for several large national organizations. His artwork has been published as limited edition prints, the most popular being paintings and prints of cadets at the U.S. Army Military Academy at West Point, New York.

Paul retired from Federal civil service in 1994, after thirty years of service as an artist, art director, writer, public affairs officer and supervisor.

He and his wife Annette are volunteer English Second Language teachers to recent immigrants each week. They also volunteer each week to teach an art class at the Olympia West retirement home.

A large selection of Paul's and Annette's artwork is available for purchase via the digital printing process. See the Ordering section of his web site at www.paulsteucke.com .

The artist is no longer affiliated with his previous publishers, Vladimir Arts USA, and Masterpiece Publishing, both of Kalamazoo, Michigan.

Appendix seven: Awards

1959:Cash competitive fellowship, Virginia Museum, Richmond,
1960:Award of Excellence, Richmond Art Directors Club
1961:Cash competitive fellowship, Virginia Museum, Richmond,
1964:U.S. Patent #335466, Slide Transparency Viewer
1967:Award of Excellence, Society of Federal Artists & Designers
1976:National Award of Excellence, Eastman Kodak Company
1982:Certificate of Appreciation, Office of the Federal Inspector
1982:Award of Merit, Public Relations Society of America, Alaska
1985:Sustained Superior Performance Award, cash, FAA, Alaska
1986:Award of Excellence, Society of Federal Artists & Designers
1986:Distinguished Service Award, KAKM Public Television,
1986:Federal Employee of the Year, Alaska
1987:"Golden Nugget" Award, Alaska Press Woman
1987:First Place, Community Relations, Alaska Press Woman
1987:Outstanding Performance Award, cash, FAA Alaskan Region
1988:Exceptional Performance Award, cash, FAA Alaskan Region
1989:Exceptional Performance Award, cash, FAA Alaskan Region
1990:NTSB Regional Award for Public Service in aviation safety
1990:Alaska Air Traffic Control Division Appreciation Award
1990:Honorary special Agent, FAA, Anchorage CASFO
1990:Federal Women's Program Appreciation Award
1990:FAA Alaskan Region, Meritorious Service Award
1991:Exceptional Performance Award, cash, FAA Washington, D.C.
1992:Outstanding Performance Award, FAA Washington, D.C.
1992:Special Achievement Award, cash, FAA Washington, D.C.
1992:Member Achievement Award, FAA Employee Association
1992:Outstanding Service Award, EPG, FAA, HQ
1993:Exceptional Performance Award, cash, FAA Washington, D.C.
1993:Special Achievement Award, cash, FAA Washington, D.C.
1993:Certificate of Commendation, FAA, HQ
1994:Retired from Federal Civil Service after 30 years of service.
2007:"Best of the Northwest" juried art show award, Ocean Shores

Appendix nine: U.S. Patent #3354566

United States Patent #3354566 awarded
To Paul Steucke, Sr. on November 28, 1967

Granddaughters Courtney and Ashley, 1987, Anchorage, Alaska

Appendix ten: Snowy Good-byes

Little hands reach for bright, green candies,
and loud voices clamor loving good-byes.
Thumping boots and jangling car keys
can barely be heard over the din.
A soft kiss and warm hug envelope me,
along with the reassuring aromas
of dinner remnants
and my grandma's gardenia scent.
Grandpa's safe arms swing me up to his chest;
on the other arm, my sister perches lightly.
We each choose a hat from the peg.
I pick my favorite, a jaunty, white sailor's cap.
Courtney grabs the straw cowboy hat.
Cold winds brush my cheeks
when Grandpa steps outside.
Closing my eyes and sticking out my tongue,
I hope for one of
the glittering, white fairies to fall in,
but they always seem to
glide safely out of harm.

Ashley L.

The above verse was written by my granddaughter, Ashley, at the age of fifteen, and was given to me, along with the photograph (left, previous page) for Christmas, 2000. The photo was taken in 1987, Anchorage, and shows me carrying the two girls (ages five and almost three) from our condominium to their car. Courtney is now an attorney with a law firm in Olympia, WA. Ashley is a master's level biologist employed with the U.S. Army's environmental program at Fort Lewis, Washington.

Appendix eleven: Community Service

President: Inlet Cluster Homeowners Association, Reston, VA
President: National Society of Federal Artists & Designers
President: Public Relations Society of America, Alaska
Chapter
Vice President: Eagle River Homeowners Association
Vice President: Toastmasters International, Club 3122
Board Member: Anchorage Citizen Review Committee, HUD
Board Member: Anchorage Metro Transportation System
Council
Board Member: St. Christopher's Episcopal Church,
Anchorage
Board Member: Hampton Condo Association, Anchorage
Treasurer: Kihei Kapu Ke Ao Hulili Ka Maluhia Dance troop
Musician: Kihei Kapu Ke Ao Hulili Ka Maluhia, Hawaiian
Treasurer: Appointed by the Governor, Alaska Safety Council
Member: Governor's Alaska Safety Council (appointment)
Member: Federal Women's Program, Alaska
Member: Women's Press Club, Alaska Chapter

Left: Volunteer teacher for English as a second language to
Chinese emigrants, Olympia, WA.
Right: Volunteer art teacher to students at Olympia West
Retirement Home, Olympia WA.

Appendix twelve Timeline of 20th century ©2011

1900: Brosnan paper clip, seismograph, Zeppelin, escalator

1901: Electric typewriter, erecter set, President McKinley killed, Teddy Roosevelt succeeds, Gillette safety razor

1902: Air conditioner, crayon, hair dryer, spark plug, teddy bear

1903: Airplane, barbiturate, reinforced concrete-skyscraper

1904: Crash helmet, Novocain, offset printing, vacuum tube, Russo- Japanese War.

1906: Animated cartoon, freeze drying, sound broadcasting, Food and Drug Act, Picasso invents cubism, Kellogg cornflakes

1907: Plastic, tungsten filament lamp, vacuum cleaner

1908: Cellophane, electric razor, paper cup, TB skin test, Model-T Ford, Jack Johnson first black heavyweight champ.

1909: Cigarette lighter, IUD, President Taft

1910: Chemotherapy, iodine disinfectant, electric washing machine.

1911: Gastro scope, superconductivity.

1912: Cabin biplane, electric heating pad, sewer sludge treatment, Mexican Revolution, Titanic sinks, Life Saver candy

1913: Artificial kidney, brassiere, crossword puzzle, diphtheria vaccine, Geiger counter, mammography, modern assembly line, Stravinsky's "Rite of Spring", crossword puzzle

1914: Opening of the Panama Canal, teletype, 35 mm camera, traffic light, zipper, start of WW I

1915: Heat-resistant glass, radiotelephone, sonar, tank, C. Chaplin's "the Tramp".

1916: Windshield wipers, general theory of relativity, idea for auto highway cloverleaf patented by Arthur Hill, stainless steel

1917: US enters World War One, Russian Revolution, mustard gas.

1918: End of WW-I, electric food mixer, fortune cookie

1919: Andrew Carnegie created 2500 libraries, Enigma Encoding machine, shortwave radio, cure for sleeping sickness.

1920: US women's right to vote, band-aid, tea bag, submachine gun.
1921: Cultured pearl, lie detector, microsurgery, R. Valentino
1922: Muzak, self winding watch, J.Joyce "Ulysses", J.C. Nichols first shopping mall (Kansas City), first use of white center line on roadways
1923: Bulldozer, TB Vaccine, Whooping cough vaccine
1924: Frozen food, gas chamber, portable radio, spiral notebook
1925: Commercial fax service, quantum mechanics
1926: Liquid fuel rockets, pop-up toaster, talking movies
1927: Lindbergh's flight, antifreeze, iron lung, tape recorder, artificial rubber, electric jukebox, Farnsworth TV, quarts clock
1928: bubble gum, pap test, penicillin, electric shaver
1929: 18th amendment brings prohibition of liquor, Wall Street crash, start of the great depression, Yo-Yo(toy)

1930: Discovery of Pluto, jet engine, cyclotron, diesel engine, tampon, first office copier, scotch tape, sliced bead, supermarket, typhus vaccine
1931: Electric guitar, FM radio, Freon, stereo recording
1932: FDR elected, car radio, color cartoon film, defibrillator, first sulfa drug.
1933: Hitler starts rise to power, end of probation, day-glow ink, electron microscope, "monopoly" game
1934: Drive in theatre
1935: Beer can, cortisone, heart lung machine, Kodachrome film, paperback books, VHF television, Gershwin's "Porgy"
1936: Jesse Owens wins at Berlin Olympics, helicopter, Sodium pentothal, Spanish civil war, Edward 8th abdicates throne, British invent radar used to locate aircraft
1937: Antihistamine, binary circuit (computers) nylon, radio telescope, xerography, yellow fever vaccine
1938: Artificial hip, ballpoint pen, first working computer, fluorescent lighting, instant coffee.
1939: Hitler invades Poland, start of WW II, automatic clutch, bra-cup sizing, DDT, electric carving knife, Paul Steucke born, "Gone with the Wind" and "Wizard of Oz" films debut, first broadcast of commercial TV at Worlds' Fair, Sikorsky helicopter

1940: Color television, Dacron, freeze dry foods, Pennsylvania Turnpike opened, Jeep vehicle

1941: Japan attacks US at Pearl Harbor, US enters pacific
war, aerosol can, cardiac catheter, television
advertising
1942: Bazooka, nuclear reactor
1943: Kidney dialysis, LSD, scuba diving gear, musical
Oklahoma
1944: Aureomycin, V-I & V-2 rockets, bombing of London
1945: Germany surrenders, end of WW II Europe, FDR dies,
U.S. drops atomic bombs on Japan, end of WW II in
pacific, 2-4-D herbicide, President Harry Truman
1946: Disposable diaper, ENAC computer, bikini, mobile
phone microwave oven
1947: Transistor, India Independence, Williams "Streetcar",
Tupperware, mobile phone (AT&T) –cell phone came
in 1983
1948: Israel established, cable television, Scrabble game,
Jackson Pollock's "drip" painting, Velcro by George
de Mestral, Frisbee (toy)
1949: Super music amplifier, Mao (China) comes to power,
auto seat belts (Nash), atomic clock invented,
commercial cake mix

1950: Korean War: McCarthy hearings, credit card, embryo
transplant, first national credit card
1951: "I Love Lucy" TV show, power steering, super glue,
video tape recorder
1952: Mr. Potato Head, 3-D film, amniocentesis, polio
vaccine, fiber optics, telephone answering machine,
sex change operation,
hydrogen bomb test
1953: DNA discovered, kidney transplant, radial tire,
President Eisenhower
1954: Nonstick cooking pan, oral contraceptive, TV dinner,
Thorazine, vertical takeoff airplane, "Brown Vs Board
of Ed.", McDonald's fast food
1955: Rosa Parks refuses to give up bus seat, Lego,
hovercraft, field ion microscope, optic fiber, synthetic
diamond, tetracycline, Tylenol, optic fiber
1956: Computer hard drive disk, DNA biosynthesis, human
Growth hormone
1957: Elvis Presley performs on The Ed Sullivan Show,
Fortran computer language, high speed dental drill,
ICBM, Sputnik, Paul Steucke graduates from
Annandale High School.
1958: External pacemaker, Hula Hoop, ultrasound exams,
Computer modem

1959: Electrocardiograph, internal pacemaker, Barbie Doll
1960: John Kennedy elected President, breast implant, fiber
      tip pen, halogen lamp, Paul Steucke marries Annette
      Hagaman

1961: USSR Gagarin first in space, nondairy creamer,
      Valium
1962: Marylyn Monroe commits suicide, audiocassette,
      laser eye surgery, Paul Steucke graduates from RPI,
      College of William & Mary
1963: JFK assassinated, instant color film, liver transplant,
      Lung transplant, measles vaccine, navigation satellite,
      videodisc
1964: Acrylic paint, permanent press fabric, touch tone
      telephone, Civil Rights Act, Beatles in America,
      permanent press fabric
1965: Vietnam War (1965-73), Astroturf, Basic computer
      language, Dolby sound system, hologram, Kevlar,
      miniskirt, NutraSweet, portable video recorder, soft
      contact lenses, virtual reality
1966: Rubella vaccine, auto fuel injection, Masters and
      Johnson sex study
1967: Coronary bypass, handheld calculator, heart
      transplant, L-dopa, Apollo-1 ground fire kills three
      astronauts in capsule
1968: Computer mouse, computer integrated circuits, King
      and RF Kennedy murdered
1969: Actress, singer Judy Garland died, Neil Armstrong
      steps on the moon, artificial heart, ATM, bar code
      scanner, ibuprofen, in-vitro fertilization, Unix
      computer system, President Nixon

1970: Kent State shootings, daisy wheel printer, floppy disk
1971: Dot matrix printer, food processor, space station,
      liquid crystal display monitor

1972: Nixon visits China, compact disc, Landsat, Pong
      Computer game, word processor
1973: Gene splicing, "Roe vs. Wade", OPEC oil embargo
1974: Watergate, President Nixon resigns, Post it notes,
      President Gerald Ford, First use of UPC bar code
1975: Ethernet computer network, laser printer, personal
      computer,

1976: Ink jet printer, VHS system for video recording,
T.P. Pearsall creates, based on other earlier research,
the first bright LED light.
1977: Apple II computer, fiber optics, linked ATM's,
neutron bomb,
1978: Disco fever, test tube baby, Pope John Paul elected
1979: Jerry Falwell founded The Moral Majority group,
artificial blood, Rubik's cube, 24 bit microprocessor,
roller blade, Sony Walkman

1980: R. Reagan elected President, gene transfer, hepatitis-B
vaccine
1981: AIDS identified, Sandra D. O'Conner first women on
Supreme Court, aspartame, MS-DOS, space shuttle
1982: Human growth hormone from engineered bacteria,
insulin made from bacteria
1983: Cellular phone network, computer virus, LISA
(Macintosh computer), human embryo transfer
1984: Computer animation, CD Rom, fetal surgery, Mac
computer, RAM (Random access memory).
1985: Oprah Winfrey launches TV show in Chicago, USSR
Gorbachev takes power, genetic fingerprinting (DNA),
Windows computer system, PageMaker software
system
1986: AIDS epidemic becomes national health problem,
digital audiotape, USSR Chernobyl accident, Iran
Contra scandal, space shuttle Challenger explodes
1987: Gene gun, Prozac approved, soy milk, 3-D video
game, disposable camera
1988: Chicken feed to make low cholesterol eggs, disposable
contact lenses, Doppler radar, positron microscope.
RU-486 birth control pill in Europe
1989: Berlin wall falls, Tiananmen Square protest (China),
Global positioning system, high definition television,
stealth bomber, President H.W. Bush elected

1990: World Wide Web started (www), Hubble space telescope
launched.
1991: Breakup of USSR, digital answering machine, plastic
explosive detector, Gulf War, Bosnia War
1992: Baboon human liver transplant, crystal holograph
memory, instant language translator, taxol cancer
drug
1993: Apartheid ends in Africa, mapping of male
chromosome, Pentium computer processor, Mideast
peace accords
1994: English Channel tunnel opened, HIV positive
inhibitor, "Amazon.com" started

1995: Gene for obesity discovered, Oklahoma City bombing
1996: Antimatter created in law, Web TV, EVI electric car.
       First traffic intersection   camera installed in England.
       first U.S military GPS system fully operational. Second
       nationwide toll free telephone number, 888, introduced.
       Phillip Kahn makes the first modern camera telephone by
       combining his digital camera and cell phone.
1997: Princess Diana and Mother Teresa die on same day,
       Gas powered fuel cell. First DVD player on market
1998: Erection drug Viagra approved, "Google" file retrieval
       system started.
1999: Atomic clocks begin operation. NASA sends a $63
       million lunar prospector into crater at South Pole to
       detect water , (None found.) Wi-Fi created.

2000: Laser goes faster than light, computer 0000 year flops,
       Cartoonist Charles Schultz ("Peanuts")dies.
2001: George W. Bush (#2) elected President, (Inherits no
       national debt from Clinton), N.Y. Twin
       Towers (9-11), President Bush abandons global
       warming treaty, Anthrax scare, Apple Corporation
       introduces the iPod MP3 player. Kodak and Sony
       invest $350 million to make flat screen color display
       for hand held devices.
2002: The euro currency debuts in 12 countries, Elizabeth II
       Queen of England for 50 years, President Bush
       abandons 31 year old antiballistic missile treaty,
       North Korea develops nuclear bomb, Braille glove. In
       China a German designed magnetic levitation train
       hits 260 mph.
2003: Iraq War started, Sec.State Powell makes Iraq war
       case to UN, President Bush on aircraft carrier says
       War over, (It went on another 8 years), National
       deficit over $200 billion, space shuttle Columbia
       explodes, war in Iraq costs $4 billion a month.
2004: Mars rovers (2) successful, Iraq weapons inspector
       quits, Martha Stewart guilty of perjury, gay marriage
       in Massachusetts, translucent concrete
2005: Asian tsunami leaves over 8,000 dead, White House,
       contrary to Colin Powell UN statement, says no
       weapons of mass destruction found in Iraq, President
       Bush begins second term as a war hero President.
       European spacecraft lands on Saturn moon,

national deficit under Democratic party President
Clinton was $00, under Republican party President
Bush $427+ billion, Pope John Paul dies,
   women vote in Kuwait, 10th planet discovered.
2006: Hurricane Katrina hits New Orleans
2007: Amazon.com starts selling electronic book reader
   "Kindle" which sells for $399, and will hold 200
   books.
2008: Hadrons Collider, worlds largest particle collider
   passed first test and then shut down for repairs ,Google
   and T-Mobile telephone unveiled T-Mobile G1 phone.
2009: Mattel (Toy Corporation) creates a toy that is
   controlled by brain control interface technology.
   June 25, Entertainer, singer, dancer, Michael Jackson
   died
2010: U.S. Military, using a laser gun aboard a Boeing 747
   jet shoots down a target missile in midair

2011: March 11: A 9.1 earthquake near Japan sets off a
   monster tsunami that devastates Japan coastal cities,
   over 15,000 dead, Japan nuclear power plants heavily
   damaged. Boeing Corporation's new "Dreamliner"
   lightweight composite material international class jet
   made first commercial flight on October 26, Seattle
   to Hong Kong. Attempted assassination of
   Congresswoman Gifford.
May 2011; Osama bin Laden killed in Pakistan by
   U.S. military.
   October 22, Dictator, Libya, Moammer Kaddafi killed
   by rebel Forces
July, NASA's last space shuttle, "Atlantis" lands
   ending the U.S. NASA Shuttle program.
   November, CERN test with Neutrinos breaks speed
   of light theory

#

Appendix thirteen: Letters of Commendation

STEVE COWPER
GOVERNOR

STATE OF ALASKA
OFFICE OF THE GOVERNOR
JUNEAU

August 2, 1990

Mr. Paul T. Steucke
3909 Hampton Drive
Anchorage, AK 99504

Dear Paul,

I have received your letter of resignation from the Alaska
Safety Advisory Council (ASAC). On behalf of the citizens
of Alaska and this administration, I want to thank you for
your service as a member of the Council.

Participation on a state board or council requires a
dedication of personal time and energy, and a commitment to
the public. You demonstrated these attributes by accepting
a position on this Council, and I appreciate your efforts
during your membership.

Through your efforts the ASAC began formal fiscal
administration of their funding. The establishment of
procedures covering annual independent audits, criteria
setting for annual budgeting, and responsible financial
liabilities management reflects your expertise and
professionalism. The procedures you have set will continue
to benefit ASAC for years to come.

In addition to your work as Treasurer, you were an able
spokesman for the Council. The other members relied on your
professionalism and dependability. I know that you will be
missed, both on the Council and in Alaska.

Best of luck in your future endeavors.

Sincerely,

Steve Cowper
Governor

National Transportation Safety Board
Anchorage Regional Office
222 West 7th Ave., Box 11
Anchorage, Alaska 99513

July 21, 1989

Mr. Franklin L. Cunningham
Regional Administrator
Alaskan Region, FAA
222 West 7th Avenue
Anchorage, Alaska 99513

Dear Mr. Cunningham:

    I wish to express to you my appreciation for the outstanding support and service that your Public Affairs officer, Paul Steucke, has provided to this NTSB Regional Office.

    Paul's personal dedication and professionalism is a significant part of this inter-agency relationship because I know I can trust him to accurately represent both agencies' viewpoints, he is willing to respond to our needs on a 24 hour basis, and we are able to enjoy the positive rapport that he has developed with the Alaskan news media.

    This inter-agency cooperation benefits the public by providing timely information and by significantly reducing the amount of personal and staff time that I would otherwise dedicate to this task.

    Thank you for providing this assistance.

                    Sincerely

                    James Michelangelo

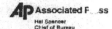

AP Associated Press
Hal Spencer
Chief of Bureau

February 20, 1985

Franklin Cunningham
Regional Director
Alaskan Region
Federal Aviation Administration
701 C Street, Box 14
Anchorage, Alaska 99513

Dear Mr. Cunningham:

In behalf of this office I wish to express our appreciation
for the effort that Paul Steucke has made to provide aviation
information to The Associated Press. For example, without his
thoughtfulness, we and therefore the nation would have had to
spend many hours the next day playing catch up on the recent
Soldotna Air Commuter airline crash. His efforts helped us
provide the national media with information about this crash
in a timely manner. It saved considerable time and resources
for all the news media, including the major national networks.

His consistent effort to provide information and his courteous
and timely response to our needs has been outstanding and a
credit to the Federal Aviation Administration.

Sincerely,

Hal Spencer
Chief of Bureau
Anchorage

HS/dh

Appendix fourteen: Annette's Cookbook

Over 50 years of good Cooking!
288 pages, 8.5 x 11
Over 500 family and friend tested recipes from the kitchen of Annette Steucke, plus a smorgasbord of drawings and paintings and a delicious kaleidoscope of food and cooking quotations

Appendix fifteen: Burbia Boy

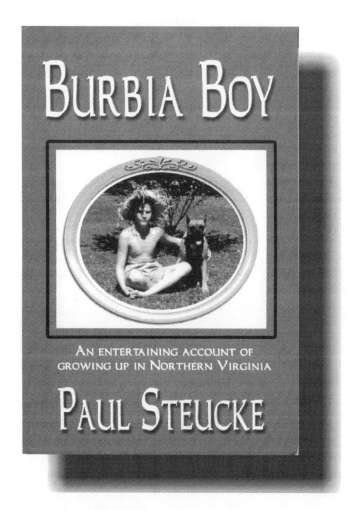

357 Pages: Available from Amazon.com
Or your local bookstore.

Appendix sixteen: Courtney's Kona Memoir

In 1994, our son Paul Junior, his wife Stacy and their four daughters came to visit us in Hawaii. One morning Annette and I took the two older girls to a lava beach area near the old deserted Kona-Kailua airport. Six years later Courtney wrote a description of that morning and gave it to us as a present. Here is what she wrote.

"Courtney, wake up," whispered my grandma's soft voice.

I arose from my bed, which consisted of a jungle hammock perched on the lanai. The air was humid for an early November morning in Kona. The sky glowed a dusky lavender, waiting for the golden sun to come brush the sleep off my dreaming eyes. My grandparents, my younger sister Ashley, and I piled into the minivan and took off down the road. We had planned a special sunrise excursion.. Our destination happened to find us on a secluded beach.

The sun peeped over the stony cliffs to show its fiery orange face, lighting the cloudless skies to pale blue. Gazing at the beach gave me an inner sense of peace.

Fine sand caressed my bare toes. The aquamarine water gently lapped at the coastline. Ebony boulders, reminders of past volcanic eruptions, jutted from the azure water. Those once, destructive rocks now contained tide pools of life. Many days of warm sunshine had heated the tepid, shallow water. Tiny brown sea anemones clung to the rough surface. Dark violet mussels clamored for breathing space. I examined domed chalky barnacles waving their tentacles, waiting to catch small bits of plankton.

On the sandy shore, my grandpa, forever a photographer, snapped pictures of my sister and me. My grandmother, with her dyed platinum blonde hair and purple eye shadow, embraced her youthful spirit by playing in the white sand. Ashley and I joined her on the beach, and we decided to create a grand sand castle. Little gray stones decorated the outside, and a pool made an impressive entrance. The tides slowly ate away and destroyed our work of art.

Hunger gnawed at my stomach from the morning's exploration. Sugary doughnuts and strawberry guava juice made up a grandma approved breakfast. Before our absence had been noticed from home, we deserted this isolated paradise. I glanced one more, wishing each moment in life could be as extraordinary as this one.

Courtney

Made in the USA
Charleston, SC
22 March 2012